UNDERSTANDING
BRITISH AND EUROPEAN
POLITICAL ISSUES

UNDERSTANDINGS

Series editor **DUNCAN WATTS**

Following the review of the national curriculum for 16–19-year-olds, UK examining boards introduced new specifications, first used in 2001 and 2002. A-level courses are now divided into A/S level for the first year of sixth-form studies, and the more difficult A2 level thereafter. The **Understandings** series comprehensively covers social science syllabuses of all major examination boards, featuring dedicated A/S and A2 level textbooks. The books are written in an accessible, user-friendly and jargon-free manner and will be essential to students sitting these examinations.

Understanding British and European political issues

Second editon

NEIL McNAUGHTON

Manchester University Press

Manchester and New York

distributed in the United States exclusively by Palgrave Macmillan

First edition published 2003 by Manchester University Press

This edition published 2010 by
Manchester University Press
Oxford Road, Manchester M13 9NR, UK
and Room 400, 175 Fifth Avenue, New York, NY 10010, USA
www.manchesteruniversitypress.co.uk

Distributed in the United States exclusively by
Palgrave Macmillan, 175 Fifth Avenue, New York,
NY 10010, USA

Distributed in Canada exclusively by
UBC Press, University of British Columbia, 2029 West Mall,
Vancouver, BC, Canada V6T 1Z2

British Library Cataloguing-in-Publication Data
A catalogue record for this book is available from the British Library

Library of Congress Cataloging-in-Publication Data applied for

ISBN   978 0 7190 8073 9 paperback

This edition first published 2010
Reprinted 2011

Typeset
by Graphicraft Limited, Hong Kong
Printed and Bound in Great Britain
by Bell & Bain Ltd, Glasgow

Contents

List of tables

Preface to the second edition

It is in the nature of books on current political issues that they become out of date all too quickly. This was never more the case than when the credit crunch struck Britain and most of the developed world in 2007. Almost at a stroke all our assumptions about how economic policy is made, and about what are the main levers operated by governments, were destroyed. Although this is less the case with topics such as law and order or Northern Ireland, it remains true that books like this need regular updating. This is the main reason for the production of this second edition. Fortunately, though much of the ground is constantly shifting, many fundamental principles of policy making remain in place. Examples include the basic philosophy and operation of Britain's Welfare State, the nature of the sectarian divide in Northern Ireland and the fundamental operation of the European Union. These permanent features are reflected again in this edition.

A second reason for a new edition concerns the main examination for which this book has proved popular. This is Edexcel's Route A specification. In September 2009 teaching began on this new specification, examinations for which have been set for June 2010. In particular there is a new topic – Environment – while the issue of race and ethnicity has been removed, as has Northern Ireland. There is also to be slightly less emphasis on individual aspects of the Welfare State, notably health and education, though these still remain as key topics. The European section of the specification remains very similar to its predecessor so relatively few changes have been made.

But a book like this is not written purely for examination candidates. It is to be hoped that there is much here for general readers who wish to bring themselves up to date on many of the great political issues of the day, as well as acquainting themselves with the recent historical background. For this reason, Northern Ireland and women's issues have been retained as chapters in their own right.

I have tried in this edition to add more political context in the accounts of policy making. It is all too easy to forget that public policy, in both Britain and Europe, are subject to the influence of the broader party and group politics going on around it. Decisions are clearly not made in a political vacuum. It is therefore vital that students of political issues should take into account the shifting political ground when analysing and assessing policy initiatives and developments.

At the end of each chapter a number of examination questions are suggested. These are based on the kind of questions which may be expected at Advanced level study. In each case there are a number of 'short' questions as well as full-length essay questions.

They range over the full extent of the specification content and reflect the key issues which arise in relation to each topic. The book contains enough information for the reader to be able to answer these questions. Nevertheless, for those readers who wish to delve further, there is also at the end of the book a short suggested further reading list for each section.

A number of people have helped with the production of both editions of this book, but I would wish to single out four in particular. Duncan Watts has been a writer colleague for many years. He has provided both encouragement and copious useful comments on the text and it is much the better for that. Tony Mason at Manchester University Press removed any doubts I had about a second edition of the book and I am glad he did. He reassured me that the task was worthwhile and I hope that readers will agree. Jacquie Grice from Woodhouse College must surely be one of the most knowledgeable experts on the European Union in the teaching profession and I have benefited hugely over many years from her advice and sharing of experience, with a great deal of valuable 'inside information' thrown in for good measure. Finally my erstwhile colleague Jacqueline Heaton has helped by removing many of my everyday work burdens so that I have had the time and energy to produce this edition.

Neil McNaughton
London

Economic policy

1

FISCAL AND MONETARY POLICY

Before examining the basis of modern economic policy making in the UK it is essential to understand the basis of two of the main types of management which have been used. These are fiscal and monetary management.

Fiscal policy refers largely to the use of the government sector of the economy to control economic activity. The term 'fiscal' strictly relates to taxation, and certainly varying the level and distribution of taxation is an important element. But fiscal policy also refers to the government expenditure side of the equation. So fiscal policy means the combination of manipulating taxation and government expenditure in the interests of economic management. We can also say that the level difference between the two – i.e. a *deficit* if the government spends more than it raises in tax, or a *surplus* if it raises more in tax than it spends – is a key aspect of fiscal control. In general terms fiscal policy can be used in this way:

First, if there is an economic slowdown when growth in output slows or even turns negative,

interventionism

A style or tendency in economic policy where government tends to intervene in economic activity to achieve certain goals. Prominent examples of intervention include manipulation of taxes and/or public expenditure, selective government subsidies, controls on prices and incomes and full-scale nationalisation of industries. Keynesiansim (see below) is an example of interventionism. It is associated mainly with socialism and left of centre politics.

unemployment rises and business activity declines, an *expansionist* fiscal position may be taken by government. This usually means reducing taxes to stimulate spending, raising government expenditure to create more economic activity or to put more money into the pockets of those receiving benefits from government, such as pensions, income support and child benefit; and therefore running a *budget deficit* where spending exceeds taxation. When this occurs government must borrow money, either from banks or from the general public (in various forms of national savings and investment schemes). Such borrowing adds to the National Debt and interest must be paid on that, taken from general taxation in the future. When the government does this it is hoped that the economy will be stimulated, business activity will increase and unemployment will fall. Fiscal expansion of this kind carries the danger of creating inflation, as an over-stimulated economy can result in excessive demand over supply. It also has the drawback of creating public sector debt which is a burden on future taxpayers.

Second, if the economy does 'overheat' and inflation becomes a major problem, fiscal policy can be used to dampen economic activity. This is described as *deflationary* fiscal policy. Taxes may be raised and public expenditure reduced. There may well be a public sector surplus in this case. Clearly deflationary policy may solve inflation but, if overdone, may result in falling growth and rising unemployment. On the other hand the resulting surpluses can be used to pay off National Debt.

Third, tax and public expenditure can also be varied to produce other economic or *social* effects. For example the tax burden may be shifted away from the poor towards the rich (e.g. by raising income tax rates on higher incomes and reducing them for low income groups). Taxes on business may be reduced to stimulate domestic investment and encourage inward investment from abroad. Similarly the distribution of public expenditure may be manipulated for similar ends. More may be spent, for example on benefits for pensioners or poor families. Some expenditure may be redirected towards small businesses to promote growth in that area.

Monetary policy is considered to be less interventionist. It involves the manipulation of purely monetary levers in order to influence economic activity. The word *influence* is important here, as those who support the use of monetary policy usually believe that government should play a limited role in economic management. For

monetarism

A movement which became popular in British and US politics in the 1980s. It is associated with free market policy and laissez-faire. It is most attributed to the American economist Milton Friedman. Monetarists suggest that inflation is caused solely by rises in the total supply of money. It is therefore only necessary for governments to be responsible in not allowing money supply to go out of control in order to prevent inflation. Other forms of economic intervention are opposed by monetarists.

supporters of monetary policy – often known as *monetarists* – fiscal policy is too interventionist and gives government an excessive role. Monetarism is, therefore, supported by those who believe that the economy should be left as free as possible and that government should operate a 'light hand on the tiller'. Monetary policy has two main instruments.

First, by controlling the central bank's (Bank of England in the UK) rate of interest, which is a guide to all other interest rates operating in the financial economy, government can seek to influence economic activity. High interest rates will dampen down economic activity, especially consumer spending (because interest rates affect the use of credit cards and other loans). This may be used when inflation becomes a threat. In other words, raising interest rates can be a substitute for using fiscal deflationary policy, as described above. Conversely reducing interest rates will encourage spending and business investment when there is a need to stimulate the economy. As with fiscal policy, such expansionary measures carry the danger of rising inflation. As we shall see, the control of interest rates became a key issue in economic policy between the mid-1990s and the recession of 2008–9.

Second, monetarists argue that government has a responsibility to keep sound public finances. This means avoiding excessive borrowing and keeping a lid on the size of the National Debt. Excessive government borrowing, they say, has a number of adverse effects. Among them, it creates economic instability which hampers business investment, it results in the need for taxpayers to pay large amounts of interest on the debt, and it can be inflationary since the extra money generated by borrowing raises the total amount of money in circulation and causes prices to rise as a result of rising demand in the general economy.

All governments use a combination of fiscal and monetary policy from time to time. But, as we shall see below, different governments, influenced by different economic theories, have tended to concentrate on one or the other at different times.

Macro- and micro-economic policy

Before moving on we also need to examine briefly the nature of macro- and micro-economic management. Here again all governments use a combination of both.

Macro-economic policy refers to management of the *whole economy*. In practice this means influencing such key elements of economic activity as the general level of unemployment, the rate of inflation, the rate of general economic growth and the level of international trade. Fiscal and monetary policy, described above, are the main instruments of macro-economic policy.

Micro-economic policy refers to attempts to manage specific *sectors* of the economy rather than the economy as a whole. This may involve, for example, targeted aid to a particular industry or industrial sector such as technology, agriculture or engineering. It may also involve specific measures directed at specific forms of activity such as the financial sector of the economy, or industrial training or research and development. It may also refer to attempts to influence labour markets and industrial relations through policy towards wages, pensions and welfare benefits.

Micro-economic policy tends to create only limited political controversy so the examination of economic policy which follows concentrates largely on macro-economic policy. Nevertheless it should always be borne in mind that governments have micro-economic measures at their disposal and are constantly using them in one way or another.

ECONOMIC POLICY 1979–97

Here we examine the nature of economic policy making from the election of Margaret Thatcher as Prime Minister in 1979 to the arrival of the New Labour government in 1997.

It is normal for economic commentators to take 1979 as a watershed year in British history, and this is certainly logical as it saw the election of perhaps the most radical prime minister of the twentieth century. Nevertheless, that year did not mark a dramatic change in the nature of economic policy making. There were two main reasons for this.

First, and perhaps most importantly, the country was entering a deep and enduring recession. Both inflation and unemployment were rising alarmingly (which economists at the time thought to be impossible, believing that a rise in one should lead to a fall in the other). This meant that radical measures were not feasible. Second, Margaret Thatcher herself was far from politically secure in her first three years in office. A number of senior members of the Conservative party were firmly opposed to a departure from traditional policies. These were the so-called 'wets' and they included such key figures as Lord Carrington, Francis Pym and Peter Walker. However, her victory in the Falklands conflict in 1982 gave her the political confidence to remove her opponents from the cabinet.

So the real watershed came in 1982–83 as the economic climate began to improve and the Prime Minister was more able to dominate the political scene. By then, however, the seeds had been sown and it is important to identify those seeds. The main element was the increasing popularity of monetarism, which is described above.

So it was that at the beginning of the Thatcher era the government largely withdrew from active economic management. Unemployment rose unchecked; but it did eventually have a positive effect. Wage increases moderated as workers faced intense competition for scarce jobs. The influence of the trade unions also began to wane. The level of strikes and other forms of industrial unrest fell and industrial activity began to pick up. In other words, unemployment became a 'price worth paying', as Thatcher claimed, though those on the dole queues certainly did not agree!

But it was not until 1982–83 that the next phase of the 'Thatcher revolution' was to begin. We may describe this stage as the 'supply-side' phase. Indeed, supply-side economics was to dominate economic policy making for many years to come.

Supply-side economics

Fiscal policy, as devised by John Maynard Keynes, the great British economist, was characterised by the need for government to control the level of aggregate demand, notably through the levels of taxation and expenditure. Supply-side economics returns to the 'classical' principle that such control is counterproductive and that there is a natural process whereby such problems as inflation or high interest rates will correct themselves automatically. However, this process depends on the ability of the economy to adjust to those mechanisms. In particular the 'supply side' (i.e. production and distribution of goods and services) needs to be both flexible and dynamic.

Margaret Thatcher and her advisers were of the opinion that the long-term problem of the British economy was that the supply side was neither dynamic not flexible. She therefore saw the role of her governments as being to correct these faults. The main objectives of policy were the following:

Keynesianism
Named after John Maynard Keynes, the most celebrated British economist of the 1920s–40s. Keynes argued that governments should intervene to manipulate economic activity (see **interventionism** above). When an economy is slowing down and in decline, he recommended reductions in taxation and rises in public expenditure, financed by borrowing, to stimulate the economy. This kind of interventionism is known as 'Keynesianism' and was out of favour in the 1980s and 1990s but was revived in the post-2007 recession.

- To make labour markets more flexible. That implied that wages could freely rise or fall according to market conditions, workers would be able to adapt quickly to new technologies and growing industries, and there would be real incentives to work and to improve output.
- To create more incentives for entrepreneurs. By making it an attractive proposition to set up new businesses or expand existing ones, it is assumed the economy can expand quickly.

- To create more free competition as a means by which businesses will be forced to become efficient.
- To reduce regulation by the state. Too much control over such factors as wages, prices, profits and production systems is believed to stifle business expansion. The most dramatic form of regulation occurs in nationalised industries, so they became a major target for reform.

free market
This refers to markets – usually product, labour and financial markets – which are free from government interference. So called laissez-faire politics has the effect of leaving markets free. The result is that prices, wages and interest rates will find their own level according to market forces. It is associated most with conservatism and neo-liberalism.

Most economic policy from the 1980s onwards was, therefore, directed at achieving these ends. As we have seen above, most of the practical measures could not be implemented until after the 1983 general election when the Conservative Party was returned to office with a huge parliamentary majority.

It should be noted that such supply-side policies have sometimes also been characterised as 'neo-liberalism'. They were, in some senses a throwback to the classical liberal economic outlook of the nineteenth century when government was seen as an inhibition against economic dynamism. The main character-istics of supply side, or neo-liberal policies, as practised by Thatcher govern-ments are shown below.

Taxation

One decision had already been made four years before the 1983 election land-slide. This was the reduction in the level of income tax, implemented in 1979. The basic rate, as paid by most people, fell from 33 per cent to 30 per cent and the highest rate (paid only by the very wealthy) was brought down from 83 per cent to 60 per cent. Reductions continued and by 1988 there were only two rates of income tax – 25 per cent and 40 per cent. These were almost the lowest rates in Western Europe. The reductions in tax revenue which resulted were made up by an increase in the rate of value added tax (VAT) from 8 per cent to 15 per cent, and this was later supplemented by increased tax revenues from North Sea oil and the proceeds of the privatisation programme described below.

The purpose of this change was to create greater incentives by allowing entrepreneurs and their employees to retain a much higher proportion of their incomes. The idea that business activity is crucial to wealth creation and must be encouraged through generously low rates of tax on incomes and profits has remained central to economic policy making by both Conservative and Labour administrations. Indeed, as we shall see, Labour governments after 1997 have continued the process of reducing the basic rate of income and corporation tax for just this reason.

There was also a general reduction in other forms of direct taxes such as inheritance and capital gains taxes. But Conservative governments after 1979 failed to achieve their greatest ambition, which was to seriously reduce the *overall* level of taxation. Indirect taxes, such as duties on petrol, alcohol and tobacco, continued to rise while taxes on incomes were falling.

The incentives were only the first element in the change in policy direction. More radical measures were soon to follow. Among them was a programme of privatisation.

Privatisation

The process of transferring industries from public ownership and state control to private ownership (i.e. from nationalised industries into public limited companies owned by private shareholders) was seen in the 1980s to incorporate four main advantages.

privatisation
During the 1980s and 1990s a large number of British industries which had been in public ownership and under state control (so-called nationalised industries) were sold off into the private sector. This process was known as privatisation. Prominent examples were the coal, telecommunications, steel, gas, electricity, water and railway industries.

First, it was expected that they would become more dynamic as their managers pursued higher profits to satisfy the shareholders and to further their own career interests. These incentives had been lacking when the industries had been state-run. Second, privatisation presented an opportunity for a wider range of the population to own shares, including the workers in the privatised industries themselves, thus giving them a vested interest in their economic success. Third, the sale of these industries would bring in much needed revenue to the government, which could use it to either to pay off some accumulated national debt or to finance higher public spending without having to raise taxes. By 1990 the sales of publicly owned assets had yielded £20 billion.

Above all, however, this disengagement of the state from economic life was very much at the heart of what has become known as 'Thatcherism'. Classical economics (also often described as neo-liberalism) assumed that state interference was nearly always negative in its effect. Margaret Thatcher considered herself to be a modern heir to that classical tradition.

The most celebrated privatisation was also the first – that of British Telecom in 1984. It was greeted with loud opposition from the Labour Party, but the public's imagination was caught by the prospect of owning shares in this huge,

growing industry and by the promise of cheaper phone calls as fresh investment was to pour into the new private enterprise. When the new shares began
to be traded freely on the Stock Exchange, their price rose sharply. The public were hooked and ready for more. The high point of national excitement
was reached when the gas supply industry was put up for sale. Thousands of
new shareholders were created in British Gas and the value of their shares rose
quickly. The privatisation of electricity supply and generation, water, coal, steel,
British Petroleum, Rolls Royce Engines and British Airways followed. Under
John Major possibly the most significant – and most controversial – of all the
privatisations took place when the railways were sold off in 1996.

As we shall see below, privatisation was not only a policy of the 1980s. It is a
process which continued into the twenty-first century. The Labour governments
after 1997 were converted to the benefits of privatisation and so one of the
most cherished principles of socialism – the common, public ownership of
the means of production – was finally abandoned. Until the credit crunch of
2007–8, that is.

Competition and liberalisation

The nationalised industries, apart from being state-controlled, were also
mostly monopolies. Serious competition was forbidden by law in such industries as coal, steel, electricity generation and supply, telephones, gas and
water supply. After privatisation, therefore, there remained the problem of how
to ensure that the industries remained competitive when they did not have to
contend with normal market forces. Two kinds of response were introduced.

The first was, simply, to introduce competition. Other private firms, including
foreign companies, were allowed to enter the market and compete on an equal
basis. In enterprises such as British Airways and public transport, competition
was perfectly natural. In others, such as water and railways, there is a natural
monopoly – it is simply not feasible to have several firms competing. In these
cases, regulatory authorities were created, such as OfWAT (water), OfGAS
and OfCOM (telecommunications). These authorities ensured that natural
monopolies would not take advantage of their position and would behave *as
if* there were competition. Eventually, too, methods were found to introduce
real competition, so that suppliers of gas, electricity and telephones are now
forced to compete. The regulatory bodies remain, however, to prevent an
collusion among firms to fix prices.

Second, in the existing private sector, steps were also taken to increase
competition. Most importantly, financial services were deregulated in 1986,
allowing greater genuine competition among banks, building societies and
other financial institutions. It became easier for new enterprises to enter these

markets. As a result there were more banks to choose from, a wider range of financial products became available and the terms offered to savers and borrowers improved substantially. Of course it was the deregulation of the financial sector which was to become so controversial after 2007. The near meltdown of the banking system and the financial crisis were seen as the result of the deregulation of the 1980s. At the same time the professions, such as law, opticians and dentists, were forced to open themselves up to new entrants, increasing competition.

Third, laws on competition were strengthened, with practices designed to keep new companies out of markets being outlawed. The European Union helped with this process by introducing its own competition rules throughout the community. The Office of Fair Trade was granted wide, powers to investigate and prevent anti-competitive behaviour among firms.

Fourth, many government services were opened up to competition by the private sector. This was known as Compulsory Competitive Tendering (CCT, later changed to 'Best Value'). CCT was a system whereby many services provided directly by local and central government should be tendered out to the best bid from the private sector. Thus, such services as parks and gardens maintenance, road repairs, prison services and public sector housing maintenance were all made competitive by introducing CCT.

Labour markets

Supply-side economics demands that wage levels should be free to rise and fall according to employment conditions. When unemployment rises, wages (at least in 'real' terms) should fall, and vice versa. The same applies to regional variations in economic activity and regional variations in wages. In the 1980s Conservative governments under Margaret Thatcher saw high and inflexible wage costs as perhaps the most difficult problem to overcome. Their perception of the problem was that organised labour, mainly in the form of trade unions, was simply too powerful. They therefore aimed to alter the balance of economic power between employers and employees.

The first solution was very much of Thatcher's own creation. She made it clear to workers' leaders that she believed that excessive wage demands simply led to rising unemployment. This was particularly true in economically depressed areas such as Merseyside, the North-East, central Scotland and the South-West of England. Unlike previous governments, however, she asserted that her governments would not take measures to combat unemployment. Unemployment was the price workers had to pay for excessive wage demands. In other words, she insisted that the cure for rising unemployment lay in the hands of the workers themselves. They needed to moderate their expectations of wage levels.

Second, her government abolished most of the wages councils after 1986. These councils, made up of union and employer representatives, operated in a variety of industries. One of their tasks was to set minimum wages. This naturally prevented wages falling when the economy was suffering and so wage flexibility was prevented. The government's view was that minimum wage levels in some industries were causing persistent regional unemployment. So their abolition struck a blow for flexible labour markets.

Third, levels of social security benefits, notably for the unemployed, were reduced in real terms. Over-generous social security was seen as a disincentive for people to seek work. In other words it meant that workers were reluctant to offer themselves for employment in lower-paid occupations. This method – of using a 'stick' to force people into low-paid work – was successful but was to become a major aspect of political conflict in the 1990s.

But the real battle to create more flexible and efficient labour markets was fought out when Margaret Thatcher decided she felt secure enough to challenge trade union power.

Trade unions – battles with government

There can be little doubt that the outcome of the conflict which occurred between the trade unions and the governments of the 1980s dramatically altered the economic and social landscape of the country. It was also to set the scene for the transformation which was to take place in the Labour Party after 1987. There were two strands to Thatcher's attack on trade union power. One was a generalised confrontation with their leadership. The other was a programme of legislation designed to curb their power.

Thatcher was fond of lecturing union leaders and workers in general about the realities of supply-side economics (as described above). She also looked for opportunities to set the forces of the state against those of organised labour. Many conflicts occurred, but two are worthy of note. The first involved the newspaper industry, where traditional unions were resisting the introduction of new technology. Printers' unions feared that the new printing methods would mean fewer jobs and that members of rival unions would be employed. Newspaper proprietors, such as Rupert Murdoch, responded by bringing in non-union labour which had the skills needed to work the new equipment. The traditional unions attempted to resist this, but the government backed Murdoch and newspaper owners like him, ordering the police to ensure that the new workers should be able to get to work against union picketing.

The other conflict was more traumatic. The state-controlled coal industry was suffering from competition from cheap coal imported from abroad. The miners' union, led by the radical socialist Arthur Scargill, campaigned for protection for the British industry. Margaret Thatcher, naturally supporting free competition, insisted that many pits would have to close. The miners went on strike, engaged in mass demonstrations and aggressive picketing to prevent non-unionised labour from breaking the strike. The police were heavily involved in controlling the demonstrations and picketing, while the courts were willing to convict miners' leaders of various public order offences. In the end the miners were defeated, the strike was broken and a programme of widespread pit closures was implemented with great hardship to workers and mining communities.

These two battles were symbolic of wider conflict. The fact that the government 'won' both battles meant that it was also liable to win the wider war against union power. But, to complete victory, legislation was also needed.

Trade unions – legislation

The story of legislation was as follows.

1980 The Employment Act forced unions to hold secret, democratic ballots in order to take industrial action (mainly strikes). It also introduced compulsory secret ballots for union leadership election. Before this Act union leaders were able to force reluctant workers to take industrial action even though they had never been democratically elected.

1982 The Employment Act made it more difficult for unions to enforce 'closed shops'. Closed shops were systems which allowed unions to control who was employed in an industry, and how many. Closed shops reduced free competition for jobs and tended to keep wages high by restricting the supply of labour. Most closed shops came to an end and so labour markets were more flexible.

1984 The Trade Union Act was the main legislation. Before the Act trade unions could not be sued by companies who were adversely affected by strike action. This gave unions legal immunity, a right they had jealously guarded for over fifty years. The Act meant that unions were more reluctant to take strike action for fear of incurring huge compensation awards against them from companies who had lost business. It certainly ended 'unofficial' strikes – action for which there had not been a democratic vote within the union.

1986 The Wages Act reduced the use of wages councils in setting minimum wages in some industries.

1988 The Employment Act gave protection for workers who wished to defy a call to industrial action. The rules for closed shops were further tightened and they virtually disappeared as a result. Trade unions were no longer allowed to use their funds for political campaigning.

1990 The Employment Act made it almost impossible for a union to call a strike for political reasons (e.g. in protest at government policy). Strikes had to be directly in the interests of the workers in the industry concerned.

1993 The Trade Union Reform and Employment Rights Act (John Major was by now prime minister) abolished the last remaining trades councils and gave workers the right to join any union of their choice, not just the main union in their industry.

This blizzard of legislation under Thatcher and Major had a number of effects. Among them were these:

- Union membership began to fall rapidly, especially when closed shops were abolished.
- Over-employment in many industries declined (causing some unemployment). With much of their control restored, employers were keen to reduce their wage costs by saving on labour. With weaker trade unions they were better able to do this.
- The incidence of strikes and other forms of industrial action fell dramatically. As a result, productivity in many industries rose.
- Trade unions lost funding as their membership rolls declined. This further reduced their power.
- The new legislation forced the Labour Party to re-evaluate its strong relationship with the trade unions.
- The Conservative Party could claim it had won its war against union power and had created more flexible labour markets.

A summary of the Thatcher reforms

- A more laissez-faire attitude to industry and employment. Free markets were allowed to make their own, natural adjustments.
- Control of inflation the first priority.
- Privatisation of many major industries.
- Little reliance on fiscal policy in favour of monetary measures to influence the economy.
- Reduction of trade union power and more flexible labour markets.
- Reduction in a range of direct taxes, replaced by higher indirect taxes.
- Reductions in many welfare benefits as an incentive to work.
- Stricter controls on monopoly power and encouragement for competition.

Labour's reaction to Thatcherism

The Labour Party's reaction can be divided into two phases: 1979–88 and 1988–97.

Internal conflict and a split 1979–88

There was fierce debate in the party concerning how to react. Put simply this was a left–right split. The left of the party, led, for example, by Michael Foot and Tony Benn, argued that the shift to the 'right' in British politics should be countered by a shift to the left within Labour. They therefore campaigned for a raft of socialist proposals such as:

- The re-nationalisation of the privatised industries and the further nationalisation of most major infrastructure companies.
- The restoration of full trade union powers.
- The restoration of a highly progressive tax system to redistribute wealth from rich to poor to a radical extent.
- An additional wealth tax on the very rich.
- Introduction of minimum wages in most industries.
- Restoration of generous welfare benefits.
- An extensive system of centralised state planning for industrial output.

These proposals formed the basis of two Labour election manifestos in 1983 and 1987, though the former was the more radical of the two. Labour was heavily defeated at both elections, adding strength to the arguments of the moderates in the party.

The moderate members had two reactions. Some, led by four leading members of the party including Roy Jenkins and Shirley Williams, formed a breakaway party, the Social Democrat Party (SDP), a moderate version of Labour. This party fought both the 1983 and 1987 elections in co-operation with the Liberal Party, wining nearly a quarter of the votes, but very few parliamentary seats. The SDP argued that many of the Thatcher reforms were positive and should be retained. Their main argument with Thatcher was that her policies, especially on tax and welfare, had created too much social and economic inequality.

Other moderates, such as Denis Healey, stayed in the party to try to defeat the left-wingers. Among the younger element among the moderates were Tony Blair, Gordon Brown, Peter Mandelson and Robin Cook, the architects of New Labour. Neil Kinnock become leader of the party in 1984 after the disastrous 1983 election defeat. In his leadership, which lasted until 1992, he first attempted to keep together the two wings of the party, but after 1988 he decided to start a process of radical reform of the Labour Party.

The creation of New Labour 1988–97

As we shall see below, three successive labour leaders – Neil Kinnock (1984–92), John Smith (1992–94) and Tony Blair (1994–2007) – created New

Labour, a considerably more moderate version of the old party. To a large extent they accepted the Thatcher reforms, for example proposing:

- Trade union power should not be restored.
- The privatisations should be retained.
- Direct taxes, especially on incomes and company profits, should remain relatively low.
- Economic management should be based largely on monetarism rather than fiscal control.

They remained opposed to some of the neo-liberal measures of Thatcher and Major, notably promising to reform the welfare benefits system and to introduce a national minimum wage. But most commentators are agreed that New Labour had become itself neo-liberal by inclination. We shall see below what happened when New Labour won government office in 1997.

NEW LABOUR AND THIRD WAY ECONOMICS 1997–2007

Background to New Labour

Most of the Thatcher reforms had been completed by the time John Major won an unexpected election victory for the Conservatives in 1992. But, despite the victory, all was far from well with the British economy. Britain was coming towards the end of serious recession which had been characterised by high inflation, rising unemployment, falling house prices and high interest rates. Furthermore the policy of fixing the exchange rate of sterling into a European system of exchange rates (the ill-fated European Exchange Rate mechanism or ERM) was proving problematic. Britain's trading position, despite the many successes of economic policy, was deteriorating. The British economy was simply not competitive enough, and as a result international speculators began to sell sterling, seeing it as a potentially weak currency. As a result Britain could not remain in the fixed, ERM system and humiliatingly was forced to leave it in September 1992 (a day known as 'Black Wednesday'). The Conservatives' record of economic competence was destroyed almost overnight. What was seen as a foolish attachment to the ERM had, critics argued, caused the recession to be worse than it needed to be.

In the next few years the Conservatives lost further credibility when the tax cuts they promised in 1992 failed to materialise. In fact taxes were rising, while, at the same time, the public services were deteriorating. In fact the economy did begin to pick up after 1993. The recession receded and Britain enjoyed an export-led recovery as the international value of sterling fell significantly in the mid-1990s, making British exports much cheaper. Inflation began to fall, unemployment subsided and the government was able gradually to reduce interest rates. The housing market also recovered.

Yet, whatever the evidence, the Conservative Party lost its economic reputation in this period, a position from which it was not to recover for over fifteen years. It was blamed for the recession of 1989–92, for poor management of exchange rates and a confused policy on taxation. The electorate soon forgot the boom years of the mid-1980s when Thatcher's neo-liberal policies seemed to be working well. New Labour, led by Tony Blair after 1994, therefore had an open goal to shoot at in the 1997 general election. It won a landslide victory.

Third Way economics

Labour's policies in 1997 were often described as 'Third Way', a middle path between the socialist policies of the Labour left, which had been discredited by the late 1980s, and the neo-liberal policies of Thatcher and Major. The fundamentals of the Third Way can be seen as follows.

Supply-side policies were supported. Like the Conservatives, New Labour understood that Britain needed to be competitive and, to be competitive, it needed flexible labour markets. Labour therefore largely followed Conservative labour market policies. The only major departure was the introduction of a minimum national wage.

The **social security system** was understood to be a disincentive to work and endeavour if benefits were too high and indiscriminate. But, rather than reducing benefits to create incentives, Third Way economics involved targeting benefits on those in most need and reforming the system so that these benefits became an incentive to seek work, rather than a disincentive.

Economic management should be largely non-interventionist. This had two strands. First, fiscal management was largely to be ignored. Like the neo-liberals, New Labour saw such intervention as counterproductive. Monetarism was, therefore, to be followed. But, rather than putting monetary levers into the hands of politicians, who might use them for short-term political advantage, New Labour was determined that they should be in the hands of independent bodies and subject to fixed rules. In other words monetary policy was to be taken out of the hands of politicians and effectively 'depoliticised'.

Like the neo-liberals, believers in the Third Way thought that **markets** should be as free as possible and competition should be protected and promoted.

Overall, it was the objective of the Third Way in economics to eliminate the excessive fluctuations which had afflicted the British economy since the 1960s. This was known as the end of **boom and bust.** By hopefully ridding Britain of its habitual tendency to inflation, by pursuing neo-liberal policies and responsible monetary management, Third Way supporters believed that this aim could be achieved.

We can now compare the Third Way economic policies of New Labour with the policies pursued by neo-liberal Conservatives in the previous eighteen years (Table 1.1). New Labour, not surprisingly, claims that Third Way policies are a significant departure from the policies of previous Conservative administrations. Many commentators, however, especially on the left of politics, argue that the Third Way represents confirmation that there developed a consensus on economic policy (i.e. the continuities considerably outweighed the differences) in Britain, based on neo-liberal ideas, which lasted from the mid-1990s to the onset of recession again in 2008.

Table 1.1   New Labour's Third Way and neo-liberal Conservatism

Continuities	Divergences
• Free market capitalism is the best way to create wealth and economic growth. • Measures to stimulate the 'supply side' of the economy are more effective than management of the 'demand side'. • Inflation is seen as the most serious barrier to economic progress and prosperity. • Excessively high levels of tax on personal incomes and company profits are a disincentive to work and enterprise and so should be avoided. • Both saw relatively weak trade unions as an essential feature of free, competitive labour markets.	• New Labour was more concerned about those on low incomes. Conservative see low wages as a natural aspect of free market capitalism, New Labour opposes very low wages and is willing to intervene to prevent them. • New Labour was content to depoliticise monetary policy while Conservatives wished to keep it under political control. • Conservatives have been more concerned to keep down the *overall* level of taxation in the economy. The Third Way believes that taxes are needed to maintain good-quality public services. • Labour sees Britain's economic future to be within the European single currency system while Conservatives are firmly opposed on the grounds that Britain would lose control over its own economic policy if it entered the eurozone. • The Conservatives have a general view that welfare benefits are a disincentive to work and employment. The Third Way belief is that benefits can be used to incentivise work.

LABOUR'S ECONOMIC MANAGEMENT 1997–2007

Monetary policy

As we have seen, New Labour followed the Conservative lead in concentrating on monetary methods of influencing economic activity. Gordon Brown, the Chancellor of the Exchequer, made two key decisions in 1997.

First, control over the key Bank of England interest rate was transferred from the government (albeit in open consultation with the Bank of England) to a new, independent **Monetary Policy Committee** (MPC). The committee, made up of a mixture of economists, bankers and business leaders, met once a month to set the interest rate. In so doing they published the reasons for their decision and other key economic data. The MPC had only one task – to control the level of inflation. A target corset of between 1.5–2.5 per cent was set (in January 2004 this corset was adjusted to 1–2 per cent) and it was expected that the committee would keep inflation between the floor and the ceiling. It had no other objectives. When inflation began to rise (or was threatening to rise in the near future) the committee would tend to raise interest rates to reduce credit and therefore spending. Conversely, as price rises began to abate or the signs were that future inflation would fall, rates would be reduced.

The purpose of the committee was twofold. First, it took decision making out of the hands of politicians who might have been tempted (and certainly had been in the past) to adjust interest rates for short-term political advantage rather than for the good of the economic health of the country. Second, it concentrated solely on inflation. This placed the control of prices at the centre of policy, with all other objectives becoming secondary.

As we shall see below, the MPC retained its independence until 2008, when the credit crunch threatened to overwhelm Western capitalism. In concert with the governments of other developed countries, the UK government was forced to order interest rate cuts, whatever the MPC might have preferred. It remains to be seen whether the MPC's independence will be restored in future.

The MPC was remarkably successful in its single objective. Between 1997 and 2006 UK inflation remained between 1.3 per cent and 3.2 per cent and was virtually always within the target corset. Historically these rates were very low and compared favourably with other developed economies. For the most part, too, it was able to do this without raising interest rates excessively. From a peak of 7.5 per cent in July 1998, the trend in interest rates has been generally downwards, again comparing favourably with the USA and the rest of Europe. However, a remarkable rise in the international prices of oil, food, metals and other commodities (outside UK control) resulted in rises in inflation above the target and there was little the MPC could do to stop it without raising interest rates to prohibitive levels. This, together with the severity of the post-2008 recession, demonstrated the limitations of the MPC. It seemed to have been effective in periods of economic growth and stable world trading conditions, but could not cope with world inflation and recession.

Gordon Brown's second key decision was that he would subject himself to what he called the **Golden Rule** (officially known as the 'Code for Fiscal Stability'). The Golden Rule stated that the government would not borrow money in order to finance general expenditure *over the course of the economic cycle*. Borrowing to finance investment (for example in permanent assets such as schools, hospitals or roads) was permissible. This effectively meant that over a period of about four years (an economic cycle) the government should 'balance its books'. A budget deficit in some years would have to be balanced by surpluses in others. At the same time the size of the National Debt (the country's total accumulated debt) was to be kept within 40 per cent of the annual Gross Domestic Product (GDP – the annual value of all output of goods and services within the UK).

In general terms the Golden Rule was a self-imposed control on government finance. What Brown called 'prudent' public finance was a key element in monetarist policy. To demonstrate how serious he was, Brown resisted the temptation to raise public expenditure during his first three years in power and paid back large portions of the National Debt. Under the rules, this allowed him to spend much more freely on public services during the following years. The early surpluses were balanced by later deficits.

Two factors weakened Brown's obedience to his own rules. One was the overwhelming need to spend lavishly on improving services, notably health and education. Conservatives claimed, after 2001, that he was beginning to break his own rules, largely by redefining the 'economic cycle'. But far more seriously, the credit crunch and recession from 2007 onwards forced the government to increase public expenditure dramatically, first to bail out the banking system and then to stimulate the economy in the recession which followed. Thus, after 2007, the Golden Rule had certainly become a thing of the past. Like the independence of the Monetary Policy Committee, it remains to be seen whether it will be revived in the future.

Fiscal policy

There had been very little use of fiscal policy in the years between 1979 and 1997. Labour's Chancellor followed this trend. His golden rule effectively prevented him from using fiscal measures – the combination of taxation and public expenditure – to influence the economy. Furthermore Brown was constrained to some extent by the rules operating in the European Union's eurozone. Though Britain was not in the eurozone Brown sought to follow the rules so that, if Britain did enter the single currency system, it would already be obeying the fiscal rules.

Fortunately for the government Britain experienced steady growth until 2007 so there was no need to use fiscal policy to expand the economy. Similarly the absence of serious inflation meant that deflationary measures were not needed. The monetary measures used by the MPC proved quite sufficient to maintain control.

All this changed, as we shall see below, when economic recession arrived in 2008. In that year growth in the UK, along with virtually all developed economies, turned negative and unemployment and business closures began to grow alarmingly. Monetary controls were simply inadequate, even though interest rates were reduced to extremely low levels. There was, therefore, a return to the use of fiscal stimuli. These are described below.

Taxation

New Labour's policies on taxation were similar to those of the Conservatives. Brown gradually reduced both income tax and company taxation, though these were partly offset by rises in national insurance payments (paid by those in work and their employers). Nevertheless the tax burden in the UK did rise under Gordon Brown and Tony Blair. Thus Labour's reputation for being a 'high tax party' was partly restored.

Brown had reduced tax from 41.2 per cent of GDP in 1996 (under John Major) to 38.8 per cent in 1999, thus gaining a reputation has an 'Iron Chancellor', determined to show his neo-liberal credentials. Since then, however, the incidence of taxation in the UK has crept up again towards 42 per cent by 2008.

A more detailed analysis of tax policy demonstrates certain principles.

First, Labour has not effected any major redistribution of income through the tax system.

Second, there is a preference for indirect rather than direct taxes (taxes on expenditure rather than on incomes). Thus Labour under Blair and Brown gradually reduced income tax, with the standard rate falling to 20 per cent by 2008 (having inherited a standard rate of 25 per cent in 1997). A similar reduction on business taxation has taken place. Inheritance tax was significantly cut (to legacies above £600,000 only). On the other hand a number of other taxes have been increased, notably on fuel, car purchases, private pensions and local authority services (council tax). At the same time there have been rises in national insurance payments for employees and employers.

The incidence of many so-called 'stealth taxes' is a feature which Conservatives and Liberal Democrats have opposed. They argue that many 'headline' cuts in direct tax under Labour since 1997 have disguised rises in other, less obvious forms of tax. The argument of Labour governments has been that reductions in income and company taxes have created greater incentives. The so-called 'stealth taxes' were needed to retain a good level of government revenue.

Third, Labour has tended to keep taxation close to 40 per cent of GDP over the period since 1997. Though taxation crept up in 2006–7, Labour remained anxious to confine to history its reputation as a high tax party.

Until 2007 Gordon Brown had been reducing taxation for poor families – a policy to keep people out of a 'poverty trap' and to relieve poverty. Indeed in 1997 a band of 10 per cent, instead of 25 per cent, was introduced for low income levels. It was, therefore, a huge surprise when Brown abolished this tax band, costing poor families about £200 per annum. He did reduce the standard rate of tax from 22 per cent to 20 per cent at the same time, but the policy reversed the process of helping poor families. Brown was forced ultimately to admit he had made an error in abolishing the 10 per cent band and was forced to introduce a compensation package for low-income families.

These principles and policies were pushed into the background when recession struck in 2008. This change is described below.

Labour markets

New Labour accepted the need for flexible labour markets and restraint on union wage demands, and refused to restore the powers of unions, which had been severely reduced by Margaret Thatcher. Though the rights of *individual workers* were greatly strengthened, mainly by adoption of the the EU Social Chapter, unions remained weak.

The most dramatic initiative was the introduction of a national minimum wage in 1997. Opponents of the minimum wage claimed it would make employment too expensive in low-paid jobs and that unemployment would therefore result as many firms would reduce their workforce to pay for the higher wages. This did not occur, however. Employment held up and few businesses were unable to pay the higher minimum. Labour therefore succeeded in compensating workers for weak trade unions without causing unemployment.

The EU Social Chapter also extended rights to company pensions, sick pay, holiday entitlement and protection from unnecessary dismissal. Here again the new measures showed few signs of creating inflexibility in labour markets. The Conservative party claimed otherwise, but there was no evidence that the Social Chapter and minimum wage were causing problems for employers. The government was helped, however, by the inflow of migrant workers when ten new members of the EU, mostly in Eastern Europe, gained access rights to UK labour markets. The extended work force increased competition for jobs and so prevented wages from falling too low and maintained good productivity levels.

Thus, the UK's traditional problem of excessively high wage levels and low worker productivity seemed to be receding. But it still remains true that trade unions play a relatively limited role in influence over labour markets.

Competition policy

In 1999 the Office of Fair Trading was further strengthened, allowing it to investigate a wide range of anti-competition policies being operated by large companies. But the main thrust of this policy lay in the provision of public services.

Post-1997 Labour governments have been enthusiastic about subjecting public services to competition between the public and private sectors. In particular Private Finance Initiatives (PFIs) were encouraged and expanded. Here private sector companies were invited to compete (often with central and local government set-ups) for contracts to build and maintain assets in the public sector. These included schools, hospitals, prisons, roads and state-owned subsidised housing. The policy was designed to give better value for money, to promote competition within the private sector and to ensure quality.

New Labour has also promoted greater competition among public utility companies. Such enterprises as gas and electricity supply, telecommunications and energy production have traditionally been controlled by monopoly suppliers. So-called liberalisation policy, however, has forced companies in these fields to offer consumers a choice of supplier. Even parts of the railway network, very much a natural monopoly, are now subject to some competition. In co-operation with international organisations, there has also been greater competition introduced in air transport.

In summary, therefore, New Labour has proved to be even more active in the promotion of competition than its neo-liberal political opponents, mainly the Conservative Party.

POVERTY REDUCTION

The elimination of poverty, especially child poverty, in the UK has been a major objective of New Labour since 1997. We will examine the question of poverty in more detail below, in the section on welfare, but the issue of poverty has also had economic implications.

The main economic policies which have had some (it is debatable how much) impact on poverty have been:

- The control of unemployment and the creation of more jobs in the economy.
- The introduction of a low 10 per cent tax band as an anti poverty measure, though, as we have seen, it was abolished in 2007–8.
- A system of tax credits introduced to help poor families. Tax credits are effectively income subsidies, given by the tax authorities to a number of categories of claimants. These include poor pensioners, working single parents, workers who are willing to accept low wages and those who are seeking work actively. Such tax credits are especially targeted at families with young children. Tax credits are designed to reduce the need for excessively high welfare benefits.
- The national minimum wage, introduced in 1997, which had a significant impact on sections of the workforce earning very low wages.

THE IMPACT OF THE POST-2007 ECONOMIC CRISIS

The origins of the crisis

There are two perspectives to be brought to the causes of the economic problems which engulfed most of the world after 2007. One is a long-term view, that is: what were the fundamental, structural causes of the crisis? This also asks whether there have been any weaknesses or contradictions within the world's capitalist system which made such a situation inevitable. This is not considered here as it is beyond the scope of this book, while it is also too early to undertake any meaningful analysis. That said, some initial conclusions can be drawn and are proposed below. When the economic crisis has finally unravelled it will be possible to undertake more measured considerations. The second perspective is inevitably short-term. This takes the form of a narrative of events demonstrating how the crisis developed and the way in which one problem led to another. At the same time we can examine how governments reacted to each successive development. The account which is offered here is largely based on this second kind of perspective. The main events of the growing recession are described in the next section.

The collapse of the US sub-prime market

During the early years of the twenty-first century American banks and other lenders had increasingly advanced mortgage loans to home buyers who had, in the past, been considered unsuitable for such loans. This was known as the 'sub-prime market'. To some extent they had been encouraged to do so by the US government as a means of helping members of the poorer sections of the community to purchase a home. These were high-risk loans mainly on the basis that the borrowers had low incomes and insecure employment. Some also had poor credit records and already had large debts, for example on credit cards. Furthermore, the mortgage loans were based on valuations of properties which had been over-inflated by a short-term property price boom.

Because sub-prime loans were high-risk – carrying the danger that the borrowers would default on the loan, the property would have to be repossessed and sold to pay off the loan, but with no guarantee that enough money would be raised from the compulsory sale to cover the initial loan – the big banks were reluctant to hold these so-called 'toxic debts'. Many of the sub-prime loans were, therefore, sold off to secondary financial institutions who were wiling to take the risk. The reward was that the interest rates on high-risk loans were relatively high. So they were high-risk, high-return loans. All was well as long as enough of the payments were being made by borrowers and as long as property prices held up in the USA.

In 2007 the sub-prime market began to collapse. House prices began to fall and increasing numbers of sub-prime borrowers were defaulting on their mortgage loans. The collapse gathered momentum until American banks began to fail. They failed because the value of their assets (represented by the loans they owned) was falling and could not meet their liabilities (the deposits of their customers). Put simply, if the banks' customers asked to reclaim their bank deposits, the banks would not have the money to cover them. When this occurs (as it had done in 1929 and in Japan in the early 1990s), there is a danger of panic setting in and the whole financial structure falls into danger. Sadly, a number of British and European financial institutions had purchased some of the loans or had borrowed heavily from American institutions which were now collapsing. One of these was the Newcastle-based bank Northern Rock. The crisis was quickly named as a *credit crunch*.

Northern Rock

In the summer of 2007 it was revealed by the BBC that the Northern Rock bank had asked the government for funds to meet its liabilities, which had been hugely degraded by the collapse of the American sub-prime market. The effect was catastrophic. Panic set in among Northern Rock depositors who feared their money was in danger. Long queues outside Northern Rock branches created an air of fear and all bank depositors began to fear for their savings. The government had to act quickly. Its first reaction was to offer a guarantee of up to £35,000 per person, reassuring Northern Rock depositors that their money was safe. This halted the immediate problem, but long-term solutions were needed as it became apparent that Northern Rock could not survive as a bank. The British government therefore took the dramatic decision to nationalise Northern Rock. It became a publicly owned bank. The depositors were given a full guarantee of the safety of their deposits.

While the Northern Rock crisis was unfolding, similar events were occurring in the USA and parts of mainland Europe, with banks failing or having to be supported by governments. Great American financial institutions such as Bear Sterns, Lehman Brothers and Citibank all failed and were closed down and sold off in sections to other banks. It was now becoming apparent that events unfolding in the USA would have major repercussions all over the world. In other words it was clear that financial markets were globally connected to a much greater extent than had been appreciated.

The British banking crisis

Though Northern Rock was saved, it was increasingly apparent that many British banks and building societies were also in financial difficulties. The causes are complex, but, put simply, too many banks had been lending money (mostly in the form of mortgages) which was high-risk. Furthermore they had been lending more money than could be covered by the value of the deposits which they were holding on behalf of customers. Some banks had also bought loans from the sub-prime market in the USA and these were proving to be almost worthless. Such leading institutions as HBOS (Halifax Bank of Scotland), RBS (Royal Bank of Scotland including the NatWest Bank), Alliance and Leicester and Bradford and Bingley were all seen to be in danger. The British government's reaction to these problems was to use a variety of devices. Among them were these:

- The government guaranteed that no depositors would lose their money if a British-owned bank were to fail.
- The government purchased parts of some banks by buying shares and so adding to the capital balances of the banks (in other words British taxpayers became major shareholders in some banks). The most striking example was RBS, 60 per cent of which became publicly owned. Where the government purchased shares, it required that the banks should behave in a responsible manner in the future. In most cases government-appointed directors were appointed as internal regulators.
- The government arranged for some stronger banks to take over weaker banks. In particular HBOS was taken over by Lloyds-TSB, probably the soundest of the major British banks. The failed Bradford and Bingley Building Society, together with the shaky Alliance and Leicester Bank, was brought into the safe Spanish Santander group (which already owned the Abbey

bank). Thus the banking structure was consolidated around a smaller number of strong institutions.

- The government flooded the banking system with liquidity. This effectively meant that, if any bank were in need of short-term funds to meet the demands of customers, the Bank of England would make funds available. These were, in practice, short-tem loans to the banking system whenever needed.

Yet despite all this activity by the British government (and by governments in the EU, the USA, Japan and other developed countries), the banking system remained weak.

The decline of the inter-bank market

Though, by the summer of 2008, the immediate dangers to the banking system had been averted, there remained a major problem. It was normal practice for the major banks to lend money to each other on a short-term basis. This is necessary as banks prefer to lend as much money to customers as they possibly can, as this is the principal way in which they make profits. Since banks are never certain how much money they will collect and retain in the form of customers' deposits, they sometimes run temporarily short of funds to meet the demands of customers who need cash. The banks therefore agree to lend to each other so that they can continue to operate effectively. This inter-bank market is vital as it enables banks to lend money to customers (especially business customers) without fear of running out of funds. In 2008, however, the inter-bank market was failing.

The reason for this failure was, simply, that banks did not trust each other any more. So many were in fragile circumstances that there was no guarantee that such short-term loans would be paid back. The result was twofold. First, the interest rates demanded by banks lending to each other became prohibitively high. Second, very few funds were made available at all. The results of this failure had wide consequences. Three immediate effects were felt. First, banks became reluctant to grant mortgages to all but the safest borrowers. As we shall see below, this had a disastrous effect on the housing market. Second, businesses found it difficult to borrow money from banks to fund investment or to deal with variations in their cash flows. Third, consumers found loans becoming scarce and expensive. This particularly adversely affected the markets for more expensive goods, such as cars, kitchen equipment and electrical goods. As we shall see below, this was one of the key links between the financial crisis and the wider economic recession.

The reaction of the British and other governments was to pour more liquidity into the banking system to keep the flow of funds moving. There was then a concerted reduction in world central bank interest rates in the autumn of 2008.

However, the inter-bank bank market failed to react positively. Despite exhortations from governments, the banks refused to lend to each other in significant quantities.

The collapse of the British housing market

As we have seen above, the severe contraction in bank lending of all kinds had a serious effect on the housing market. This occurred in all developed countries, but was especially important for Britain and the USA where home ownership is more common and house prices are relatively high. Mortgages became expensive and difficult to obtain and were offered only to the soundest of borrowers. Demand for housing fell dramatically and, as the law of economics clearly dictated, that led to falls in house prices lasting into 2009.

While falling house prices were good news for home purchasers, especially lower-income first-time buyers, the fall had a negative impact on the wider economy. This is traced further below.

Implications of the banking crisis for economic policy

It remains relatively early in the banking crisis and economic recession to draw firm conclusions about British economic policy making. However, a number of initial lessons can be drawn out. Among them are these.

First, the deregulation of the financial system, which was largely developed in the mid-1980s, had led to a number of problems. In effect the independent regulatory authorities – mainly the Bank of England, and the Financial Services Authority (FSA) – operated a very light control over the way banks operated. Credit became increasingly easy to give and receive. New financial institutions found it easy to set up in business and were allowed to operate in ways which involved high risks. It was therefore clear that regulation would have to be more thorough in the future.

Second, questions were increasingly being asked whether deregulation had gone too far. The implication of this analysis included a need in the future for governments to operate *legal* controls over credit, to prevent high-risk financial businesses from establishing themselves and possibly to eliminate such practices as the selling of mortgages from one bank to another, which tends to disguise the true risks involved in such markets.

Third, the Bank of England and its offshoot, the Monetary Policy Committee, had been granted 'operational independence' in 1997 by the incoming Labour government. In effect this gave them control over interest rates without any political interference. In times of sound economic growth, this had been remarkably successful. However, the avalanche of problems which appeared in 2007 demonstrated that the powers of the Bank of England were too puny to cope with the crisis. Effectively, therefore, from 2007 onwards, the government exercised control over the monetary operations of the Bank of England. In particular the setting of interest rates effectively was passed back to the Treasury and therefore government ministers.

Fourth, faced with the need to provide liquidity for the banking system and to purchase bank shareholdings, the government's determination to control its own borrowing (i.e. the public sector deficit) had to be relaxed. In other words, in order to lend money to banks, the government needed to borrow money from taxpayers, present and future. As we shall see, the growing economic recession accelerated this process markedly.

Table 1.2   The credit crunch – a chronology of key events

Period	UK	USA	Rest of Europe
2006–7		House prices decline sharply	
Summer 2007		Collapse of 'sub-prime market'	
September 2007	Northern Rock bank failed and was financially supported by the Bank of England. Customer deposits guaranteed by the government		
February 2008	Northern Rock bank nationalised		
March 2008		Two largest mortgage providers, Fannie Mae and Freddie Mac, fail and are taken over by the US government	
		Bear Sterns (USA's fifth largest bank) fails and is sold to J. P. Morgan Chase	
July 2008	Oil prices peak at £145 per barrel	Oil prices peak at £145 per barrel	Oil prices peak at £145 per barrel

Table 1.2 *(countined)*

Period	UK	USA	Rest of Europe
August 2008	US, UK and European banks inject $90 billion into banking systems	US, UK and European banks inject $90 billion into banking systems	US, UK and European banks inject $90 billion into banking systems
September 2008	HBOS (Halifax–Bank of Scotland) fails and government brokers a takeover by Lloyds-TSB	Lehman Brothers merchant bank fails and closes USA's fourth largest bank, Wachovia, fails and is taken over by Citibank	Germany's second biggest bank, Hypo Real Estate, collapses and is rescued by government Giant Belgian-Dutch bank, Fortis, fails
October 2008	All central banks of major economies agree a half percent cut in interest rates Government pumps £400 of liquidity into the banking system European Summit agrees a concerted rescue programme for banks and for growing economic recession Government takes 60 per cent (later increased to 70 per cent) of shares of RBS (Royal Bank of Scotland–NatWest) into public ownership	All central banks of major economies agree a half percent cut in interest rates President and Congress agree a $700 billion rescue package for the ailing economy	All central banks of major economies agree a half percent cut in interest rates European Summit agrees a concerted rescue programme for banks and for growing economic recession German Government pumps €500 million into its banking system All three major Icelandic banks fail, threatening large deposits from European investors

Table 1.2   (*countined*)

Period	UK	USA	Rest of Europe
November 2008	Government announces a package of £20 million tax cuts to stimulate the declining economy		
December 2008		Federal reserve cuts interest rate to zero	Eurozone interest rate cut to 2.5 per cent
January 2009	Bank of England cuts interest rate to 1.5 per cent Government announces it has taken a 43 per cent stake in the merged HBOS/LloydsTSB bank Government announces plans for direct subsidies to industry to create new jobs Government announces a £20 billion loan guarantee scheme for small and medium-sized firms £50 billion made available for the government to invest in ailing private firms A government guarantee scheme announced for banks, insuring them against losses incurred from lending to bad debtors	Announcement that unemployment has reached a 16-year high at 7.2 per cent New President Obama announces a major economic reflation package	Spain announces it is in deep recession and 3 million are unemployed Germany also announces it is in recession

Table 1.2   *(countined)*

Period	UK	USA	Rest of Europe
March/ April 2009	Bank of England announces it will start 'quantitative easing', effectively pumping new money into the economy Alistair Darling's budget signals some tax increases, notably a new 50 per cent rate for earnings over £150,000, but also a number of measures to stimulate the economy including subsidies to the motor industry		The European Central Bank follows Britain's lead in injecting a further €50 billion into the eurozone economy through the banking system
November 2009	Government announces that two banks – Northern Rock and Lloyds-HBOS – will be split into smaller units The Bank of England introduces a further quantitative easing of £25 billion British housing market begins to recover Stocks in London have risen by over 20 per cent from the low point in 2008	USA comes out of recession though unemployment is still rising	EU comes out of recession though not Spain and the UK

From credit crunch to economic recession

The term 'recession' strictly means that a country's economy has experienced negative growth (that is a fall in its output of goods and services) for two quarters; in other words for six months. But this strict definition simply expresses a broader idea that an economy is experiencing decline for a substantial period of time. By the beginning of 2009 virtually all the developed economies in the world were in recession. Even the rapidly expanding economies of developing countries such as India and China were growing at a much slower rate than before.

The causes of any recession are complex, but the recession which began in 2008 was certainly directly linked to the credit crunch which preceded it. There were four main linkages between the financial crisis and the recession:

- The banks severely reduced their lending. This meant that businesses suffered and began to fail because so little credit was available. It also restricted credit available to consumers, who therefore spent less, adversely affecting consumer industries.
- The collapse in house prices reduced consumer confidence and meant that there was less value in houses, which were often used as security against loans. Thus, here again, consumer spending fell rapidly.
- The general uncertainty about the banking system further reduced consumer confidence as people became uncertain that their savings were safe.
- As this was a world recession, there was a decline in world trade generally which affected all exporting nations.

One other set of factors can be identified. These were only indirectly affected by the credit crunch. This was the rise in the price of energy, especially oil, basic commodities and food during most of 2008. The increasing costs experienced by businesses and consumers further depressed economic activity. Though these world prices had fallen back by the end of 2008, the after effects were long-lasting.

The reaction of the British government to the recession

While various countries adopted their own anti-recession measures, we will concentrate here on the British circumstances. It is worth reminding ourselves of the bases of policy *before* the crisis. These included the following.

- Policy was mainly directed towards the control of inflation.
- Governments operated a policy of fiscal 'prudence'. That is, there was a reluctance to allow the public finances to fall into excessive debt.
- The main instrument of economic policy was variation in interest rates. These were independently controlled by the non-political Monetary Policy Committee of the Bank of England.
- Free markets and competition were seen as essential to maintain efficiency and competitiveness. This meant that government rarely intervened in the operation of such free markets.
- A level of general taxation representing approximately 40 per cent of the National Income was the appropriate level. Taxes on companies and personal incomes should be kept as low as possible within constraint of the 40 per cent overall level. 'Excessively' high levels of tax on the very rich were to be avoided as they were seen as wealth creators who attract inward investment to the UK.

These principles had served Britain well since Labour took power in 1997. There had been steady growth, better than most of the rest of the developed world, with low inflation, little unemployment and low interest rates. House prices had risen steadily over the period, home ownership expanded and the country attracted healthy levels of inward investment from abroad. But the crisis which emerged in 2007–8 removed all these certainties and changed the economic landscape drastically.

As we shall see, most of the policies which had been successfully pursued since 1997 (and to some extent before, under the Conservatives) had to be re-examined and, in some cases abandoned.

The main features which characterised the recession in the UK were as follows:

- From mid-2008 unemployment began to rise alarmingly. Estimates for 2009 varied between figures of two million and three million.
- Business failures increased. Some 'household names' such as Woolworths and MFI furniture stores went out of business.
- Consumer confidence sagged and retail sales suffered, with many retailers following Woolworths out of existence.
- House prices continued to fall. Estimates for the fall in house prices during 2008 varied from 15 per cent to 20 per cent. House sales declined and a number of large building companies went out of existence. Further falls were forecast for 2009, although by the end of 2009 house prices were beginning to rise, albeit at different rates in different parts of the country. There was also a steady rise in the number of repossessions – where defaulting borrowers were forced to sell their homes to pay off debt.
- Credit continued to be difficult to obtain, for mortgages as well as for general borrowing to fund consumption.
- The value of the pound sterling fell dramatically. Against the US dollar, the pound fell from a high of $2 in the summer of 2008 to $1.46 at the end of the year. Against the Euro, the pound stood at €1.04 at the end of 2008, from a high of €1.42.
- Though the fall in the external value of sterling made British exports considerably cheaper, the world recession made exporting problematic.
- The value of shares on the London Stock Exchange fell by 31 per cent during 2008. This was not a direct economic problem, but caused a large fall in the value of corporate and private pension funds (pension funds usually invest heavily in company shares). This also adversely affected consumer confidence. At the same time many people's savings were declining in value if held in the form of shares.
- The necessary cuts in interest rates during 2008 reduced the incomes of those who rely on interest on savings as part of their income (often the elderly). This again had an adverse effect on consumer spending.
- Nevertheless, the end of 2009 saw positive signs that the UK was about to follow the USA and the rest of Europe out of recession.

The immediate impact on UK government economic policy making

The immediate responses of the British and other governments to the credit crunch and economic recession which followed after 2007 can be seen as fire-fighting actions, necessary measures to try to prevent economic disaster. However, these events were of a different character to previous economic downturns in the early 1980s or the late 1980s and the early 1990s. They raised serious questions about the nature of the world economic structure, how the major economies of the world were interconnected and the relationship between finance and the wider economy. In some quarters the very basis of capitalism was being examined closely, including the morality behind the actions of many of the players involved. Two overall questions had, therefore, to be asked. The first was how to put in place long-term remedies to prevent similar events happening again. The second was whether the very basis of modern capitalism should be reformed. The possible remedies included these:

- To exercise much tighter controls over the international banking system. This would ensure that banks behave responsibly, only lend on a solid basis and curb their uncontrolled pursuit of profit in favour of providing long-term economic stability.

- Relatedly, to establish more *international* controls over finance. It is clear that actions by individual governments are increasingly futile in the face of globalization.

- To encourage more saving. Savings had, by 2007, fallen to extremely low levels, especially in the UK. Savings provide funds which the banks can use to channel funds for investment. Without high levels of saving, lending for investment is inevitably more speculative.

- To encourage a more responsible attitude to borrowing among the general public.

- To stimulate new house building. The volatility of the housing market has presented a major problem, so a programme of large-scale house building would help to dampen down fluctuations in property prices.

> **economic globalisation**
> A tendency for markets to become global, that is to be influenced by global rather than merely national forces. The most prominent examples of industries which are affected by global forces are finance, services, commodities, energy and currencies. In these and similar cases purchasers and sellers operate on a global scale. A key implication is that economic regulation must also therefore be global in nature as such markets are out of the control of national governments.

- To restore responsibility in public finances. It is a matter of political controversy whether the UK government had acted irresponsibly during the boom years after the mid-1990s. Conservatives believe that excessive government borrowing over the period meant that there was insufficient public funding available to ride out the storm. Conservatives also argue that Labour ministers had failed to curb excessive private debt and paid too little attention to saving. Their remedies would, therefore, include reform of the public finances and greater incentives for saving. Labour disputes this analysis, claiming that it had been prudent with the public finances over the medium term and that the recession had its origins elsewhere.

- To promote growth in the economy. Above all the Labour and Liberal Democrat parties have argued that the short- and medium-term remedies should include so-called *fiscal stimulus*. This means returning to the traditional solution to economic recession of increasing government expenditure, reducing taxation, supporting some sectors of the economy and adding to social security benefits to encourage spending. This inevitably means greater borrowing by government (and thus a charge on future taxpayers), but it is seen as a price worth paying for economic recovery. Conservatives remain considerably more suspicious of such fiscal measures, preferring to support a more responsible attitude to public finance involving reduced public expenditure to pay for tax cuts.

The fall in the value of the pound sterling during the second half of 2008 presents few policy implications. First, it has to be said that the UK government has little power to do anything about it. Second, in many ways, it benefits the British economy by making exports cheaper and imports more expensive, thus boosting many British firms. Normally a fall in the value of the currency creates inflationary pressure as the country is forced to pay higher sterling prices for imports which it cannot avoid (food and energy, for example). In the case of the 2008–9 recession, however, inflation is not a problem for the UK as it has been characterised by falling inflation. Indeed the spectre of *deflation* – falling prices – is almost as feared as inflation as it can cause a very severe businesss downturn, as Japan discovered in the early 1990s recession. Nevertheless the volatile nature of currency markets (the US dollar, for example, became very unstable) is a concern which may need longer-term remedies.

Long-term implications of the credit crunch and recession

Having looked at the shorter-term implications of the recession, we may speculate about much longer-term issues. It remains to be seen, however, whether policy makers will address them. To some extent they concern political ideology rather than short-term governing matters. Nevertheless, we can consider some of these fundamental implications.

There are questions to be asked about the very nature of capitalism. Some commentators have suggested that modern capitalism is driven by greed and that this was the basic cause of the crisis. Lured by the prospect of ever increasing returns, the managers of financial institutions were drawn into engaging in ever more speculative and risky ventures. The far left thinkers question, therefore, the whole basis of capitalism and would replace it with various forms of common ownership of the means of production. More moderate thinkers have argued that capitalism needs to be subject to much greater controls, largely by curbing the availability of excessive profits which are the result of purely speculative activity (implying that those who create *real* wealth might be allowed to retain greater rewards).

It is very clear that capitalism is now highly globalised. This was already known, of course, but its extent had perhaps been underemphasised. Since capitalism is fully international, it follows that financial institutions will also have to be international. Thought will certainly therefore be given to their creation in the future. Such institutions would need to include a financial regulatory authority and possibly a system for regulating the exchange rates of various currencies to create a stable basis for international trade.

The international banking system may need complete reform. Some have even suggested a system of national or even international ownership of banks in order to ensure that funds flow freely into investment and business activity generally. This would also protect and guarantee the savings held by individuals and organisations in financial institutions which proved to be so fragile during the credit crunch.

On a more general level the question should be asked whether the age of 'neo-liberalism' is over. The neo-liberals, who dominated economic policy making theory from the 1980s onwards in the UK and USA, insisted that markets, including financial markets, should be as free as possible. Government intervention was seen as counterproductive, and free market, largely uncontrolled capitalism, was considered the way to future, unlimited prosperity. With the collapse of the Western banking system and the major recession following it, it became apparent to many that neo-liberalism had been carried too far and that a more interventionist approach was needed. If capitalism is to survive, it is now increasingly argued, it cannot be relied upon to regulate itself through the 'discipline' of free competition. Governments, at an international level, may have to take a considerably more active role in management at both macro- and micro-economic levels.

In terms of British government and politics it is still not clear whether these fundamental issues will become a serious aspect of political debate. This question may well depend upon how deep and critical the world recession becomes.

Party politics and the 2008–9 recession

For much of the crisis, there was a tense truce between the main parties. While the Labour government under Gordon Brown and Chancellor Alistair Darling (and the background presence of Lord Mandelson, surprisingly brought back into cabinet as Industry Secretary) fought to save the banking system, the other main parties mostly gave qualified support. By the end of 2008, however, consensus had broken down again. Essentially the party positions on how to deal with the recession and its aftermath were as follows.

Conservatives are naturally suspicious of too much government interference. They therefore opposed most proposals to intervene directly in attempts to save major businesses. They also came to the conclusion that the fiscal stimulus given to the economy during 2009 was excessive. It led to far too high a level of public debt which would result in much higher taxes in the future, when the debt would have to be paid off. Their preference was to reduce public expenditure in order to prevent too much debt and to allow for tax cuts in the future. A new and radical policy initiative was also unveiled. This was a plan to reduce taxes for the poorer sections of the community so as to boost consumer spending and, at the same time, create more social justice. Normally seen as the 'friend' of big business, the Conservative leadership also proposed measures to curb the excessive rewards being offered to high earners in the financial sector. Despite their dislike of government intervention, they also proposed much stronger regulation of the banking system.

Liberal Democrats claimed the moral high ground. Their financial spokesman, Vincent Cable, had foreseen the disastrous effects of the collapse of the American sub-prime market and had campaigned for earlier intervention. When the crisis unfolded they were the most interventionist of the main parties, proposing some bank nationalisations even before the government introduced them in the autumn of 2008. They largely supported the fiscal stimulus of the economy, but proposed that there should be higher taxes on the wealthy and significant tax reductions for the poor. Like the Conservatives they wished to combine rescue measures with the introduction of fairer taxes. But the Liberal Democrats were more radical than either of the two parties on the issue of taxation. Liberal Democrats also supported intervention to save major businesses such as the ailing Jaguar–Land Rover company.

Labour were, of course, in government. We therefore have to consider the attitude of the wider party as well as the government which was having to deal with the crisis. Certainly those on the left of the party took a similar view to the Liberal Democrats. They wished to extend bank nationalisation, intervention to save major failing companies and increases in taxes on the rich to pay for government economic intervention. Most of the tax cuts and expenditure rises should be directed, they argued, at the poorer sections of the community, notably old age pensioners and working families with children.

Not surprisingly the government took a more moderate view. It relied very heavily on so-called *Keynesian* policies (named after John Maynard Keynes, the economist who had, in the 1930s, proposed such fiscal intervention to deal with the Great Depression of that decade). Essentially this meant that Britain should 'borrow its way out of recession'. By raising public expenditure and cutting taxes they hoped to boost the economy so that it would come out of recession as quickly as possible. Tax cuts were, to some extent, targeted on the poor, and a future higher rate of tax of 45 per cent on those earning over £150,000 per annum was announced in late 2008 (increased to 50 per cent in April 2009), but on the whole there was only a moderate redistribution of the tax burden. Labour still clung to the neo-liberal belief that excessive direct taxes were a disincentive to wealth creation and inward investment to the UK. The government accepted that taxes would rise in the future to pay of the mounting public sector debt, but, by then, the economy would be growing again.

SAMPLE QUESTIONS

Short questions

1 Explain how the British government attempted to deal with the credit crunch of 2007–9.

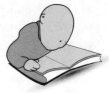

2 In what ways did financial control of the economy fail in Britain after 1997?

3 How were Keynesian policies used by the British government after 2007?

4 Why is taxation a key issue in contemporary British politics?

Essay questions

1 To what extent has neo-liberal, monetarist economic policy been abandoned in Britain?

2 To what extent does British government control the state of the national economy?

3 To what extent was Gordon Brown's claim to be a prudent Chancellor exaggerated?

4 How much political conflict exists between the main British political parties over the future of economic policy?

The Welfare State

2

Two matters need to be clarified before looking at welfare policy in the UK. The first is to define the Welfare State, establishing what is included within it. The second is to describe the principles of the Welfare State that distinguish it from other kinds of provision. Although elements of the Welfare State developed before the Second World War, it is generally agreed that it came into existence from the mid-1940s on, inspired by the report on postwar Britain produced by Lord Beveridge, a leading liberal policy maker.

COMPONENTS

We can generally agree, certainly for the purposes of this book, that the UK Welfare State includes the following:

- The provision of personal **health services** and medical research. This includes *primary care –*

Welfare State
The provision of state welfare developed after the Second World War. The term 'Welfare State' refers to the plan that a number of welfare services should be provided solely or largely by the state and that all citizens should participate. The Welfare State was and still is largely funded from general taxation and all citizens are entitled to benefit from its services free, or on a subsidised basis. The Welfare State was also very comprehensive and included health care, education, social security, pensions, social housing, social services, child services, care of elderly poor people and mental health provision.

the doctor service, dentistry, minor procedures etc. as well as hospital treatments.

- **Public health** provision such as protection from virulent diseases, mass inoculation, services for the unborn child and very young babies, normally provided by local authorities.

- **Social services** at local government level. These deal with such issues as family support, care of children in danger or orphaned or needing to be put into care, support for elderly people and for those with low-level mental illness.

- **Subsidised housing**, again at local level. This is known as council housing. Homes are rented to residents and maintained by local authorities.

- **Education** from nurseries through to universities. Universities are not strictly part of the welfare state, but the funding of students in higher education certainly is.

- **Social security**, which involves financial support for those in need, including lone parents, the unemployment, the disabled, those on low incomes and, above all, **pensioners**. The Welfare State benefits system also provides maternity allowances to all mothers, sick pay for those unable to work, grants for school uniforms and free school meals for children from low-income families etc.

social rights

A general term referring to the principle that all citizens of a modern state should be entitled to a number of welfare and social services as of right. These include the right to health care, education, care in old age and to employment.

social security

That part of the Welfare State which deals with state aid to those who are in particular need. Social security is available to all in the form of child benefits and the state pension, and to those in need of unemployment benefits, maternity and sickness pay, help when disabled, family income support, residential and nursing care of the elderly and provision for lone parents. Effectively it is a compulsory state insurance scheme which pays benefit when the need arises.

We can see that the system is universal in its scope. It also has to be said that the services supplied within the Welfare State are very much what they were when the system was first developed in the 1940s.

PRINCIPLES

It is crucial to understand the principles upon which the Welfare State was founded. In doing so we can understand the political ideology behind the system and can make judgements as to whether these principles have been eroded. These principles were as follows.

First, the system is **compulsory**. This means that it is not possible to opt out of the Welfare State. All those who pay tax and/or National Insurance must contribute to the Welfare State through those payments whether they wish to or not. Since some people rely very little on the Welfare State, especially those who buy private education or health care or have no children, or enjoy excellent health and never fall into financial hardship, they are effectively subsidising those who *do* rely on welfare services. This makes the Welfare State *redistributional* in nature and constitutes an important element of social justice (some might also call this an aspect of *socialism*).

Second, the system is **universal**. This simply means that all are entitled to the benefits of the Welfare State. No groups are excluded from contributing or from benefiting.

> **universalism**
> A principle relating to the Welfare State. It is a feature which implies that all the services of the Welfare State should be available to all those in similar need. The state old age pension and child benefits are examples, as are the services of the NHS and the state education system.

Third, the system should apply **equally** to all. This means that the Welfare State treats everybody in the same way, whatever their circumstances and wherever they live. It does not mean that everyone will benefit equally. What it does mean is that the needs of individuals will be assessed on an equal basis. As we shall see, this principle has come under threat, especially since devolved government was introduced in 1998 for Scotland, Wales and Northern Ireland. Control over many welfare services was passed to devolved governments so there is some variation in provision, especially in Scotland and Wales.

Fourth, the services of the Welfare State should be supplied **free** at the point of delivery. Again, this principle has been eroded as we shall see below. However, the majority of the Welfare State is free to its users.

Having established the nature and principles of the Welfare State in the UK, we can examine typical political attitudes to the system. These are as follows.

Socialists, mostly on the left of the Labour Party, are very strong supporters of the Welfare State. They see it as a form of socialism and a means by which prosperity and living standards can be equalised. They defend its principles staunchly and would prefer to see further extensions in its scope. They strongly oppose any involvement by the private sector in the provision of welfare services.

Liberals are also strong supporters of the Welfare State. Indeed, the founder of the system, William Beveridge, was a liberal. Like the socialists, liberals see welfare as a means of achieving social justice. They also believe that a strong Welfare State underpins greater equality of opportunity and makes for a more moral society.

Neo-liberals, largely 'Thatcherite' members of the Conservative Party, are suspicious of the Welfare State. They see excessive welfare as a disincentive to work and enterprise. High social security and other benefits inhibit people from seeking active employment. It can also create what they describe as a 'dependency culture'. This implies that, if people become used to relying on welfare, they will lose the ability to be self-reliant. As supporters of individual freedom, neo-liberals also resent the compulsory nature of the system. They also believe that the Welfare State denies people choice in what services and what kind of services they consume. Most who hold this view realise that the dismantling of the Welfare State, as we know it, is not politically realistic, But if the climate were different, they would certainly wish to see the compulsory system replaced by a voluntary one.

Traditional and 'social' conservatives, who have dominated the Conservative Party leadership since 2005, support the Welfare State. For them it is an essential and traditional part of British society, strongly supported by its people. It is also a uniting force, around which all the people can express a sense of community. They are not as enthusiastic about devoting resources to it as liberals and socialists have been, but remain committed to protecting it. They do share with neo-liberals a suspicion of welfare benefits which are too high or too easy to obtain, but accept most of the provisions available. They also wish to see more choice within the services provided (for example of schools or hospitals), but agree that there should be equal quality throughout.

Social democrats, the best description for most members of the current Labour Party, have championed high levels of welfare provision. Like social conservatives they see the Welfare State as an expression of Britain as a single community. However, they recognise that many families wish to make their own provision for welfare and so support the idea of private provision (for example in pensions, housing and health care) alongside state provision of services. They also accept today that the private sector can play an active role in providing welfare services in partnership with the state. As a mark of its support New Labour radically increased expenditure on many aspects of the Welfare State from 2000 to 2008, notably in education, pension provision, poverty relief and health care. It has also attempted to target welfare benefits more precisely on those in real need and to make them an incentive, rather than a disincentive, to self-reliance.

Having described the main principles of welfare in the UK we can examine four of its main branches. These are education, health, social security including pensions, and housing.

EDUCATION

Background

It should be noted at this stage that the discussion of education which follows concentrates on England and Wales. Scotland has its own education system which is distinctive and controlled separately from the rest of Britain. Indeed, since 1998 it has been fully under the control of devolved Scottish government.

The comprehensive system had been gradually introduced into English and Welsh secondary education during the 1960s and 1970s. There was a consensus in that period around the comprehensive principle – that all children at 11-plus should be offered places in schools which were designed to cater for all ability levels. A small number of selective grammar schools remained in parts of the country such as Kent, Buckinghamshire and Greater Manchester. The grammar schools were permitted to select the more academically able children who applied. However, they remained very much in a minority. Attempts to abolish the grammar schools by Labour governments in the 1970s had failed.

Primary education, from 5 years to 11, remained very much as it had been for most of the twentieth century. Higher education by the 1980s was providing places for an increasing number of post-18-year-olds. There was a mixture of universities, polytechnics (18-plus colleges offering some degree courses along with a number of other, largely technical qualifications below degree level), technical colleges and further education colleges offering A levels and other vocational course.

But it was not the *structure* of education which caused political controversy. Rather, it was the *standards* in education which became the subject of conflict from the late 1960s onwards. The early shots in the battle were as follows.

In 1968 a group of right-wing academics published a series of reports which became known as the 'Black Papers'. These reports blamed the comprehensive system for falling standards. The group also pointed the finger at left-wing ideas and 'progressive' teaching methods. The Black Papers received little support within education circles, but did have some influence within the Conservative Party, not least with one of their education ministers of the early 1970s, Margaret Thatcher.

In 1976 another report, known as the 'Yellow Book', was published. It recommended measures to improve school discipline, the restoration of a conventional curriculum and a return to traditional teaching methods. Once again this reactionary report had an influence on the Conservative Party which found itself again out of power.

The Conservative Party, which was elected to power in 1979, began to question how schools were being run and examined some of the fundamental problems with the structure. In particular, the Conservatives believed that schools were suffering too much interference by local authorities (most of which were Labour-controlled) and that standards of education varied too much in different parts of the country.

The neo-liberal leadership of the Conservative Party believed that free market competition was always preferable to state monopolies. They therefore set about planning ways in which competition could be introduced into education without privatising the whole system.

The Labour Party for much of the 1980s was dominated by left-wingers. They believed that the reason why standards were low was that the grammar schools and private education were 'creaming off' the best resources. Their answer was to abolish grammar schools and possibly even abolish private education altogether. They also proposed that education resources should be concentrated on deprived inner-city areas where standards were particularly low, for economic and social reasons rather than educational ones.

It can therefore be said that, certainly until 1988, there was considerable political conflict over education provision and, furthermore, that much of the debate was conducted along ideological lines. The Conservatives wished to see competition and variety in secondary education, with little political control. Labour, meanwhile, wished to extend comprehensive education, create equality of provision with some positive discrimination towards deprived areas, and to exercise more political control.

It was not until 1988 that the Conservative government had formulated its education plans. Their reforms were contained in the Education Reform Act (ERA) of that year.

The Education Reform Act, 1988

This act was the most radical reform of education in Britain since comprehensive schooling had been introduced in the 1960s. Its main provisions were as follows:

- A **National Curriculum** was introduced. This prescribed the subjects to be taught in schools between the ages of 5 and 16. It also specified how much time was to be spent on each. Special emphasis was given to traditional subjects such as English, Mathematics, Geography, History and Religious Studies. This had the effects of 'crowding out' more modern subjects such as media studies and design. However, it was believed that these basic subjects would improve general standards.
- Four **key stages** were established. These were at the ages of 7, 11, 14 and 16. By those ages pupils were expected to have achieved certain levels of attainment. These levels of attainment were specified in the National Curriculum.
- Schools were taken out of local authority direct control. This meant that schools themselves, notably their head teachers and governing bodies, were given considerably more autonomy. This system was known as **local management of schools (LMS)**.

- Schools were given the option of opting out of local authority control altogether. This would depend upon a vote among current and prospective parents at the school. Opted-out schools would be 'grant-maintained' and would receive funding directly from government rather than from their local authority. This also meant that they would be able to pursue their own education policies within the constraints of the National Curriculum.

The ERA of 1988 had a number of significant effects. It created a system of national standards by which pupils, teachers, schools and local authorities could be judged. It changed the nature of the curriculum towards a more conservative structure, at both primary and secondary level. It also had the effect of making all schools, to a greater or lesser extent, independent. In fact, power over schools moved both upwards and downwards. The National Curriculum placed the teaching and learning aspects of education under *central* control. On the other hand LMS moved some power downwards, especially in terms of staff recruitment and the distribution of education funding. The losers were, therefore, the local authorities, who lost control over the curriculum and the management of schools. This achieved an important Conservative objective, which was to take many schools out of the direct control of left-wing Labour-controlled councils.

The 1988 reforms were, to some extent, ideological in nature. Certainly they reflected a very conservative attitude to the curriculum. They also symbolised opposition to liberal, sometimes radical, attitudes to education. It was assumed that the National Curriculum and the introduction of attainment standards would eliminate more 'permissive' types of teaching. It also represented part of a wider ideological conflict between the New Right Conservatism of the 1980s and the leftward-drifting Labour Party, represented by some radical local councils.

The Major reforms

When the Conservative successor to Margaret Thatcher, John Major, came to power in 1990 he was determined to build on the reforms made in 1988. Two particular reforms were introduced. First, SATs (standard attainment tests) were introduced. These were standard examinations for all children in state schools at ages 7, 11, 14 and 16 (key stages 1–4). SATs were designed to meet a number of objectives:

- They would be a means by which children's performance could be monitored.
- They would be a means by which the performance of schools and teachers could be compared.
- They would help to ensure that the standards established by the National Curriculum would be met.
- They provided parents with a means by which they could compare different schools' performance.
- They would promote competition between schools.

Alongside the introduction of SATs, league tables for schools were to be published.

New Labour: 'Education, education education'

On his election in 1997 Tony Blair declared that education was to be one of New Labour's flagship policies. The three priorities of the party, he asserted, were to be 'education, education and education'.

First, he argued that Britain needed a well educated, flexible workforce, if Britain was to be competitive in a rapidly globalising world. Second, he felt that education was a key weapon in the war against such evils as crime, unemployment and poverty. Third, he argued that education was a key element in the achievement of greater equality of opportunity. In this last sense he was simply building on the objectives adopted by Liberal and Labour governments since the late nineteenth century.

As a 'New', rather than 'Old', Labour politician, Blair was certainly not going back to the left-wing agenda of local government-controlled education and 'modern' teaching methods operated by radical educationalists. He accepted that some of the Conservative reforms should be retained, while his neo-liberal instincts led him to believe that competition between schools was a positive feature.

It was the Education Secretary David Blunkett who was responsible for New Labour's early reforms. The main features were these:
- Schools were given targets to achieve. The targets required a minimum number of pupils to achieve the four attainment levels at the four key stages.
- Literacy and numeracy hours were introduced. These were designed to ensure maximum performance in two key subjects – English and Maths.
- There was increased expenditure on Information and Communication Technology (ICT), with all schools supplied with large numbers of computers and network systems.
- 'Beacon' status was introduced for schools which achieved a level of excellence. Such schools were rewarded with more resources and higher salaries for senior staff.
- Sanctions were imposed on failing schools. The most serious failures could result in the transfer of management to inspectors or private management companies and, in extreme cases, closure. In such cases heads and senior staff were likely to lose their jobs.
- Parental choice of schools at secondary level was introduced to increase competition between schools.
- A limited form of payment by results was introduced for teachers. Better-performing teachers could apply to have their salaries placed above a higher threshold.

- Trainee teachers were guaranteed an additional payment of £6,000 per annum to encourage high-quality entry to the profession.
- In general terms teachers' pay was raised above average levels of wage increases to make the profession more attractive.
- More recently there have been added incentives to attract scientists and mathematicians into teaching, with 'golden hellos' offered. A 'Teach First' programme was also introduced in 2006 to attract potential teachers from other professions, offering a 'fast track' into a teaching qualification.

Change and consensus

Education policy in 2009 is the subject of both political consensus and conflict, though an overall judgement must be that the areas of consensus are greater than those which divide the main parties. The key issues include the following.

SATs and league tables. SATs are supported by both the Labour and Conservative parties, but are opposed by Liberal Democrats. Supporters see them as vital ways of ensuring good standards in the core subjects of Maths, English and Science. They are designed to ensure that all children receive a similar quality of education, have access to the basic curriculum and are measured, in terms of attainment, by the same yardstick. SATs, and the league tables on schools which are based on them, also enable parents, communities and political decision makers to assess the performance of individual schools. Nevertheless they have encountered a good deal of opposition, mainly from the teaching profession itself and the Liberal Democrat Party.

Opponents claim they interfere with education by testing children too often, that they are too rigid in terms of what is taught, are open to abuse and 'coaching' solely in the interests of good SAT results, favour middle-class schools and pupils and, perhaps above all, are an unreliable method of measuring the performance of pupils, teachers and schools. Some of these arguments prevailed when the SAT tests at key stage 3 (mainly 14-year-olds) were abolished. However, the two main parties remain committed to testing at key stage 2 (11 years) and 4 (GCSE year).

Academies. It became apparent in the early years of the twenty-first century that the existing provision for secondary education was failing in these areas where there were particularly challenging problems in terms of social deprivation, high levels of recently arrived immigrant populations and persistently low levels of educational attainment. In the main this applied to city-centre areas. The experiment of converting many comprehensive schools to 'specialist' schools, with an individual emphasis on such education sectors as business, IT, sport, the arts and languages, had achieved partial success with improving performance and popularity with parents. There were, however, many schools where the fundamental problems were so great that a more radical change was needed.

In 2000 the **Learning and Skills Act** established the city academies (now known only as academies). With private sponsorship and independence from local authority control, academies can set their own education agendas and policies (within the constraints of the National Curriculum) and may adopt a particular speciality of their own, such as business, citizenship, science or ICT. Operating in difficult social and educational circumstances as they do, many academies have adopted a 'zero tolerance' stance on behaviour and have high rates of temporary and permanent exclusions. By early 2009, 133 had been established, with plans for a total of over four hundred.

The academies have resulted in a high degree of political consensus. The Conservatives support them enthusiastically and propose even more than the Labour government plans, possibly extending the principle to primary schools. The Liberal Democrats also support academies, though less enthusiastically than the other two parties. To some extent they see them as divisive and are suspicious of too much private sector involvement.

Examinations. As with academies there is a good deal of consensus over the future of school examinations, though there remain disagreements over detail, if not principles. Consensus between parties includes the following ideas:
- Post-sixteen provision should be widened so that it caters for the much more varied intake that sixth forms and colleges are experiencing. This will become more acute as the school and training leaving age is extended in the future to 17 and then to 18 years.
- There is support for the greater provision of vocational courses, including the vocational element in the 14–19 diplomas. Such courses will better cater for those who do not have traditional 'academic' strengths.
- Though no party yet proposes to scrap A levels, there is agreement that there should be some competition to A levels, notably from the International Baccalaureate which is increasingly being adopted by schools and colleges.

Nevertheless, despite the wide consensus on examinations, there remains a suspicion among opposition parties that there has been some devaluation in standards, notably of GCSEs and A levels. Apparent year-on-year improvements in educational attainment at 16–18 have, therefore, been challenged.

Post-11 selection. This is another area of general consensus. Indeed, David Cameron's decision in 2006 to distance the Conservative Party from the principle of greater selection at 11 and the provision of more grammar schools caused a great deal of consternation among Conservatives. Nevertheless Cameron and his leadership group believe that selection at 11 is largely divisive and should not therefore be encouraged.

No party proposes the widespread closure of selective secondary schools, but not do any suggest that the sector should be expanded. Indeed, all the parties are committed to an education system which creates equality of opportunity, as well as variety and high standards.

Higher education. It is perhaps in the area of higher education that most political conflict has occurred in recent times. While all main parties subscribe to the belief that a strong higher education is essential, important distinctions have arisen between the parties. Among them have been the following.

First, disputes over how higher education is to be funded have been one of the principle issues. The Labour government policy has been to raise tuition 'top-up' fees and to allow some universities to charge higher fees than others. These fees are paid by the students themselves, normally through the provision of low-interest loans, to be paid back when the graduate's earnings reach a certain level. The Liberal Democrats oppose top-up fees and wish to return to a system where higher education is largely free, paid for by taxpayers in general. Conservative policy changed in 2008. The new policy proposes that top-up fees should be abolished altogether, restoring the principle of free higher education. However, this would involve much loss of revenue from fees. This is to be 'clawed back' by charging normal commercial rates of interest on student subsistence loans. Thus students will still feel the burden on higher education expenditure, but will pay in a different way.

Second, while Labour and the Liberal Democrats in 2008–9 support the expansion of the university sector, with the Labour government supporting a target of 50 per cent of all 18-plus-year-olds on degree courses, Conservatives take a different view. They believe that too many 18-year-olds are being encouraged to pursue degree courses. They favour a smaller university sector (perhaps catering for only 40 per cent of 18-plus students), but with many more vocational courses available, as well as practical training in trades and manual occupations.

Third, conservatives challenge the very nature of many degree courses. They argue that quality has been sacrificed for quantity. They therefore propose the abolition of many courses which they consider to be 'inferior', such as film and media studies, some social sciences and sports management. Labour defends such courses on the grounds that they widen opportunities and offer many more students the chance to obtain a degree-level education.

Has education improved since 1997?

The measurement of educational performance is notoriously difficult and controversial. However, some statistics can first set the scene (Tables 2.1–2.3).

Table 2.1 Literacy levels: proportion of children reaching 'acceptable' levels of literacy for their age (%)

Age	1996	2007
Key stage 1 (7)	78	82
Key stage 2 (11)	57	80
Key stage 3 (14)	61	74

Table 2.2 GCSE performance (% achieving)

	5-plus passes at grades A–C	A–C grade in English
1996	43	54
2007	62	62

Table 2.3 Average class size in primary schools

1997	27.5
2001	26.7
2005	26.2
2008	26.2

Exclusions and truancy

Despite government plans to reduce exclusions from schools there was a rise of 28 per cent in exclusions from large secondary schools between 1997 and 2007. However, this disguises a 28 per cent fall in permanent exclusions but a rise in temporary exclusions at *all* secondary schools over the same period. Truancy rates, which are difficult to measure accurately, appeared to reach new record high levels by 2008.

Table 2.4 Expenditure on education, as percentage of Gross Domestic Product (GDP)

1997–98	4.5
2000–01	4.6
2004–05	5.3
2006–07	5.5

The overall picture suggests a distinctly improving position on attainment levels, little progress on primary class sizes and some deterioration in the truancy picture. The exclusions rates, indicating behaviour levels in schools, show a contradictory picture. However, there is much dispute over the effectiveness of such statistics. Among the concerns are the following.

- Though there have been improvements in literacy levels, Britain remains relatively low on attainment scales in comparison with much of Western Europe.

- There have been suspicions that the standards of examinations – both in SATs and in GCSE – have fallen so that more pupils appear to be doing well.
- Though there have been some impressive achievements it could be said that they do not represent a good return on the huge increases that have been made on expenditure on education.
- Critics suggest that the problems being faced by schools in terms of the prevalence of English as an additional language, of special educational needs and of problem families, have been increasing. This would suggest that schools may be achieving well under worsening circumstances.
- Supporters of government policy argue that there are considerable time lags between rises in spending or reform and educational outcomes. In other words, improvements will be seen in the future.

The political context

In the 1960s and 1970s education was subject of significant ideological conflict. It reflected a major conflict between democratic socialists in the Labour Party who saw education as a means of creating greater equality, and conservatives who believed that the education system had to reflect the natural inequalities in society. Thus, the Conservative Party supported the principles of selective education where the most able went to academic grammar schools and the less able attended secondary modern schools to learn basic literacy and numeracy plus practical skills.

The dominance of Labour in this period led to major changes in education, notably the replacement of most of the selective system by a comprehensive scheme, the basis of which still exists today. Subsequently the primacy of comprehensive schools became a matter of political consensus and even the neo-conservative Margaret Thatcher did not attack the comprehensive system in any significant way.

After 1988 attention shifted away from the *structure* and *philosophy of education* towards the issue of how to improve standards. Since then there has been a growing consensus, the principles of which are that:
- Competition between schools is healthy, breeds efficiency and promotes higher standards (though Liberal Democrats disagree with this principle).
- The publication of performance tables for schools gives parents vital information and enables them to make rational choices (here again Liberal Democrats disagree).
- It is crucial that a National Curriculum is followed, with national standards imposed.
- The school system should not, on the whole, differentiate between pupils purely on the basis of academic ability.

- The truly comprehensive schools should offer a range of provision to cater for all abilities and all aspirations.
- There should be some variety in the nature of secondary schools to offer choice and to differentiate between the different social circumstances of each school.

This adds up to a distinct lack of ideological conflict. Political controversy is largely confined to issues concerning the nature of examinations, how higher education is to be funded, what part performance targets and tables should play and how best to deal with the social problems that many schools face. In other words they are issues of administration, competence and efficiency rather than of educational principle.

HEALTH

Background

The National Health Service (NHS) came into existence in 1946 after a prolonged period of negotiation between the reforming Labour government of the day and the various sections of the medical profession. It rapidly became known as the 'jewel in the crown' of postwar Labour's achievements. It also attained a unique place in British culture. Though it is often criticised and has been the subject of political controversy throughout its existence, the British people, on the whole, consider it to be a central aspect of British life. The NHS came under immediate pressure in the 1940s when it became apparent that it was underfunded. The main problem was its popularity. People began to use their doctors more frequently – not surprisingly as it was now seen as a 'free' service. This meant that there was a huge increase in the number of prescriptions being dispensed. In 1950, therefore, charges were introduced for prescriptions (though young, elderly and very poor people were exempt). Prescription charges were needed to discourage too many unnecessary treatments and to help fund the service.

The issue of prescription charges has dogged the service ever since. It also illustrates the perennial problem of the NHS. The charges were needed because the NHS was successful. Demand for health care naturally rose, as did expectations of what the service can provide. Ever since the 1940s, as new treatments in the form of drugs and medical procedures have become ever more available, the costs of providing health care have risen. Furthermore, demands for service have accounted for an ever increasing proportion of National Income to be devoted to health care.

Signs of strain

The greatest strain emerged in the 1970s. Governments were confronted by a squeeze on health. On the one hand there were major advances taking place in treatments, notably for cancer, heart conditions, arthritis and other joint problems, diabetes and other common ailments. On the other, government revenues were falling in the face of economic stagnation in the later 1970s. The indications of problems were clear. Waiting lists and times for operations began to grow alarmingly, longer waiting lists to see general practitioners (GPs) appeared and the medical professions complained of staff shortages and excessive pressure of work. Thus, faced with rising expectations and falling revenues, the NHS began to suffer. These were the problems which Margaret Thatcher inherited in 1979.

Policy under the Conservatives 1979–97

Faced with major problems in health provision, the neo-liberal Conservative leadership of the 1980s considered a number of alternative plans. The main four were as follows:

First, go to the American model. This would essentially mean that most people would be expected to make their own arrangements for health care by taking out private health insurance. The poorest and most vulnerable in society might be protected by what Americans usually call 'medicare', essentially free health care, but this plan was, effectively, privatisation. Its main problem was that many would be 'priced out' of the market and thus suffer greatly, and there would be great inequality among individuals with differing abilities to pay. Its greatest advantge was that it would reduce taxes greatly. It was also assumed that, by placing health provision into private, competitive markets, its quality would improve. It was rejected for being too radical. Even if it had been accepted by the medical profession, the general public would certainly not have tolerated the destruction of a cherished aspect of British life.

Second, adopt the French model. This was a subsidised insurance scheme combined with a nationalised scheme which would provide some of the services. In other words a 'hybrid' system. It was rejected, partly because health practitioners opposed it and partly because the French experience was that the quality of the service had become 'patchy'. Primary health care – mainly the GP service – was relatively poor, while the more 'heroic' or fundamental forms of medicine, such as heart and cancer care, were impressive.

Third, encourage more people to take up private health care and so take pressure off the NHS. This could have been achieved by offering tax breaks on private health insurance – effectively 'subsidising' private health care. This was very attractive, but was felt to be too politically attractive as it appeared to be a subsidy for the better-off.

Fourth, leave the NHS as it was, but raise charges for some of its services. At the same time, major restructuring of management might create greater efficiencies.

The fourth option was clearly the most attractive and was the only one which would have received enough public support. A report produced by a committee led by Roy Griffiths, the CEO of Sainsbury's, was published in 1983 and formed the basis of a new management structure.

The essential criticisms of the Griffiths report were as follows:
- The NHS was extremely inefficiently run when measured against normal business practices.
- Management was poor and indecisive.
- Spending decisions were made in a haphazard way. They took little account of value for money and were not allocated on a rational basis.
- Doctors were taking too little part in management. They had a great deal of freedom in making *clinical* decisions (those directly affecting the treatment of patients), but took no responsibility for the wider implications of their decisions.
- Future management of the system was to be rationalised and was to operate business principles rather than the confused system as it existed.
- Management should be a combination of externally recruited executives and practising doctors.

The Griffiths *principles* were adopted but failed to render any fundamental improvements. They have formed the basis of the system ever since, but they did not address sufficiently the perennial problem of funding. There remained too little funding to meet demands, and the distribution of funding remained difficult and controversial. It was therefore decided to introduce a *market* system into health provision.

The internal market

The essential problem of the NHS, apart from shortages in funding, was that it was inefficient and did not allocate resources in a rational way. The solution was believed to be to introduce a market system in health provision. But this posed the question, how can one introduce competitive markets into a publicly funded system, whose services are mostly supplied free of charge at the point of delivery? The apparent answer was produced in a 1989 report entitled *Working for Patients*. The key to the proposal was to divide the NHS into **providers** and **purchasers**, thus imitating the circumstances of private sector markets.

There were three types of **provider**:

- **NHS trusts** were made up of groups of hospitals, clinics and other medical services. Trusts were run by professional managers. They were to 'sell' services to purchasers at a negotiated price. Those trusts which failed to compete or were unable to supply services at reasonable prices would therefore decline, jobs would be lost and they would be forced to become more efficient and effective. This circumstance effectively mimicked the operation of free markets.
- **Special Health Authorities** were specialist services such as blood transfusion units (obviously supplying blood products) or teaching hospitals (training medical staff).
- **Non-fundholding GPs** were family doctors who chose to stay outside the system. They were given fixed contracts depending on how many patients they treated.

> **marketisation**
>
> One of the problems of any state-run provision is that it is not subject to the 'disciplines' of the free market. That is, it does not need to be efficient because there is no competition and it has few incentives to produce high-quality services. To combat this, either state-run services can be forced to compete with private sector service providers or state-run providers should be forced to compete with each other. Thus schools and hospitals may be required to compete for scarce resources provided by the state. This process is often known as marketisation.

There were two kinds of **purchaser**:

- **Health authorities** received their funding from government. They purchased services from providers as shown above. They would be able to search for the best and most efficient (usually cheapest) provider. Here again they were imitating the actions of consumers in a private free market.
- **GP fundholders** were those doctors who opted *into* the new system. They were given budgets by government which they could use to purchase services from providers. The salaries of doctors would come from these budgets. Thus, if they were able to achieve value for money in their purchasing, they could top up their salaries and even expand their operations. This made them extremely independent and they were the driving force in creating an efficient internal market system.

The system was introduced in 1990 by the NHS and Community Care Act. A reluctant medical profession was slow to implement the reforms, and many doctors chose to remain non-fundholders. However, the internal market was gradually introduced over the next three years.

The Act also introduced extra charges for eye tests and for dental checks. This was designed to reduce the 'funding gap'. Some community health services were also transferred to local authorities. Most notoriously, this included responsibility for care of patients with low-level mental health problems. This policy, known as **care in the community**, was highly controversial as it placed huge burdens on local communities, who were to take over care of such patients from NHS psychiatric units. It was not just a financial issue. Care in the Community also led to a great deal of vagrancy and homelessness as councils were unable to support enough hostels for such individuals. Though it reduced the financial burden on the NHS, it simply transferred it to local taxpayers.

A summary of Conservative policy

Nobody could accuse the Conservative governments of 1979–97 of not attempting to reform the NHS. Their changes could also be described as a radical set of policies, certainly not timid. They were, to some extent, ideological in nature as they sought to introduce the disciplines of the free market into health provision. They also sought to create efficient, rational and professional management. On the other hand the Conservatives had succeeded in preserving the basic *principles* of the NHS. Most of its services were still free at the point of delivery and the main funding came out of general taxation. The new structure has formed the basis of the NHS structure ever since, suggesting it is a successful model. Future governments were to make further reforms, but the basic principles of Conservative reforms endured.

Labour opposed the reforms on the grounds that they were really the prelude to full-scale privatisation. There remained problems with waiting lists and the general performance of the NHS remained mediocre in comparison with other comparable countries. Labour suggested that the fundamental problem of the NHS lay not in management or structure but in lack of funding. They therefore entered the 1997 election campaign with the slogan '*24 hours to save the NHS*'. It proved to be an effective message.

New Labour and health

New Labour had come to power in 1997 with a promise to 'save the NHS'. However, it was relatively slow to start the reforms. Chancellor Brown was constrained by his own promise to keep the previous government's spending plans for three years. The government also quickly decided that the internal market, though flawed, should not be dismantled. Instead it was to be reformed to retain its strong features while rejecting its problems. By 1999, however, plans were set and reforms began. The main features of reform have been the following:

The principle of dividing the NHS into purchasers and providers was retained. However, the relationship between the two was changed. Instead of negotiating prices and seeking the best deal, purchasers were to buy services at set prices. Emphasis moved away from price and centred more on quality and efficiency.

The purchasers were Primary Care Trusts (PCTs). These included the general practitioner practices, dentists, opticians, other health specialists and clinics which undertook minor procedures. The PCTs were organised into a number of Strategic Health Authorities. In 1999 there were 300 PCTs and 28 Strategic Health Authorities. These were later reduced in 2006 to 156 and 10 respectively. This created a federal system within the NHS. The providers were Hospital (or 'Acute') Trusts. These dealt with in- and out-patient requirements. By 2008 there were 172 such trusts.

The Primary Care Trusts were free to determine their own priorities, to allocate funds as they wished and to purchase services from any of the Hospital Trusts. Overall policies were determined by Strategic health Authorities, but the PCTs were granted a remarkable degree of freedom of action. The principle behind the system was to allow the trusts to be able to respond to local needs.

The government was aware that the decentralised nature of the system was likely to cause inequality in health services, in particular in relation to the development of new drugs and treatments. Therefore the National Institute for Clinical Excellence (NICE) was set up. NICE was independent of political influence and was given the central task of determining which drugs and treatments should be approved for use by the NHS. Nevertheless NICE could not force PCTs or Hospital Trusts to adopt new treatments and drugs as they controlled their own allocation of resources.

After 2000 the government freed itself from its restraints on public spending. This signalled a steady, substantial increase in expenditure on health.

The practice of using targets for health care improvement, which had been adopted for schools, was extended to health care. The main targets were the reduction of waiting lists for treatments in hospitals, shorter waiting times for medical procedures, faster service in A&E departments and shorter waiting times for appointments with doctors.

In 2003 it was announced that Hospital Trusts could apply for *Foundation* status. Applicants would have to pass various tests of excellence and efficiency. The process of granting foundation status began in 2004 after a prolonged political battle to introduce them (see below). Foundation Trusts are freed from direct control by the Department of Health. Though funded by government, they are run by trusts (also described as 'co-operatives') which can make their own decisions as long as they remain within the principles of the NHS (for example they would not be able to charge for services). The members of the management trusts include staff, patient representatives, members of local community groups, health professionals and local politicians. Though they are not elected, it is assumed the trusts would be more accountable to local communities.

In return for their quality, the Foundation Trusts are free to determine their own policies, can raise finance on the open market, can control their own budgets and can use the private sector for major building and maintenance contracts. They are also more free to expand and to apply for additional funds from government.

General practitioner services were reformed with the introduction of a new contract for doctors in 2004. In return for reducing workloads and out-of-hours services, GPs agreed to improve the management of their practices (effectively turning them into businesses) and to concentrate more on excellence and on widening the services available at primary level (for example, including minor operations and other procedures). GPs also accepted the need to concentrate more on prevention. Instead of being paid merely fror treating patients, they were to be rewarded for improving the general health of their patients. In 2008 the contract was modified to persuade GPs to provide out-of-hours services (evenings and weekends) in return for financial rewards. It was also envisaged in 2008 that increasing numbers of practices would be amalgamated into 'polyclinics' which would be a combination of doctors' practices and clinics for treatment of minor conditions. The plan is to improve efficiency, through size, and to provide a wider range of treatments, taking the pressure off A&E and hospitals in general.

These changes (there have been many more of a less significant nature) may appear bewildering in their scope. We can, therefore, simplify them by identifying the main *principles* of the changes since 1997. These include:
- Vastly increased expenditure on health to raise England up to normal Western European standards.
- A decentralised system giving more local accountability.
- Driving up standards through target setting.
- Improving primary health services, seeing them as the key to better all-round health provision.
- Attempting to create more equality in health care in different parts of the country.
- Improving hospital services using the incentive of foundation status.

An assessment of health policy under Labour since 1997

There are a number of ways in which we can assess the effectiveness in health policy. One is to examine the relevant statistics. This includes considering the accuracy of the statistics and whether they may be misleading. A second is to consider the various criticisms that have been levelled at health policy. The third is to ask whether the improvements (no parties or groups dispute that there have been improvements) are proportionate to the vastly increased expenditure.

Table 2.5   NHS spending 1999–2008

Year	Spending in England (£ billion)
1999/2000	39.8
2000/2001	41.3
2001/2002	44.5
2002/2003	53.5
2003/2004	57.2
2004/2005	64.2
2005/2006	69.1
2006/2007	75.8
2007/2008	90.7
Real increase	81.9 per cent

Source: Civitas

The best place to begin is expenditure. Spending on the NHS has increased since 1999 as in Table 2.5. This is an impressive increase, to say the least. The Labour government's target to reach average European levels in terms of health expenditure as a proportion of National Income by 2007 was certainly met, though critics have argued that this has not meant improved performance which could be said to represent value for money. The evidence on waiting times for outpatients also looks impressive (Table 2.6).

Some other performance targets can be quoted to support the thesis that NHS performance has improved considerably. For example in the period 1999–2007:

- Deaths from heart disease fell by 35.4 per cent
- Deaths from stroke fell by 31.4 per cent
- Deaths from cancer fell by 13.5 per cent

On the other hand, comparisons with the rest of Europe appear less encouraging. For example, looking at mortality rates (deaths per 10,000 people) the comparison is as in Table 2.7. Other negative statistics include:

Table 2.6   Outpatients waiting more than 13 weeks for first of people appointment 1999–2008

1999/2000	497,544
2000/2001	429,342
2001/2002	393,349
2002/2003	257,612
2003/2004	160,745
2004/2005	77,537
2005/2006	39,794
2006/2007	174
2007/2008	183

Source: Civitas

Table 2.7 Deaths per 10,000 in 2007

	UK	EU average
Respiratory disease	126.1	73.6
Heart disease	344.8	421.9
Cancer	237.8	250.3

Source: Civitas

- Productivity (output per employee) fell by 2.5 per cent between 2003 and 2008.
- GP salaries rose by 58 per cent in 2002–6 but doctors worked on average seven hours fewer per week.
- In terms of patient satisfaction, the UK was seventeenth out of 29 European countries in 2007.

The overall assessment, as this selection of statistics suggests, is contradictory. Virtually all performance indicators are moving in the 'right' direction, but two serious questions remain:

- Is the UK falling behind the rest of Europe in terms of health care?
- Do the improvements represent a good return for the increases in expenditure?

The political context

None of the three major parties is considering any fundamental changes in the way that the NHS is funded. Most political controversy revolves around the management of the NHS, the degree of waste, the question of whether there is 'excessive' bureaucracy and whether there is sufficient equality in terms of treatment and quality between different regions of England and Wales.

There is a faction on the right wing of the Conservative Party which supports the restoration of neo-liberal policies, including consideration of the privatisation of some parts of the NHS. Similarly some on the left of the Labour Party oppose the use of the private sector in building and maintenance projects (mainly PFIs) in the NHS. However, the main political parties do not propose basic reform.

quasi-privatisation

A term which largely relates to welfare state provisions. Whereas full privatisation would effectively abolish the Welfare State, placing it in the private sector, quasi-privatisation refers to a policy, originating in the early 1990s, whereby some welfare provision has been contracted out to private sector companies and organisations. Thus, for example, some medical procedures may be paid for by the NHS but provided by private hospitals and medical staff. Similarly private finance initiatives (PFIs) now occur in all sectors of the Welfare State. PFIs involve private companies in capital building projects, maintenance contracts and service provision for the public sector. Quasi-privatisation does not affect the fact that welfare services are paid for by the state from general taxation.

Conservative policy in 2009 demonstrated the relatively limited nature of proposals:

- Abolition of NHS targets and so freeing-up of health authorities to create genuine improvements.
- An increase in the availability of single rooms in hospitals.
- Reductions in bureaucracy and the diversion of savings to front line services.
- Possible renegotiation of doctors' contracts to reduce costs.
- Cancellation of Labour plans to create hundreds of 'polyclinics' where a range of GP and minor hospital services will be available in one location.

Liberal Democrat policy revolves largely around proposals to make the NHS more democratic and sensitive to patient needs. This would be achieved largely by devolving control over health services down to a more local level and by the establishment of bodies staffed by local citizens and patient groups to ensure that the service is responsive to local needs. Above all, however, Liberal Democrats wish to ensure that the quality of health care should be equal and accessible to all throughout England and Wales.

SOCIAL SECURITY

Background

Much of Britain's current social security system was established in the 1940s following the Beveridge Report of 1942. The principal legislation was the **National Insurance Act, 1946**. A number of principles and features can be identified, as follows:

- It was to be comprehensive – 'from the cradle to the grave', as Beveridge expressed it. This meant there were to be benefits from conception right through to a person's death and funeral. To a great extent this is true of the system today.
- It was based on equality. This meant that all citizens were to be treated on an equal basis. It does *not* mean that everyone receives the *same* benefits, whatever their circumstances. It *does* mean that all citizens are subject to the same rules.
- It is comprehensive. Everyone must contribute either through National Insurance payments or through taxation. Employers contribute through National Insurance which they have to pay for every employee.
- It is compulsory. It is not possible to opt out of the benefits system if you are eligible to pay tax and/or National Insurance.
- It is a mixture of **means-tested** and **non-means-tested benefits**. The term 'means-tested' implies that a benefit will be paid only if applicants can

prove they are in need. For example, all the benefits which supplement income are means-tested: one has to prove that one has a very low income. Non-means-tested benefits are paid to all those who qualify, *whatever their income*. Two key examples are the state old age pension and child benefit.

- Social security benefits are subject to tax if a recipient's income is high enough.

There is a very wide range of benefits available, but the principal reasons for claiming benefit today are as follows.

Old age. Currently women above 60 and men above 65 are entitled to a state pension, provided they have paid enough National Insurance during their lifetime. The age at which the state pension is paid is likely to rise in the near future as there is a large deficit building up in the pension fund as people are living longer and so claiming pensions for longer. Britain also has an ageing population, meaning that an increasingly high proportion of the population is above retirement age. This places a larger burden on those who are in work and paying tax.

Poverty. People may be poor for a number of reasons. In any case, they may claim state benefits depending on circumstances, such as whether there are children in the home, or they are actively seeking work, are in very low-paid employment or are a lone parent.

Unemployment. This is effectively the same as poverty, though short-term benefit will be based on one's former earnings before reverting to a basic, standard level.

Disability. Disability benefits are paid to a person who can prove they are unable to work because of long-term disablement such as blindness or other physical problems. Benefits are also available for carers of disabled or long-term sick people.

Maternity. A range of benefits is available for women who are pregnant or nursing a young child.

Sickness. A regular payment is available for those who are temporarily sick and cannot work. This is normally claimed and paid by an employer.

Children. All parents are entitled to benefit for each child they have. Poor families may claim free school meals and grants for uniforms.

Short-term poverty. Where this occurs there is a variety of benefits available, including loans, benefit to pay council tax, and housing benefit, the latter being paid only for housing costs – rent or a mortgage.

There are, of course, a number of other benefits available, but those described above form the core of the system as it has existed since 1946.

Social security under the Conservatives 1979–97

Successive governments after 1946 had made various reforms to the social security system, with a tendency (only a *tendency*) for Labour governments to spend more on benefits and to extend the system. The Labour Party has tended to use the benefits system as a way of reducing the gap in living standards between rich and poor. Conservatives tend to see benefits more in terms of a 'safety net' for those who fall below a certain acceptable standard of living. But neither party made significant changes to the system until 1979. The arrival of a more radical and reforming government in 1979, however, changed Conservative attitudes to welfare.

The neo-liberal Thatcher government adopted largely ideological positions on social security. Among others were the following.

- Neo-liberal conservatives are instinctively suspicious of over-powerful government. Social security places a large amount of power and responsibility in the hands of 'big' government. It means that the government accounts for a large proportion of National Income in terms of both taxation and expenditure. This they oppose. Margaret Thatcher stated that she intended to 'roll back the frontiers of the state'. Reducing the social security commitment was part of this.

- There was also a fear of a *dependency* culture developing. This was a throwback to late nineteenth-century social Darwinism. Social Darwinism suggests that we are individuals who should be responsible for our welfare. If we depend too much on handouts from the state or charities we will lose the ability to be self-supporting. This robs society of its dynamic character which is a result of competition between individuals.

> **individual/social responsibility**
> This refers to the principle that, just as citizens are entitled to the benefits of the welfare state, so they also have social responsibilities to contribute to the system and to be responsible citizens.

- Neo-liberals oppose high taxation. High welfare benefits mean high taxation.

- As we saw in the chapter on economic policy, the Conservatives at this time hoped to make labour markets more flexible. High benefits, especially those applying to unemployment and low incomes, were, they believed, a disincentive for people to seek work, to work harder and to start up new businesses.

Irrespective of the ideology of the Conservative Party under Thatcher, there was a knowledge that the *dependency ratio* was worsening. This ratio is the relationship between those who are productive and pay taxes, and those who are dependent because of age or circumstances. As Britain has an ageing population, fewer and fewer productive members of the workforce are supporting more and more dependants. One answer, therefore, was to reduce the generosity of the benefits system. This was done in a number of ways.

The 1980 Social Security Acts. Two pieces of legislation reduced sickness benefits by breaking the link between the benefits and the sick person's earnings. But the most controversial measure was the Act which broke the link between the old age pension and the average level of earnings. Though state pensions would keep up with the rate of inflation, this was usually lower than the average rise in earnings. The result of this change was that pensioners would steadily become worse off in comparison with those still working. In other words, it increased the *relative poverty* of pensioners. The Labour opposition was furious as the maintenance of the value of the old age pension was one of its most cherished policies.

The 1982 Social Security Act forced employers to pay a higher proportion of sick pay when an employee was unable to work. The **1986 Social Security Act** reduced the general availability of housing benefits and brought down unemployment benefit for the under-25s. The **1988 Social Security Act** reduced the unemployment benefit further for young claimants unless they were willing to join training schemes. The **1989 Social Security Act** further tightened the rules for the unemployment to claim benefit.

The Statutory Sick Pay Act 1991 further reduced the amount of sick pay available from the state. The **Job Seekers' Allowance Act 1993** forced unemployed people to prove that they were actively seeking work before they would be eligible for benefits.

But the legislation does not tell the full story. Through the 1980s and into the 1990s the real value of several benefits was gradually eroded. At the same time the rules for those, including disabled people, claiming benefit were tightened up. Most controversially, the value of child benefit was reduced in real terms in that it did not rise in line with general inflation.

An assessment of Conservative policies

The principles of the Conservative reforms were threefold. First, they were designed to make it more difficult to claim benefit. The purpose of these changes was to ensure that those who received benefits could demonstrate that they *deserved* them. Second, they reduced the general level of benefit. In so doing they reduced government expenditure and, at the same time, attempted to force more people to become self-reliant, especially the unemployed. Third, the reforms were ideological in that they reduced the role of government in reducing inequality, implying that inequality is natural and it is up to individuals to improve their own economic circumstances.

The Labour Party naturally opposed the reforms vehemently. However, they were out of power throughout the period from 1979 to 1997 and were faced with a general public the majority of whom supported the changes as they were not adversely affected by them but had to pay for welfare benefits out of their taxes.

In a more general sense Labour has argued ever since that the attack on benefits under Thatcher and John Major considerably added to the level of poverty in the UK. This was especially true of pensioners and families with children, with both groups bearing the brunt of the reductions. The counter-argument deployed by the Conservative Party was that the measures, together with tax reductions had boosted wealth creation. The greater wealth created would 'trickle down' and ultimately help the poorest elements in society, mainly by creating more employment, especially at the lower end of the labour market. Meanwhile, the tighter eligibility rules were helping to ensure that benefits were more reserved to those who deserved them.

New Labour and social security

The Labour Party leadership who won power in 1997 developed a number of objectives with respect to welfare benefits:

- There was to be a general reduction in poverty and in particular attacks on child poverty and pensioner poverty.
- Benefits were to be better targeted on those in most need. This policy was known as **selective universality**.
- Too many people were in a *poverty trap*. The poverty trap was a circumstance faced by many poor people where there was no economic incentive for them to find work and remove themselves from the need to claim benefit. The problem was that, if an unemployed worker were to take on a low-paid job they would be worse off than they had been on benefits. The reason was that the person concerned would lose benefits when they found work, would have to start paying tax, and the net result was a loss of disposable income.
- New Labour wished to use the benefits system as an *incentive* for people to work, rather than a disincentive as it appeared to be.

At the heart of Labour policies have been two measures. One has been *Welfare to Work* and the other is the system of *tax credits*. Welfare to Work policy and its associated policy, known as *New Deal*, were based on the belief that benefits could be used as a way of incentivising work. It was also the most important example of the 'carrot and stick' approach adopted by the new government. On the one hand the state would offer help to the unemployed to find work in return for more generous benefits than had been available under previous governments. On the other benefits would become harder to claim and less generous for those who refused to co-operate. In effect this meant that unemployed people were offered job seekers' allowance in return for attending training sessions in finding work, attending job interviews and being willing to take low-paid employment. Of course, those who were unwilling to co-operate could not expect to receive such benefits. **New Deal** was introduced in 1998 and took the following course.

1998 New Deal for jobseekers. The New Deal for Young People was introduced for those under 25 who had been out of work for six months or more. Recipients had to be actively seeking work but were offered positive help to improve their chances of finding employment. Failure to co-operate would result in a return to minimum benefits. A similar programme was introduced later that year for over-25s who had been out of employment for at least two years.

1998 New Deal for Lone Parents. Help was introduced for lone parents who wished to return to work. This included advice, information and help with childcare, including financial grants to subsidise child minding.

2000 New Deal for over 50s. This was a similar deal to that offered to young people. Over-50s who had been out of work for six months or more were offered help and advice in return for higher benefits. Again, refusal to co-operate results in a fall in benefits.

2003 New Deal for the disabled. Disabled people were offered the opportunity to be helped back into employment as far as their disability would allow. There were, however, no threats to reduce benefits for this group if they did not enter the scheme.

The Labour government claims that New Deal has been a success. In 2008 the main claimed statistics for 1998–2008 were as follows:

- A total of 1.8 million people have been found work under the scheme.
- 500,000 lone parents have been brought into the workforce.
- 150,000 registered disabled people have found jobs.

Of course these figures have been disputed by both opposition parties. In particular they suggest that unemployment has been falling over the period because of economic growth so they cannot all be ascribed to New Deal.

Tax credits were a crucial element in providing incentives to lift people out of the poverty trap, by ensuring that there was an additional incentive to those who were willing to take on low-paid employment, even though they would lose benefits, notably the New Deal benefits shown above. There are three main groups who are entitled to tax credits.

- Child tax credits are available for those responsible for the care of children and who have a low income. Those who are not part of a New Deal programme are entitled to these credits.
- Working family tax credits are for those who are in work, but earning a low income. Those with children receive a higher level.
- Pensioners who have no sources of income other than the old age pension receive payments known as pension credits.

The principle of tax credits is to ensure that all citizens have a minimum standard of living, whatever their circumstances. Those who seek and find work will be considerably better off as a result because of the credits system. The system is also designed to reduce two special Labour targets – child poverty and pensioner poverty.

In late 2008 the government announced proposals to reform the benefits system again, especially the New Deal. The main thrust of the proposals is to tighten the rules on claiming unemployment benefit, introducing financial sanctions against unemployed people who do not co-operate with efforts to find them long-term employment. There are also to be sanctions against those who do not attend job centres regularly, mainly a requirement to undertake community work in return for benefits. Meanwhile, earlier in the same year, there was a new system of incapacity (disablement) benefit introduced. Disabled people would have to face an assessment of their abilities. Those able to take up some kind of employment would be helped back into work. Only those incapable of working at all would be offered unconditional benefit. The government called the policy 'concentrating on what people *can* do, rather than what they *cannot* do'.

Labour has, therefore, been radical in its benefits policy, introducing new ideas and attempting to disincentivise idleness and identifying the 'deserving poor' more accurately. Critics have argued the system is too complex and too much based on means-testing. Those on the left of politics suggest it does not redistribute income enough. On the right, neo-liberals have argued that it remains too generous, especially to unemployed people.

But Labour's greatest social security problem perhaps turned out to be what to do about pensions.

The pensions issue

Pensions became a major issue in British politics in the 1980s for a number of reasons.
- There was a looming problem in the country's ability to support a relatively generous state pension. The ageing population, worsening dependency ratio, growth of the use of occupational and private pension schemes and an increasing aversion to high taxes all contributed to problems with government's ability to fund the system and taxpayers' willingness to fund government.
- The Conservative government's instinct in the 1980s was to reduce the involvement of the state in welfare provision. This included pensions. It preferred to see the majority of people making provision for their own pensions. Increasing wealth in the 1980 seemed to make this more possible.

- Alarmed by these developments, the Labour opposition, mainly left-wing elements of it, insisted that the value of the old age pension should be preserved. The pension was seen as a key element in the maintenance of a socially just society and in improving equality.
- The growing elderly lobby, represented by powerful pressure groups such as Help the Aged and Age Concern (supported by trade unions), recognised its potential power, notably at the ballot box. When the value of the pension began to be eroded, especially when its link to average earning was broken, this section of society became increasingly concerned and vociferous.
- To make matters worse, after 1999 an increasing number of private pension schemes run by large companies were running into trouble. As with the state pension, they were finding it difficult to fund pensions as the recipients' life expectancy was rising so rapidly. Generous schemes which had been started in the 1960s and 1970s found themselves very underfunded. The firms which ran the schemes found themselves having to subsidise pensions, with an adverse effect on profits. This meant an increasing number of schemes actually collapsed, leaving retired people with little or no private pension, while most existing schemes had to be made less generous. This produced a greater demand for government to ensure that the state pension could provide for those whose private schemes had disappeared or were inadequate.

When Labour won office in 1979, pensions were a key issue. But Chancellor Gordon Brown faced three problems. First, he was committed to holding down public expenditure to pay back National Debt. Substantial pension increases would place a large burden on the public finances. Second, the erosion in the relative value of the pension during the 1980s meant that it would be extremely expensive to return to its value in 1982. Third, Labour and Brown's commitment to 'targeting' welfare made him reluctant to give substantial increases to *all* old age pensioners, whatever their private means. He attempted to placate his own left wing, the age lobby and the unions by arguing that, while he did not wish to restore the earnings link and give the pensioners large rises in their pensions, he would target benefits specifically on poor pensioners – those in genuine need. In other words he wanted to make some – not all – of state payments to pensioners means-tested. These appeals by Brown failed. All the concerned groups insisted that the state pension should not be means-tested and should grant a decent standard of living to all those who had reached retirement age.

The debate on pensions became especially intense when, in 1998, the state old age pension was increased by only 75p. This was, in fact, in accordance with the rules, that the pension should be increased by the annual level of inflation. In that year inflation stood at just 1.2 per cent, so that was the scale of the rise. Though the government was observing the rules, the political impact of such a tiny increase was immense. The government was jolted into offering compensatory measures such as cold weather payments, winter fuel allowances, annual Christmas bonuses for all pensioners (not means-tested) and free TV licences for the over-75s. The level of attendance allowances – paid to old people with special mobility problems – was also substantially increased. To make matters worse, Chancellor Gordon Brown had also cut the tax allowances on private pension schemes (effectively making them more expensive to operate). So the impression remained that New Labour had lost interest in the welfare of old people. Certainly, since 1998, the package of benefits and tax credits available to pensioners has been significantly improved.

As a companion to the principle of targeting poor pensioners, a **stakeholder pension** scheme was introduced in 1998. This was a system to give everybody the opportunity to start their own personal pension. All employers above a certain size were required to arrange for a stakeholder pension to be available for their workers. Those not in work were also encouraged to start a pension. Though administered by private sector firms, stakeholder pensions were guaranteed by government and enjoyed tax allowances for those taking part. The plan was to encourage as many as possible to make *their own* provision for old age and so reduce the burden on the state pension system in future.

By 2005 Labour had restored some of its reputation as the party for pensioners, but political controversy has remained. Issues have included the following.

- Conservatives believe the system is too complicated, as a result of which many pensioners do not receive the full pension and benefits to which they are entitled.
- Liberal Democrats and the left of the Labour Party believe the non-means-tested pension must be considerably higher and should keep pace with average earnings. This, they argue, is the only way to guarantee the elimination of pensioner poverty.
- Conservatives argue that not enough has been done by governments to encourage private pension schemes. They would restore tax concessions to make them more attractive.
- Liberal Democrats and pensioner pressure groups campaign for a greater understanding that many pensioners are in very different circumstances from younger people – disabilities, the need for carers (many pensioners are carers for their spouses) and poor housing – and that the pensions and benefit system should be more generous in recognising such individual circumstances.
- There remains controversy over how to fund a state system coming under increasing pressure. The options include:
  1. Paying the state pension at a later age, which was favoured by the Labour government of 2009.

2. Introducing a better system of private pensions to go alongside state pensions, possibly making private provision compulsory, a system supported by many Conservatives.
3. Funding a more generous scheme from the taxpayer, in particular raising more tax from higher-income earners, favoured by Liberal Democrats.

Has poverty been substantially reduced under New Labour?

Labour adopted a number of measures whose purpose was to reduce poverty. Most of these have been described above. In addition, there were a number of other devices used:

- The minimum wage, introduced in 1997, helped to improve the living standards of those in low-paid jobs.
- In 2005 every child was given a £250 'bond' which had to be invested and could not be used by its parents for any other use. The invested bond could be added to by parents and would be redeemed when the child reaches the age of 18, by which time it should have considerably increased in value.
- The real value of child benefits was increased, with a large and sudden one-off increase in 1999.
- Pensions have been substantially increased and a number of other benefits, such as winter fuel allowance, have been granted to pensioners.
- Education Maintenance Allowances (EMAs) were made available to poorer families after 2005 in return for retaining their children in full-time education or training after the age of 16. This was originally set at a maximum of £30 per week for families on incomes below £30,000 per annum.
- There have been significant increases in allowances available for paying council tax, especially for pensioners.

There has been, therefore, no shortage of measures to reduce poverty. The question is, however, how effective have the various measures been?

There are a number of problems associated with measuring poverty in the UK. Among them are these.

- It is important to distinguish between *relative poverty* and *absolute poverty*. Relative poverty refers to a person's or family's economic position in relation to changing average earnings. In other words it measures how well or badly off a family is in comparison with normal living standards in the country. Absolute poverty ignores what is happening to average incomes, but simply identifies a low level of income which is seen as poverty. Clearly, therefore, if incomes generally are rising, but a poor family remains 'on the poverty line' it is becoming *relatively poorer,* but is *not* becoming poorer in the *absolute* sense. It is a matter of political controversy as to which measure should be used.

- There are problems deciding what level of low income constitutes *poverty*. For example, different organisations argue it should be 40 per cent, 50 per cent or 60 per cent of average household incomes. This assumes, of course, that we are using a *relative* measure of poverty.
- How should we measure income? Should it simply be gross income before taxes and housing costs are deducted, or should it take into account tax and housing costs including council tax?
- Statistics are difficult to collect and tend to be at least 12 months out of date.

There is always a tendency for the government (whichever party) to use statistics which favour its own case on poverty figures, and opposition parties and those pressure groups who champion the cause of poor people tend to use measures which underpin their arguments. Nevertheless some conclusions can be drawn about Labour's period in office for ten years after 1997, a period when the reduction of poverty was a major objective.

In June 2008 the Department for Work and Pensions (DWP) issued an assessment of poverty in the UK. The DWP uses 60 per cent of average income as its measure of poverty. The main conclusions were as follows:

- The number of children in the UK experiencing low income *and* material deprivation – in families who can't afford basic things such as sending their kids on a school trip – fell by 100,000 between 2005–6 and 2006–7.
- The number of children in relative poverty rose by 100,000, both before and after housing costs are taken into account, to 2.9 million (before) and 3.9 million (after) respectively between 2005–6 and 2006–7. Between 1998–99 and 2006–7 the number of children in relative poverty fell by 600,000 (before housing costs) and 500,000 (after).
- The numbers of pensioners in relative poverty rose by 300,000 to 2.5 million (before housing costs) and by 200,000 (after) to 2.1 million between 2005–6 and 2006–7. Between 1998–99 and 2006–7 the number of pensioners in relative poverty fell by 200,000 (before housing costs) and 900,000 (after).
- Between 1997 and 2007, 1.9 million pensioners were removed from *absolute* poverty and 500,000 children were taken out of *absolute* poverty.

These statistics suggest that the government enjoyed a high degree of success in reducing poverty for children and pensioners (the two main target groups) in the earlier years in office, but that the improvement has dried up more recently. The child poverty figures are also a disappointment in that they represent an achievement of only half the government's own target of bringing one million children out of poverty in the first ten years in office. The figures show *relative* poverty, which suggests that the figures for *absolute* poverty will be more impressive as this was a period of rising prosperity in the UK.

The leading pressure group dealing with child poverty is the Child Poverty Action Group. Its reaction to the figures is threefold. On the one hand it accepts that considerable progress has been made. On the other, it argues that the measure of poverty is not realistic and does not reflect 'normal' standards of living. They also argue that 3.9 million children in 2007 (after housing costs are removed) in poverty is too high a number. Help the Aged and Age Concern, the two main pressure groups representing pensioners, accept the government figures, but claim that the measure of poverty for pensioners does not reflect reality. This is because pensioners face disproportionately high costs compared to younger people, notably in terms of heating fuel and council tax, both of which represent a high proportion of their incomes.

The Conservative Party also accepts the broad conclusions of the figures, but points out that *severe* poverty (applying to those earning less than 40 per cent of average earnings) has risen by 600,000 since 1997. It also points out that the poorest 10 per cent of the income scale are worse off than they were at the beginning of the century. The general drift of Conservative criticism is, therefore, that the degree of *inequality* is growing. This is a serious argument for Labour, traditionally the party most committed to greater equality.

Liberal Democrats are mainly concerned about relative poverty and social mobility. They argue that the figures look good in terms of absolute poverty, but that relatively there is too much poverty. Of course, as Britain has been more generally prosperous than most of the rest of Europe, it is difficult to reduce relative poverty. It must also be pointed out that the Labour government has given itself tough targets, notably be setting the poverty level at below 60 per cent of average earnings. Liberal Democrats also argue that social mobility is poor in Britain, suggesting that too many people are in poverty for too long and with too little prospect of escaping.

The overall verdict by 2008, therefore, appeared to be 'has done well, but could do much better'. Absolute poverty in Britain has been greatly reduced in the UK since 1997, but too many people are relatively poor and the target of reducing child poverty to zero by 2020 looks distinctly over-optimistic. The post-2008 recession may create further problems in reducing poverty too, as unemployment rises and increasing numbers of people lose their homes.

The political context

Policy on social security in the UK has moved from a position of great political conflict during the 1980s to fundamental consensus after 2005. The ideological conflict between New Right Conservatives under Thatcher and Major, which were inspired by neo-liberal philosophy, came into complete conflict with the view taken by Labour before the mid-1990s. While neo-liberals saw excessive social security as a threat to economic dynamism and flexible labour markets, the traditional Labour Party saw it as a means by which greater social justice could be achieved. This was fuelled by a basic difference in beliefs about how people are motivated. Neo-liberals believe that state support will simply make people less able to be self-reliant, while supporters of redistribution of income believe that greater equality will be an incentive for people to become more productive. Both main parties have moved away from these original positions.

As we have seen, New Labour takes a 'Third Way' approach, seeing state benefits as potentially both an incentive and a means by which people can be forced back into productive roles and less reliance on the state. This was the basis of Welfare to Work and the New Deal. It has taken longer for Conservatives to move. Under David Cameron after 2005, however, there has been a change. The Conservatives, notably the Social Justice Commission led by Iain Duncan Smith, identify two social priorities. One is the restoration of strong families; the other is an increase in *social mobility*. Families, the commission suggested, are weakened by poverty, unemployment and lack of opportunity. Similarly, social mobility – the ability of successive generations to enjoy a better standard of living and better employment prospects than their parent generation – can be improved if families are brought out of poverty and a lack of employment opportunity (though education remains the critical device in social mobility for both main parties).

Liberal Democrats retain some of 'old' Labour's attitudes to social security. Of the three main parties they have the greatest commitment to social justice through the redistribution of prosperity from rich to poor. For them welfare benefits form a key element in this redistribution. The party also remains the greatest champion of pensioners, insisting that they are as deserving of a good standard of living as any other section of society. The party opposes the system of discriminating between different groups of pensioners and wishes to see the restoration of the state old age pension to its relative level in the early 1980s. This would remove the need for those in special need to apply for credits.

Yes, despite the differences there is a consensus on how social security should work.

The **consensual** issues are:
- The tax credit system is, in principle, a good way to reduce poverty and distribute benefits fairly.
- Special attention should be paid to families with children.
- Unemployment benefit should be tied to requirements that claimants actively seek work, accept state help and are willing to take low-paid employment if necessary.
- Lone parents must be offered a realistic choice between finding employment and caring for their children full time.

The **conflict** issues in 2009 were:
- Liberal Democrats wish to see large-scale rises in the level of pensions.
- The opposition parties believe the tax credit system should be simplified.
- Conservatives wish to see long-term unemployed people placed on community work schemes to 'earn' their benefits.
- The Conservatives, in comparison to Labour and the Liberal Democrats, still believe many benefits are too high and are too easy to obtain.

HOUSING

Background

When the Welfare State was coming into existence in the 1940s, housing played a major part. After the Second World War home ownership remained relatively uncommon so most people were reliant upon rented accommodation. An important element of the new plan was, therefore, to make available a large stock of housing – houses and flats – at subsidised rents and with a guaranteed maintenance service. It was decided that most of this housing would be supplied and maintained by local authorities, with the costs of maintenance borne by taxpayers rather than tenants. The subsidising of rents was also covered out of local taxes. Thus there was some transfer of resources from better off people – who subsidised council housing yet who did not need to rent – to lower-income families who relied on subsidised rents. Thus, council housing became a key aspect of the ideology of the welfare state – the collective principle, greater social justice and some redistribution of wealth. The system also recognised that it was a right of every British citizen to enjoy decent housing accommodation.

For the next decade housing policy changed little. Home ownership gradually advanced, new homes were built and slum housing in inner cities was steadily replaced by new housing estates. Most of the political controversies centred upon how much of the National Income should be set aside for building what has become known as 'social housing'. The main parties engaged in a contest to see who could promise the most new houses. Targets for house building were set and routinely missed. The housing stock did gradually rise, but by the mid-1970s a crisis was looming. This was the growing incidence of homelessness. The growing population, swelled by large-scale immigration, was creating pressures which could not be met by the sluggish house building programmes of both parties. The major pressure group, Shelter, came into existence, campaigning for more houses to be built and for reforms to the law relating to the private rented sector.

The Labour government of 1974–79, however, went in a different direction. It encouraged the creation of Housing Trusts or Associations to try to fill the gap. These associations could apply to the government, through a Housing Corporation, for funding and could then build or buy housing which was then rented at relatively low rents. The associations were non-profit-making so rents were kept down, although they did aim to make some surpluses in order to build and buy even more houses. The associations, often run by churches and charities, were partially successful in reducing homelessness, but the problem remained and Labour left office in 1979 leaving a legacy of a growing problem.

The Conservatives and 'right to buy'

The Thatcher government was also concerned about housing, but in a very different way. Its approach was largely ideological in nature. The ideas behind housing policy included these:

- Margaret Thatcher was aware that council housing accounted for a huge proportion of the resources of local government. The city councils who controlled most of this council housing were nearly all Labour-controlled. This provided Labour with a considerable power base at local level. She wished to degrade this power base by reducing the resources under the control of Labour politicians.
- As neo-liberals, Thatcher and her allies believed that as much housing as possible should be returned to the control of market forces and away from government.
- The Thatcher government was committed to reducing public expenditure and taxation. Reducing the need for housing subsidies seemed an effective way of achieving both.
- As a neo-liberal conservative Thatcher believed that families should be free and enabled to determine their own lifestyles and prosperity. She understood that this drive towards a more individualistic, less collectivist, society centred largely on home ownership.
- Thatcher also recognised that subsidised council housing represented a major redistribution of resources from the more wealthy middle classes to the poorer elements of the working class. She wished to reduce this redistribution and to encourage families to become more self-reliant.

In 1980 the Conservative government announced its 'right to buy' policy. This was to prove highly controversial and set the scene for many of the ideological battles between the government and the Labour Party in the 1980s. The basis of the policy (most of whose provisions still exist today) were:

- All council tenants were given the legal right to attempt to buy their house or flat from the local council.
- The sale price was to be below the normal market price according to a set formula (this amounted to a discount of up to 30 per cent in many cases).

- Generous mortgages were made available to the new home owners, in particular allowing them to borrow up to 100 per cent of the price.
- Councils could use the proceeds from the sales to build new housing.

The Labour Party furiously opposed the policy. In the hands of the socialist left, led by Michael Foot and Tony Benn, Labour saw the policy as socially divisive (dividing those who could afford to take advantage of the scheme from those who could not), a betrayal of the principles of the Welfare State, notably its collectivism, and as a means by which an 'underclass' would be created of the very poor who relied on the state and private landlords for poor-quality housing.

But, as Labour was to be made painfully aware, the right to buy policy was a huge success. The two landslide Conservative election victories in 1983 and 1987 were partly put down to the success of the policy and Labour's determination to oppose it. By 1983 over 500,000 council houses had been purchased. Nearly one million new home owners were created in that period. In just four years, the proportion of homes which were owner-occupied rose from 54 per cent to 59 per cent. To the delight of the government, most of the new home owners became Conservative voters (research indicated 56 per cent voted Conservative against 18 per cent for Labour). Not only had the policy been a 'success' (at least in the government's terms), it had also created a whole new generation of Conservative supporters.

In 1988 a further Housing Act gave the right to private landlords and not-for-profit housing associations to purchase run-down council house estates, renovate them (using government grants where necessary) and then charge tenants market-value rents. This further eroded the proportion of housing in the control of local government.

Since 1983 home ownership has continued to increase (see below) and this can be ascribed to the continuing success of right to buy policy, as well, of course, as a being a reflection of rising prosperity. Yet one aspect of housing went less well for the Conservatives between 1979 and 1997. This concerned planning laws. Britain suffers from a shortage of land generally, building land in particular. If house building were to increase significantly, planning laws would have to be relaxed to allow building on so-called 'green field' sites. As such areas of the country tend to be populated by largely Conservative voters, such changes to planning laws could not be contemplated.

When Labour returned to power in 1997, it faced the following situation with regard to housing. First, the right to buy system was in place and very popular, and certainly could not be cancelled. Second, there had been a vast extension in private ownership of homes. Third, the stock of housing controlled by local authorities had been drastically reduced. Fourth, there was still a major shortfall in the housing stock. Finally, private house building companies were faced with tight planning laws which restricted the ability of such firms, as well as housing associations and local councils, to find suitable land for new houses.

New Labour and housing

One of the tasks facing successive Labour leaders Neil Kinnock (1984–92), John Smith (1992–94) and Tony Blair (1994–2007) was to rid the party of its own left wing's insistence that support for state-controlled subsidised housing should remain central to its policy. They pointed out that the policy of extending private ownership was undeniably popular and that there was now a new consensus that the state's role in housing should be limited to providing a safety net for the most needy. It was futile, they argued, to swim against the popular tide for the sake of an 'outdated' ideological position. These leaders won their argument and housing policy moved towards a new consensus.

New Labour policy since 1997 has centred on the following features:
- Encouragement for extensions in home ownership. Council tenants still have the right to purchase and the banking system was allowed to reduce restrictions on its lending practices (with some disastrous consequences when the credit crunch struck the UK in 2008). Helped by persistently low interest rates after 1995, growing economic prosperity and falling unemployment, an increasing proportion of families and individuals became home owners.
- Continued support for housing associations, helping them to purchase more property and reducing council housing as a result. Labour also introduced generous schemes to allow housing association tenants to buy their homes.
- Relaxation of the planning laws to release first 'brownfield' sites (derelict former industrial and commercial land) and then more green field areas and so encourage private house building.
- Some relaxation of laws relating to private landlords and tenants, making private renting of property more attractive to the owners of such homes (i.e. reducing rights of tenants).

The policies have had some success, with the incidence of homelessness falling and a gradual improvement in the house building figures. However a major problem remained. This was the persistence of very poorly maintained council housing estates with concentrations of the poorest, most deprived sections of society. This was the issue which had so exercised opponents of right to buy policy in the 1980s. Crime, low educational attainment and long-term unemployment were critical features of these estates. These multiple problems – known as 'social exclusion' in Labour circles – were proving intractable and lack of investment in new, low-cost housing was taking its toll.

THE WELFARE STATE ASSESSED

Here we ask two fundamental questions: First, how much, if at all, has the Welfare State been eroded? Second, how can the performance of the Welfare State be assessed?

Has the Welfare State been eroded?

Here we must compare the basic principles of the Welfare State, which were described at the beginning of this chapter, with the current status of the system. We can do this by referring to Table 2.8. Here we look at examples of erosions, but place them alongside some enduring qualities. There is a mixed picture in terms of principles, although, in general the Beveridge philosophy remains in force and has been extended in places.

Assessment of the performance of the Welfare State, as we have seen above, is notoriously difficult. On the face of it, most indicators suggest that welfare provision, particularly in health and education, is improving. However, there remains dissatisfaction and a general feeling that the services do not give value for money. In other words, accepting that there have been large increases in Welfare State expenditure in the last decade, there remains a question mark over whether the *outcomes* have been good enough. It is also true that the demands on the Welfare State have increased. More is expected of education and health care than ever before. With an ageing population and housing short-ages, the pressure on social security and housing provision is growing at a faster pace than resources. It is, therefore, perhaps best to leave an assessment in terms of relevant questions, for example:
- Do welfare services give value for money?
- How well is the Welfare State keeping pace with increasing demands?
- Are *perceptions* of services out of step with reality?
- Is the UK keeping pace with similar economies in Europe?
- Are the actual *outcomes* of welfare services in line with the *inputs*?

One conclusion can, however, be reached. This is that Britain still boasts a Welfare State which remains more extensive and egalitarian than in almost any other part of the developed world.

Table 2.8   **Erosion and maintenance of Welfare State principles**

Erosion	Maintenance or extension
Universality • The old age pension is no longer an income upon which people can live without further support. • A large proportion of local authority housing has disappeared. • NHS dental care has been severely eroded.	• Education for all has been maintained and extended to 4-year-olds and soon to 3-year-olds. • There has been an extension in higher education places. • Support is available for all poor individuals and families. • All remain entitled to state health care.
Equality • There is a 'postcode lottery' in health where provision varies a great deal. • Education provision varies considerably. • Subsidised housing provision varies in different localities.	• No groups have been excluded from the provisions of the welfare state. • There is now positive discrimination for areas where there is special educational need, thus improving equal opportunities.
Free at the point of delivery • University top-up fees have been introduced. • Patient contributions to dental care costs have increased. • Increases in prescription charges continue.	• All necessary medical procedures are available free. • Increasing types of medical treatment, including IVF, cosmetic surgery etc. are now available free. • Education provision is free apart from university fees.
State control • Increasing provision has been contracted out to the private sector. • Private Finance Initiatives have brought much of the creation of capital assets into the private sector. • NHS medical treatment may now be provided by the private sector.	• The vast majority of Welfare State services remain in the public sector. • The Welfare State is still totally funded out of general taxation or contributions by recipients.

SAMPLE QUESTIONS

Short questions

1 Explain the modern 'pensions crisis'.

2 How have tax credits been used in an attempt to reduce poverty?

3 In what ways did New Labour seek to target welfare benefits more effectively?

4 Why was education so important to New Labour governments?

5 To what extent has the health service been privatised?

6 In what ways has housing been an ideological as well as a political issue?

Essay questions

1 To what extent have the principles of the Welfare State been eroded since 1990?

2 How has New Labour sought to deal with social exclusion?

3 In what senses, and to what extent is the Welfare State still an ideological issue?

4 Assess the extent to which there is political consensus over the future of the Welfare State.

Law and order

3

BACKGROUND

Before examining the political issue of law and order as it has unfolded since 1979, we need to define the scope of the subject. The following elements may be included under the general heading 'law and order'.

- **The system of criminal law**. How can it be kept up to date and used to combat law through conviction and deterrence?
- **Crime and punishment**. What are the most effective ways in which the sentencing of convicted criminals can be used to deter crime, to satisfy the victims of crime, to prevent re-offending and to satisfy public demands for retribution?
- **The law courts**. How can they be organised to deal effectively and efficiently with crime?
- **The prison and probation system**. This needs to keep up with demand, to ensure security from criminals for the community and to take measures to rehabilitate prisoners and to try to prevent re-offending.
- **Policing**. How much should be spent on the service, how many officers should be employed, what equipment should be invested in and how should police forces be managed and deployed to combat crime?

> **public order**
>
> This term refers to the condition where the public feel safe from general disorder, as opposed to individual crime. In practice it relates to measures to prevent major public disturbances as a result of demonstrations or major entertainment events.

- **How to deal with potential breaches of public order**. This involves both the laws on public order and also how police are used. It also concerns the circumstances in which public meetings and demonstrations should be banned or curtailed.
- **How to deal with the social and moral causes of crime**. Such policies concentrate on how to reduce the incidence of crime by cutting off its causes at source.

From time to time all these matters come to the attention of policy makers. Some may be stressed more than others at times, but they are all facets of the same problem.

Although the maintenance of law and order is one of the oldest and most basic functions of government, it has not been one of the main subjects of partisan conflict for most of the modern era in Britain. Crime and public disorder (including terrorism) are the concern of all, but usually stand in the background of politics. This has been for two reasons:

- There was a perception that politicians do not have it in their power to control crime levels. Crime was seen as a social problem which is inevitable and whose causes are complex.
- Until the 1970s crime levels, or at least known and reported levels of crime, did not rise seriously. Nor was the fear of crime seen as a major problem. To be directly affected by crime or public disorder was rare enough for other issues, such as the economic for people to have well-being of the country, foreign policy and welfare policy, uppermost in their minds when making political judgements.

> **causes of crime**
> This general expression is commonly used by politicians to describe and debate the reasons why crime is occurring and why specific individuals become involved in crime. Traditional conservatives place the cause of crime firmly on the shoulders of the individual who must be responsible for their own actions. Liberals, social democrats and many modern conservatives, however, argue that the causes are complex, being partly economic, cultural and social rather than simply based on individual choices.

This led to a situation where there was a general consensus on law and order issues. The causes of growing crime rates were seen as social and moral, more the concern of churches, schools and courts than of governments. The way in which crime could be combated, all major parties agreed, was to reduce the social causes of crime. Prosperity, educational opportunity, high employment and better housing were all seen as the best way of dealing with crime. Breakdowns in public order were, meanwhile, rare events. There had been some race rioting in the 1950s, youth violence in the 1960s, political demonstrations in the late 1960s and some violence during large-scale strikes, but most people remained unaffected. The police, too, seemed capable of handling the outbreaks. No special legislation was seen as necessary.

During the 1970s this situation was to change. Crime levels were rising inexorably, especially crimes against property and cars as well as violent and sexual offences in general. This also meant that the fear of crime was growing. Public disorder also grew, with large-scale industrial strikes becoming more violent and football hooliganism growing.

An increasingly alarmed public turned to the politicians for solutions. Under this pressure the political consensus on law and order collapsed. The Labour Party remained committed to policies that were designed to deal with the social causes of crime. The Conservative Party, however, moved steadily towards a harder-line approach. For them the laws needed to be reviewed, police and law courts to be given greater powers and public disorder controlled more effectively. The Liberals (later Liberal Democrats) shared a social view of crime with the Labour Party, but they also emphasised the threat to human rights which was increased by the Conservatives' increasingly severe policies.

The electoral campaign of 1979 marks a clear end to the consensus. The Labour Party was still arguing that economic prosperity and reduced unemployment would solve many of the problems of growing crime. The restoration of communities, better housing and social services were also seen as potential factors in crime reduction. This was rejected by the Conservatives, who actually blamed many of the policies of the Labour government of 1974–79 for the rise in crime. Labour's 'soft' approach to trade unions led to public disorder, they argued. An extremely liberal approach to young offenders – largely replacing custodial sentences with community work, probation supervision and the involvement of social services with young offenders – was criticised for failing to deal with delinquency. The electorate seemed to agree. Conservative law and order policies were certainly one of the factors that that brought them back into power in 1979.

> **punishment**
> In modern politics punishment no longer refers simply to custodial sentencing. It also refers to so-called 'community sentences' where offenders are expected to undertake community work and to non-custodial measures such as curfews, tagging and Anti-Social behaviour Orders (ASBOs).

THE CONSERVATIVES IN POWER 1979–97

The first seven years of the administration of Margaret Thatcher saw one of the greatest onslaughts on crime and disorder ever seen in Britain. The issue was attacked at all levels. The main developments were as follows:

- There was a steady increase in the size of the police force. Police pay was raised by 16 per cent to raise morale and to boost recruitment. Between 1979 and 1984 expenditure on policing more than doubled. From 1979 to 1983 police numbers rose from 110,000 to 120,000 officers in the UK.

- To meet the demand for greater custodial sentencing, eight new prisons and four new detention centres were built between 1979 and 1984.
- The **Criminal Justice Act** of 1982 gave magistrates much greater powers to imprison offenders and to lengthen sentences. More importantly a system of youth custody for very young offenders was introduced. This policy was known as the *short sharp shock* and was based on a belief that, if a young criminal was given a short, but very strict, period of custody, it would nip their criminal tendency in the bud. The policy was highly controversial. Many sociologists were convinced that it would not work and that detention centres (sometimes known as 'boot camps') would only be breeding grounds where young offenders would learn more about crime from older inmates.
- The **Police and Criminal Evidence Act (PACE)** of 1984 marked a further considerable increase in police powers. The ability to stop and search those suspected of committing, or even contemplating, crime was extended. It also became possible to question suspects for extended periods of time with the permission of a magistrate. The compulsory recording of interviews of suspects went some way to balancing out the greater questioning powers, but the overall effect of PACE was to change the balance of power markedly in the direction of the police.
- In 1986 the **Public Order Act** was passed. This was a response to the inner-city disturbances which had occurred in London, Liverpool, Bristol and other cities in the early 1980s, and to the conduct of the miners' strike of 1984 when there was extensive violence around the coal pits and serious challenges to the police peace lines. The Act gave the police extensive powers to prevent marches and demonstrations if they believed that breaches of the peace might result. Rioting itself became a special crime and curbs were introduced on the activities of trade union pickets who might try to prevent non-union workers from entering factories and mines.
- New training was introduced for the police, enabling them to become almost a paramilitary force when facing major public disorder.

These measures, and the general climate whereby policy makers were becoming increasingly hard-line, proved popular. However, the figures suggest that they were unsuccessful. Crime figures continued to grow steadily (see Tables 3.1 and 3.2). This was to lead to a re-examination of policies after 1987.

Retreat from the hard line 1987–93

By 1987 it was apparent that law and order policies, especially those designed to contain the crime rate, were failing. Furthermore there was a complete reappraisal of the hard-line approach by policy makers. Attention switched once again to the social causes of crime and to the belief that severe custodial

Table 3.1 Crimes reported in the British Crime Survey 1981–99 (millions)

Year	Total crimes	Violent crimes
1981	11.0	2.2
1983	11.9	2.1
1987	13.3	2.3
1991	15.1	2.7
1993	18.6	3.6
1995	19.2	4.1
1997	16.4	3.4
1999	14.7	3.2

Table 3.2 Numbers of drugs seizures 1981–99

Year	Cannabis	Heroin	Ecstasy	Cocaine	Crack
1981	17,227	819	n/a	503	n/a
1991	59,420	2,640	1,735	1,401	583
1995	91,325	6,468	5,513	2,210	1,444
1998	114,667	15,188	4,849	5,207	2,488
1999	97,356	15,108	6,438	5,619	2,436

Table 3.3 Offences per 10,000 people by age range 1987

Age range	Male	Female
10–15	221	85
16–24	597	123
25–34	250	57
35 +	47	11

Source: Home Office

sentences, especially for young people, were ineffective. At the same time a new initiative was developed. This was a community-based approach to crime reduction. The changes which occurred in the period can be summarised as follows:

- Local authorities were given greater responsibility for crime reduction. Improvements in the condition of communities, neighbourhood watch schemes and the idea of **community policing** were all undertaken at local government level. Community policing was thought to be particularly important. This policy was that local police forces should become integral parts of their community, with close links being developed between officers and local agencies, schools, youth groups, tenants' associations etc. By so doing it was hoped that the police would be seen not as outsiders but as part of local society. It was also expected that local authorities would create schemes for young unemployed people and offenders which would provide employment or other projects to divert them away from crime.

- Tough sentencing policies were relaxed. The courts and probation service were encouraged to find alternatives to prison and detention centres. The main devices was to be community service and probation orders, which were to be more active in attempting to rehabilitate offenders. This policy was legislated in the **Criminal Justice Act 1991**. Judges and magistrates were required to justify prison sentences and to give them only in cases of serious crimes.
- There was a steady rise in the number of police and probation officers employed.

The course of law and order policy was hampered considerably by a lack of consensus about how best to stem the alarming rise in crime statistics and by the fact that there was too little continuity in policy. There were four different home secretaries in the period, reflecting the low profile of the issue in the government's political programme. To make matters worse, an economic recession struck the country in 1990. Rising unemployment, which resulted from the downturn, led to a further leap in the incidence of crime.

So, by 1993, Conservative policy on law and order appeared to be in disarray. Both the hard-line and the community-based approaches seemed to have failed. The party, which normally led Labour comfortably in opinion polls on this issue, began to lose public confidence. It was time for a radical initiative. This was provided by the appointment of Michael Howard as Home Secretary in that year.

The 'twenty-seven point plan' for law and order

When Michael Howard took over as Home Secretary he signalled a complete reversal of Conservative law and order policy. Cynics have suggested that this was a response to the unpopularity of the government as it struggled to overcome the effects of economic recession. A more objective explanation is that it was the result of a continued rise in crime and clear public (and tabloid media) demands for a tougher stance. Youth crime represented the main concern and Howard went a long way to addressing this particular aspect of the question.

At the Conservative party conference in the autumn of 1993 Howard declared that 'prison works' and criticised his predecessor's policies as being too soft on crime. As the title of his policy – the **'twenty-seven point plan'** – suggests, his policy was broad and comprehensive. Its main features were contained in the **Criminal Justice and Public Order Act** of 1994, as follows.

First, to tackle juvenile crime Howard announced the introduction of secure detention centres for 12–14-year-olds. This group had previously been placed into local authority care for education and rehabilitation. At the same time magistrates were given powers to give longer custodial sentences to 15–16-year-olds.

Second, it had long been a complaint of the police and the courts that the law was weighted in favour of accused persons. The main culprit was seen as the ancient 'right to silence' which allowed suspects and defendants in court to remain silent without this being allowed to be used against them in court (i.e. prosecution lawyers were not permitted to suggest to magistrates or juries that a defendant's silence was an indication of possible guilt). This absolute right was removed. Prosecution lawyers could suggest that silence might be a sign of guilt. Thus a centuries-old right had been lost and defendants would be encouraged to give evidence, evidence which might incriminate them. The police welcomed this change, though civil liberties activists were infuriated.

Third, the police were given increased powers to limit demonstrations and public meetings. Open-air 'rave' parties were effectively banned, and squatting was made a criminal offence, as was trespass on private land. These measures extended police powers greatly and, most controversially, particularly affected young people. They were designed to control the activities of groups of homeless or travelling people who were often seen as a public nuisance and seedbeds of crime.

Fourth, the rules on bail were tightened so that it became very difficult for those who committed violent crime or were persistent offenders to be given bail. This resulted in a sudden increase in the number of people being held on remand in custody. The police had requested the measure on the grounds that accused people on bail very often committed repeat offences.

The Criminal Justice and Public Order Act of 1994 was an extremely controversial piece of legislation which received widespread condemnation as an infringement on several human rights and a step backwards in the treatment of juvenile crime. But its author, Michael Howard, was unrepentant and continued his crusade to prove that a harsher regime would eventually make a positive impact on crime figures.

Also in 1994 the **Police and Magistrates Courts' Act** was passed. This made changes in the management of the police. It involved much greater central control over police policy – into the hands of the Home Office. By reducing the influence of local authorities on police matters, Howard hoped that policing could become more effective. It marked the end of the experiment in community policing. More significantly, the Act introduced performance targets for police authorities. It was hoped that a system of targets for clearing up crimes would concentrate minds and result in better detection rates.

Finally under Howard, the **Crime Sentences Act** of 1996 allowed for much higher *minimum* sentences, especially for repeat offenders and for those convicted of violent, drugs, or sexual offences. For those already in prison the parole and early release system was severely reduced. More prisoners would now serve their full term. For young offenders a system of curfews was introduced, permitting the police to impose severe restrictions on the movements of juvenile offenders.

The result of these measures was to increase the prison population from 47,000 in 1993 to 60,000 in 1997. On the positive side there were signs in 1997 that the rise in crime was slowing down and, in the case of some offences, was actually falling. Clear-up rates by the police also began to improve.

The post-1994 policies of the Conservative administration also have to be seen in the context of a marked shift in the party's moral outlook. Prime Minister John Major had announced in the early 1990s a new moral initiative which he entitled '**back to basics**.' The policy was designed to restore a stronger sense of moral responsibility and to try to re-establish Christian and family values. Criminals were seen as responsible for their own actions, and the liberal notion that the causes of crime were predominantly social was rejected. The term 'New Right', which had been applied to the more authoritarian policies of the Conservatives in the 1980s and 1990s, could be applied more directly to the law and order policies of Michael Howard.

They could also be viewed as a direct assault on many civil liberties which had been closely guarded in the United Kingdom for many years, even centuries. When added to the more draconian measures of the 1980s they also mark a significant increase in the powers of the police. Citizens could now be prevented from demonstrating in public or from forming large public gatherings as long as the police believed they might lead to serious breaches of the peace. Individuals could be routinely stopped and searched by the police. Accused persons could be held in custody for up to three days without charge (and longer if suspected of terrorist activity). If they chose to remain silent it could be held against them in court. Young people were much more likely to be given custodial sentences and these sentences could be for substantial periods. It became more difficult to obtain bail and prisoners were more often denied the opportunity for parole or early release, even if they showed signs of becoming rehabilitated. Finally, judges and magistrates lost a great deal of discretion over sentences through the imposition of minimum sentences for some crimes. Thus there was a significant shift in responsibility for the treatment of convicted criminals away from the judiciary in favour of politicians.

The Labour Party, whose law and order policies were largely formulated by Tony Blair, the shadow Home Secretary until 1994, and his successor, Jack Straw, opposed many of these Conservative policies, They, along with the resurgent Liberal Democrats, criticised the attack on civil liberties and the neglect of the social causes of crime. But it was clear that a new Labour government would not abandon all the Howard policies. Indeed, aware that a tough stance on law and order was a vote winner, Blair promised to be as hard on criminals as the

Conservatives had been. But the traditional Labour view – that crime had mainly social and economic causes – meant that Blair had to promise that these too would receive the party's attention.

Tony Blair's 1993 assertion that Labour would be 'tough on crime and tough on the causes of crime' reflected this dual approach. However, when the party unveiled its programme of action against crime in 1995, the measures looked to be as severe as Howard's had been. As the 1997 election loomed, the two main parties seemed to engaged in a contest to see which of them could be seen to have the harsher line on crime in the eyes of the electorate. Thus, in many ways, a new consensus on law and order had emerged even though the two main parties *claimed* to have distinctive policies in the 1997 campaign.

'TOUGH ON CRIME AND TOUGH ON THE CAUSES OF CRIME' – NEW LABOUR'S RESPONSE

As Labour's policies on law and order began to unfold in its early years in office, it became clear that there was a great deal of continuity between the Conservative policies of Michael Howard and those of Jack Straw, the new Home Secretary. There were, however, different emphases and it is certainly true that the Labour programme was more extensive than its predecessor's.

Much of the programme was inspired by the experience of Mayor Rudy Giuliani of New York and his conspicuous success in reducing crime. His policy was commonly described as **zero tolerance**, though it was much more than merely a drive against minor offences. The New York scheme suggested that 'low-level' crimes such as begging, minor drug dealing, drunkenness and general disorderly behaviour, if left unchecked, would soon grow into more general criminal behaviour. They also exacerbated the fear of crime and socialised vulnerable young people into a life of more serious offending. The effects on the crime statistics in New York, especially on violent crime, were dramatic, with crime falling by 15 per cent in 1995 alone. Murders fell from just over 2,200 to 990 in the period 1990–96.

Jack Straw, who became Home Secretary in 1997, set about introducing a broad-based version of the New York experience in Britain. Youth offending was to be a priority as research indicated that most offences were committed by boys and men between the ages of 15 and 25. The fact that government in Britain is able to make more social interventions than in the USA meant that a programme of attacks on the basic, social causes of crime could be undertaken in a way which was less feasible in New York or the USA in general.

If we are to describe and assess policies since 1997, a summary of the policies is best divided into two sections, as suggested by Tony Blair's 1993 declaration, 'tough on crime and tough on the causes of crime'.

The attack on crime

The New Labour programme appeared to be the most extensive set of proposals to appear in modern times. Of course, some of the plan is little more than a set of objectives, targets and pledges. But there was also a good deal of legislation and concrete action.

Youth crime

In 1999 a major experiment was introduced. **Anti-Social Behaviour Orders (ASBOs)** could be made against youths who were suspected of causing widespread crime and disorder within a particular community. The ASBO holders were ordered to cease their activities and, if they failed to do so, would be liable to prosecution for ignoring the order. This represented a completely new kind of offence, based on generalised behaviour rather than on specific crimes.

The central piece of legislation was the **Crime and Disorder Act 2000**. This was aimed very much at young, repeat offenders, who were responsible for the vast majority of crime. A **Youth Justice Board** was set up in order to co-ordinate the government's efforts and to advise on new legislation. However, immediate action was taken to speed up the legal process of bringing offenders to trial. The system of giving young offenders repeated warnings was ended. A 'final warning' system was devised after which young criminals were to receive a full-scale trial and sentence. Curfews were extended for child offenders and restrictions were placed on offenders, preventing them from enetering certain districts where they were known trouble makers.

These youth crime policies were further beefed up in the **Criminal Justice and Police Act** of 2001. The scope of curfews was further extended and more youth detention centres were announced. The main thrust of the Act, however, was an attack on what Jack Straw described as Britain's 'yob culture'. The main innovation was a system of 'on-the-spot' fines which could be levied by police on those engaged in public disorder offences. Eight such offences were identified, including actions such as public drunkenness, threatening behaviour and general violence. There was a fixed penalty fine assigned to these, rather like a parking fine. The purpose was twofold – to provide summary justice without the need for a court case, and to allow police to deal with disorder more effectively.

General crime

Although there was little evidence that serious crime among the older age groups was on the increase, there were also measures which were designed to deal with criminals of all ages. Minimum sentences were extended to include a range of crimes of violence as well as sexual and drugs-related offences. Mandatory drug testing for all suspects was introduced in the **Crime and Public Protection Act** of 2001.

The Act also forced sex offenders to submit themselves to police orders restricting their movements on release from prison. A sex offenders register had already been set up, but the new regulations gave greater discretion to the police in informing local communities of the presence of such offenders in their neighbourhood. In extreme cases, sex offenders could be forced to relocate in the interests of public safety. The laws preventing them working with children were also toughened up.

For some prisoners 'tagging' was sanctioned, an electronic system which enabled the probation service to maintain some surveillance over released criminals without keeping then in custody. It also became possible to impose curfews on repeat offenders, preventing them entering certain districts in restricted hours.

The harder line which Labour governments were taking was to be maintained into the twenty-first century and, up to 2006, the issue of crime became part of something of a 'contest' between the two main parties to see which could be seen to be 'tougher' on crime. At the same time, a number of distinct 'themes' began to emerge.

Anti-terrorism

The 'war on terror' largely began in 2001, following the attack on the World Trade Center in New York and became more urgent in the UK after the attacks on London Transport in 2005.

The **2000 Terrorism Act** had been the main piece of legislation designed to counteract terrorism. It gave wide powers to the police to arrest and hold suspects without trial. It also made incitement to terrorism an offence and gave the government powers to freeze the assets of known terrorists.

The **Anti-Terrorism, Crime and Security Act 2001** introduced the controversial measure of outlawing incitement to religious hatred. It also gave the police and security forces wide powers to access information which might be used as evidence of terrorist activity. The legislation, together with the 2000 Act, was controversial with civil liberties groups who saw it as a curtailment of freedom of speech and granting too much unaccountable power to the security services.

The **Prevention of Terrorism Act 2005** introduced the practice of placing control orders on suspected terrorists, effectively a system of house arrest and curfews. This was designed to get round the Belmarsh ruling of the House of Lords that suspected terrorists could not be held for more than 28 days without charge.

The **Terrorism Act 2006** introduced a range of new offences including acts of planning a terrorist offence, encouraging others to terrorist acts, disseminating publications about terrorism and training terrorists. The Act also gave the police almost unlimited powers to stop and search, without reason, anybody suspected of terrorist activity.

The **Counter Terrorism Act 2008** was most controversial for its proposal to extend to 90 days the period for which police could hold terrorist suspects without charge. Parliament vetoed the proposal and a later proposal to reduce the period to 42 days. The permitted period, therefore, rests at 28 days. The Act gave the security authorities greater powers to seize the assets of suspected terrorists. It also tightened the control orders introduced in 2005.

The sum total of counter-terrorism legislation since 2000 adds up to an enormous increase in the powers of the police and security authorities. It has proved to be enormously controversial with civil liberties groups who have objected to a number of developments, including:
- Ability to hold suspects without charge for excessive periods.
- Too much uncontrolled stop and search power for the police.
- Too much power in the hands of the security forces to access private information.
- The loss of freedom of speech resulting from the various anti-incitement legislation.

On the other hand there is much public appetite for the adoption of draconian measures against suspected terrorists and, notwithstanding the shooting of the innocent Jean Charles de Menezes by security forces in 2005, there has certainly been a gradual drift towards more arbitrary powers for the police services. The main point at which campaigners and parliamentarians drew the line, however, was in not granting the security forces power to hold suspects for excessively long periods without charge.

The 'surveillance state'

The gradual increase in police powers has proved to be highly controversial. The following developments have proved to be the most significant and fall under the general category of the 'surveillance state':
- There has been a massive increase in the use of closed-circuit television (CCTV) in areas where crime and disorder are common.

- Motorists are increasingly subject to camera surveillance, a development which is now being extended to illegal parking.
- Most controversially the police have, since 2001, been taking the DNA profiles of all those who have been questioned or arrested for any offence, whether or not they are subsequently charged or convicted. By 2009 approximately 4.5 million people were on the DNA database. Although this practice was declared illegal by the European Court of Human Rights in 2009, it will be 2015 before the records of unconvicted people are removed, as the government decided to obey the ruling but retain the records for six years.
- The powers of the police to stop and search suspected people have been steadily extended and are now effectively unlimited. This is especially true since additional anti-terrorism legislation was passed after 2006.
- Local authorities and the social security authorities are increasingly using camera surveillance to identify people who may be defrauding the state over benefits, housing and services.
- Police now have increased powers to trace people's movements through mobile phone records and Oyster Cards (travel cards used in London).
- The police also have increased powers to access the hard disks of computers used by suspected sex and credit card fraud offenders.

Though public sentiment in general supports these increases in the powers of the police and other state authorities, there has been much opposition among civil liberties groups, notably Liberty. At the same time, the Liberal Democrats and many Conservatives have also become concerned by these developments. Indeed, in 2007, David Davies, a leading Conservative and former shadow Home Secretary, resigned his parliamentary seat to fight a by-election on the single issue of the growth of the surveillance state. He won comfortably, adding fuel to the controversy.

Guns and knives

While concerns over the surveillance society were growing in the early years of the twenty-first century, so too were worries over the incidence of crime involving guns and knives. The issue was exacerbated by a number of high-profile cases, the fact that many of the victims were very young and a growing awareness of 'gang culture' in many inner-city districts. Thus, the development was seen as both a crime problem and a social issue.

The reality has been that gun crime has not significantly increased since 2006/7 with a rise of only 2 per cent. However firearms offences rose by 88 per cent from 1997/8 to 2007/8. These statistics suggest that there was a major problem for many years, though this has now 'flattened out'. It may well be that the introduction from 2007 of a minimum prison sentence of five years for any individual found with an unlicensed firearm has had some impact.

The incidence of knife crime is difficult to measure. This is because it was only in 2007/8 that the police began to record crimes involving knives separately from other crimes of violence. Despite public perceptions, however, knife crime was reported by the police to have fallen by 4 per cent between 2006 and 2007. Certainly there is a widespread belief and perception that knife crime has significantly grown. The incidence of murder also gives some indication of the growth of the use of guns and knives. Between 1997/8 and 2007/8 murders of all kinds (including the killing of children and spouses) rose by 5 per cent, a significant but not dramatic increase. However there was a 3 per cent increase in murders between 2006 and 2008, which suggests a growing problem.

The social problems behind the raw statistics reveal concerns about both gang culture and the so-called 'broken society' where growing numbers of male youths were seen as outside social control. This has provoked a dual approach by all political parties. They have introduced or proposed harsher treatment against those using guns and knives, but also recognise that only social solutions can hope to deal with the problem in the long term.

THE MEASUREMENT OF CRIME AND AN ASSESSMENT OF LAW AND ORDER POLICY UNDER LABOUR SINCE 1997

The accurate measurement of crime is both difficult and controversial. A number of problems can be identified, including the following.

- There are differences between recorded crime noted by the police and the incidence of crime identified by the British Crime Survey (BCS). The BCS estimates crime by interviewing a large sample of the population. Thus they include crimes which may not have been reported to the police. BCS figures are normally higher than police statistics and, in the main, they are used below as they are considered to be more accurate.
- *Perceptions of crime* can be very different from the actual incidence of crime. This may be because of a general fear of crime and may also be the result of over-reporting of crime in the media. It is also true that there may be a time lag between changes in real crime and what people believe to be the rate of crime. Thus any fall in the crime rate takes time to filter through to public attitudes.
- The incidence of crime varies considerably from place to place. Thus there are many crime 'hot spots' which may make crime appear to be more prevalent than it is.
- Methods of recording crimes can be problematic. In particular the collection of data may use different criteria. Thus the definitions of 'serious' or 'violent' may change and cause confusion. As we have seen above, knife

crime was not recorded at all until 2007/8. A particular problem was caused when drugs were reclassified in 2005 so that the definitions of 'serious' drug crime also changed.

- We will also examine below 'fear of crime', which also may not accord with actual crime. Fear of crime, for example, certainly often runs ahead of real crime. This is particularly true of the incidence of general street disorder which may not qualify as 'crime'.

With those reservations in mind, it can be said that, on the whole, crime in the UK has been falling since 1995 when it reached a peak. Table 3.4 shows falls in crime between 1995 and 2007/8. In the same period the chance of being a victim of any crime fell from 40 per cent to 22 per cent. The year 2007/8 especially saw a major fall in the crime figures since 2006/7. Two types of crime, however, increased over the same year (Table 3.5). In the same period the British Crime Survey reported that the chances of individuals being the victim of any crime fell from 24 per cent to 22 per cent.

Table 3.4 Falls in crime 1995–2007/8 (%)

Vehicle crime	66
Burglary	59
Thefts general	53
Violent crime	42
Wounding	49

Source: British Crime Survey

Table 3.5 Trends in crime, 2006/7–2007/8 (% fall)

Total of all crime	down 9
Total of all serious crime	down 2
Violent crime	down 12
Vandalism	down 10
Car crime	down 11
Wounding	down 19
Serious sexual offences	down 5
Robbery	down 16
Drug offences	up 18
Credit card frauds	up 25

Source: British Crime Survey

Fear of the use of guns remained high and this was partly borne out by the figures. Gun crime reached a peak in 2005/6 and has remained at those high levels since.

Anti-social behaviour has been a major theme since the 1990s. Much of this is unrecorded as no prosecutions ensue. This is mainly made up of minor damage to property, graffiti, public drunkenness and noise etc. However, some indication can be estimated from public perceptions, as seen in Tables 3.6 and 3.7.

Table 3.6 Proportion of British Crime Survey respondents claiming to have witnessed anti-social behaviour (%)

2001/2	19
2002/3	21
2005/6	17
2007/8	16

Table 3.7 Proportion of British Crime Survey respondents claiming to be worried about violent crime (%)

1998	25
2003	21
2004	16
2007	17
2008	15

At the high point of modern crime rates in 1995, 75 per cent of respondents reported that they believed that crime had increased 'a little' or 'a lot'. This figure fell by 2007/8 to 66 per cent. This reflects lower levels of crime but also demonstrates how fear of crime is more serious than crime itself. An interesting statistic suggests why the perception of crime does not match the incidence of crime. In 2007/8, 44 per cent of readers of tabloid newspapers believed crime had risen 'a lot'. On the other hand only 24 per cent of readers of serious broadsheets believed crime had risen a lot. The conclusions are too obvious to need recording.

Finally the prison population figures are instructive. They are as shown in Table 3.8 for recent years. The government also had plans to increase prison capacity to above 85,000 by 2010. The problem with these data, however, is that it is not clear what they indicate. They could mean that the police have been more successful in bringing criminals to justice. They could mean that magistrates and judges are sending more criminals to prison. They may also indicate that prison sentences are becoming longer. One conclusion seems unlikely, however, given the figures shown above. That is that the prison population is higher because the crime rate is higher.

Thus, on the face of it, Labour governments since 1997 have been successful in reducing crime in the UK. However, there needs to be some caution

Table 3.8 Prison population 2005–9 (April)

2005	75,228
2006	76,869
2007	79,996
2008	82,319
2009	82,773

Source: Home Office

surrounding this conclusion. First, and above all, the period 1997–2007 was one of unprecedented growth (built on shaky ground as we have discovered since). It is to be expected that, as economic growth improves and unemployment falls, crime rates are bound to fall. As economic recession bites, it may well be that crime rates will begin to rise again. Second, there remains a high level of youth offending and general anti-social behaviour. It is these realities which tend to fuel the fear of crime, especially among older people. Third, there are also a number of crime 'hot spots' in inner cities where crime rates remain very high indeed. Fourth, there are few signs that even harsher measures were getting to grips with gun and knife crime during 2008/9. Finally, the successes against crime have come at a high cost to the taxpayer. Police numbers rose between 1997 and 2009 from 57,900 to 77,900 (after a long period of decline in numbers). In addition, by 2009 there were 15,700 community support officers on duty in England and Wales.

The political context

By 2009 a political consensus had emerged between the three main parties that government policy should be based on the dual principle of attacking crime on the front line by improving police services and using greater deterrents while, at the same time, trying to deal with the causes of crime. The Liberal Democrats are the only one of the three main parties to believe that longer prison sentences are a real deterrent, but still accept that the police and courts need to bear down on serious crimes.

The Conservative Party since 2006 has come to accept that the old 'New Right' agenda of treating crime as a law and order problem rather than a social one was flawed and one-sided. Now dominated by 'social conservatives', the party recognises that the causes of crime lie in decaying communities, broken families and social exclusion. They therefore believe that better policies in welfare, family retention, education, parenting and housing will bear fruit in terms of reduced crime. At the same time Conservative policy lays great stress on reform of the police service. The main proposals in 2009 were:

- Continued growth in the numbers of police and community support officers.
- Reductions in the bureaucracy faced by police freeing up time for officers to be on the street.
- More freedom for the police to stop and search.
- Greater use of both minimum and maximum sentences with fewer prisoners released early.
- Directly elected Police Commissioners.
- Making local police accountable to local bodies staffed by representatives of local communities.

Labour policies look remarkably similar, though there is less stress on local democratic control over the police. The main thrust of policy is directed at youth crime, with greater use of a variety of specialised services to deal with youth offending, gang culture, drugs and public disorder. In other words, labour is continuing to move closer to the 'zero tolerance' policy on youth crime which it had promised since 1997.

There is little ideological conflict over law and order. The Liberal Democrats do suggest that the attack on crime should be much more focused on causes and less on punishment, but this does not represent an ideological position. Labour and the Conservatives, on the other hand, have adopted a remarkably similar stance on basic principles.

SAMPLE QUESTIONS

Short questions

1 Why has sentencing policy become a major political issue?

2 Why is it so difficult to determine whether crime rates are rising or falling?

3 Why has law and order policy come into conflict with civil liberties concerns?

4 In what ways and to what extent have judges become involved in law and order policy?

Essay questions

1 To what extent was New Labour 'tough on the causes of crime'?

2 To what extent is there political consensus over law and order policy today?

3 'The law and order policy agenda is now largely set by the media.' Discuss.

4 To what extent is the 'war on crime' now being won?

Environment policy

4

DEFINING THE TERM 'ENVIRONMENT'

The term 'environment' is a broad one and we need first to establish which aspects are covered here. For the purposes of this chapter, we will recognise the following meanings:

- Matters concerning the physical environment, including air and water quality, climate, noise, traffic congestion, health issues and the physical beauty of landscapes etc.
- Long-term concerns about bio-diversity, preservation of endangered species, the effects of earth changes which affect climate etc.
- Issues concerning the safety of foods etc., mainly dealing with the implications of genetically modified foods.
- Environmental issues which affect safety, such as the use of nuclear energy or mining.
- The question of preserving sources of energy and other resources, including the development of alternative forms of energy and recycling schemes.

These examples may omit some environmental concerns, but they represent a selection of the most important matters which have been considered by the British political system.

PRINCIPLES

Environmental policy is very different from other issues in British politics. There are a number of reasons for this.

As a policy issue, it is very densely populated with pressure groups. Greenpeace and Friends of the Earth are well known examples, but there are many others concerned with a wide range of specialised areas. Furthermore, some of these groups have extremely large memberships. The National Trust and the Royal Society for the Protection of Birds (RSPB) are prominent examples. But there are many others such as the Council for the Protection of Rural England, the Countryside Alliance and Woodland Trust. If we consider local levels of political activities, there are still more, many of them temporary in nature. Groups exist to promote or prevent traffic management measures, airport building, changes in countryside use, building developments and the like.

ecology

Literally the science of the environment, but more often used to describe a political attitude which places care and protection of the environment at the centre of public life and policy. It can imply that such a political position is ideological in nature.

Issues affecting the environment concern the political system at different levels. There are, as we have seen above, many local campaigns constantly being fought. In addition, issues may be regional or national, but, more often than not, are European and global in nature. Most environmental problems do not recognise political boundaries, so action by governments is rarely simple and cannot be conducted in isolation.

environmentalism

A more generalised term than ecology, environmentalism describes any form of general concern with the environment. It does not imply a fixed, ideological position, but rather a concern that environmental care and protection should be at the centre of any political agenda.

The environment is not normally considered to be a subject that is a vote winner or loser in elections. Although environmental issues remain on most people's list of concerns, they are not normally high and rarely influence voting behaviour. Political parties know this, so they do not consider the environment a high priority. Meanwhile, the British Green party has failed to gain a significant toe-hold in British political life, largely as a result of the first-past-the-post electoral system which discriminates against small parties. As we shall see below, some progress has been made in recent years, but this is slow and relatively modest.

THE ORIGINS OF ENVIRONMENTAL CONCERNS

Until the 1960s the environment scarcely appeared at all on the political agenda. There had been concerns about the health implications of pollution in the nineteenth and early twentieth century, but they were largely seen as isolated examples. They tended to be dealt with by the creation of inspectorates, which were set up to regulate the activities of individual industries.

Two early pieces of legislation which signalled the end of an *ad hoc* approach to environmental issues were the **Clean Air Acts** of 1956 and 1968. This legislation applied to both individual households and to industry. They were concerned solely with air quality, but were the first signs of a national policy emerging.

In 1974 the **Control of Pollution Act** marked a further step towards a more comprehensive policy, being both national and concerned with a wider variety of forms of pollution, adding water quality to air. At the same time the issue of pollution was brought on to the agenda of the European Community, with Germany leading the way in demanding European-wide anti-pollution standards.

These were some of the opening shots in the war against pollution and in the battle to bring environmental concerns to a higher place on the political agenda. During the late 1960s and 1970s a number of developments were important.

Part of the New Left movement of the 1960s, which was concerned with the alienation of marginalised groups in society, became interested in environmental issues. Left-wing opponents of free market capitalism, mainly among youth protest movements, saw it as exploiting the Earth's physical environment as well as its workers and consumers. As members of this youth movement grew older, many of them retained the environmental concerns which they had developed in the 1960s.

A larger amount of scientific evidence was emerging. Information accumulated about links between air pollution and diseases such as cancer and asthma. Concerns about the increasing danger to many animal and plant species were growing. Scientists began to suspect that long-term changes in climate were taking place and were possibly the result of environmental degradation.

The two oil price crises of the 1970s alerted the developed world to its over-reliance on a single source of energy. This led to a search for new sources of energy which would be both environmentally friendly (i.e. not fossil fuels) and renewable.

New political groups were coming into existence in this period. The British Ecology party appeared and soon transformed itself into the Green Party. Friends of the Earth appeared as a world movement and soon became a huge pressure group with extensive funds and a large organisation for campaigning, publicity and scientific research. Greenpeace soon followed. Meanwhile, existing organisations such as the National Trust were turning themselves into campaign groups.

THE ENVIRONMENT BECOMES A MAJOR ISSUE

Having drifted around the margins of British and European politics in the 1960s and 1970s, the environment moved closer to centre stage in the 1980s. The environmental concerns of the past were becoming more obviously acute and political action was clearly needed.

In Britain the issue was brought to the forefront of the agenda by the Conservative government of Margaret Thatcher. The Conservatives seemed to be an unlikely candidate as guardian of the environment. From an apparent friend of capitalism, which was seen as the main culprit in environmental degradation, one would not have expected radical policies in this area. Yet progress was made in the mid-1980s.

In 1987 **Her Majesty's Inspectorate of Pollution (HMIP)** was set up. This was the first national organisation created to deal with environmental matters. It had powers to deal with both industry and local authorities in controlling air, water and waste pollution. In 1988 Thatcher herself made a landmark speech to the Royal Society, accepting that global warming was a serious problem for the future.

The years 1989–90 proved to be landmark ones in Britain. In 1989 the **National Rivers Authority (NRA)** was set up. In 1990 the **Environment Protection Act** was passed. This was the first piece of legislation to set universal standards of pollution control. They were to be administered by the NRA and the HMIP. Private and public bodies were bound by the targets and sanctions were introduced against transgressors. Any organisation which felt it could justify breaking the targets was forced to apply for special dispensation. Also in 1990 the Conservative government published a document entitled *This Common Inheritance*, the first comprehensive policy document to appear concerning sustainable development.

While these initiatives were taking place, the European Community was placing the environment on to its agenda. In 1987 the **Single European Act** was implemented. This Act made environmental protection one of the responsibilities of the Community, with voting on the issue in the Council of Ministers requiring unanimity to protect national interests.

In 1993 John Gummer became Environment Secretary. This was a key event as Gummer was an important environmental campaigner. He wished to build on the progress made in the 1980s. Gummer introduced air pollution targets, which began the process of reducing harmful car emissions, and instituted a policy for farmers to create environmentally sensitive areas, with grants to support them. Most importantly, however, he created the **Environment Agency** in 1995 by amalgamating the NRA and the HMIP. This large powerful body was to carry forward environmental policy and had extensive powers to enforce standards. Any developments which might have environmental consequences had to submit plans to the agency for approval.

> **sustainable growth**
> The idea and belief that economic growth (i.e. rises in general prosperity) should be undertaken only if it can be sustained in the long term. The main constraint on such long-term growth is the finite nature of the Earth's resources. Thus sustainable growth means that methods of achieving prosperity must be consistent with preserving those resources. The main example is the generation of sustainable energy, such as wave or wind power.

NEW LABOUR AND THE ENVIRONMENT

Part of New Labour's 'Third Way' philosophy was to accept environmentalism as a key political issue. Although the Labour Party is committed to supporting business, it argues that this can be done only if environmental concerns are addressed. In other words, it contains a belief that industrial development and environmental concerns can be compatible, an idea which many campaigners see as impossible. The diversity of New Labour policies reflects the breadth of the issue in itself.

Global involvement

Two international treaties have set the scene of global concerns. These were the agreements at Rio de Janeiro in 1992 and the Kyoto agreement in 1997. The former was negotiated by the Conservative government of John Major and the latter by the Labour government, with John Prescott representing Britain, interestingly assisted by John Gummer who had led the Conservative environmental initiative earlier.

These two agreements aimed to make progress in cutting harmful emissions, known as greenhouse gases. The Rio accord, known as **Agenda 21**, placed a requirement on all participants to take measures to reduce emissions. However, the targets were too imprecise. At Kyoto, however, it was agreed that greenhouse gas emissions should be cut from 1990 levels by the following levels: USA: 7 per cent; EU: 8 per cent; Japan: 6 per cent.

There is little doubt that the British government representatives played a leading role in these negotiations. Furthermore, the British commitment has been in excess of the targets set. New Labour sees itself as a more internationalist government than its predecessors and has attempted to move both the EU and the USA to a more radical position on the environment. In the case of the USA this has not been successful and President George Bush junior repudiated the Kyoto treaty early in 2002. His administration also largely ignored the 2002 Johannesburg conference on poverty and the environment.

Traffic and car pollution

Although the Labour government since 1997 has claimed to be interested in reducing traffic levels and congestion in cities, its policies have failed to make significant progress. Road building programmes have not been cut back (despite fierce opposition from a variety of local anti-roads campaign groups). Indeed, when London Mayor Ken Livingstone announced the introduction of congestion charges in the city centre and proposed parking taxes, the government seemed remarkably hostile.

Labour has also dragged its feet on such issues as road tolls to reduce motorway traffic and a taxation system designed to reduce the use of large-engined cars which produce most pollution. Its **1998 Transport White Paper** promised more spending on public transport to get cars off the road, in combination with a variety of proposals to introduce charges on motorists to deter car use. By 2008 little progress had been made and a new crisis in public transport threatened to de-rail (literally!) policy.

But the government's anti-emissions policy was most severely tested in the autumn of 2000. At that time there was a sharp rise in oil prices, and therefore also petrol prices. This caused a massive campaign against the high levels of duty on fuel which the government was levying (in its defence, the government could argue that the rise in fuel taxation had started under previous Conservative governments).

Gordon Brown was now in a dilemma over how to deal with the crisis. Fuel depots were being blockaded by protesters: the farmers and other rural interests were applying huge pressure and motorists were running out of fuel as the blockades prevented petrol getting to filling stations. Brown argued that high petrol duties were a key part of an integrated emissions policy. Indeed, he added, it was part of the country's Agenda 21 commitments.

In the event Brown made concessions to the protesters. Fuel duties were reduced and he gave a commitment to hold them down in the immediate future. Environmentalists were dismayed by Brown's apparent climbdown. Motorists, however, were pleased that the crisis had passed. Most agree that the government, Brown in particular, had failed its greatest environmental test.

Farming and the countryside

The Labour government reluctantly became mired in problems with the countryside after it came to office. It was dealing with the aftermath of the BSE crisis, which had devastated livestock farming, when two further problems emerged. The first was the outbreak of foot and mouth disease in 2001. It took nearly a year before the epidemic subsided. During this period rural interests claimed that the crisis had been badly handled and was a sign that the government did not understand the problems of the countryside. The second was very much of the government's own making. It decided to allow Parliament a free vote on whether to ban hunting with hounds (mainly fox hunting). This was seen as an attack by urban dwellers on the countryside. A third problem which the government faced threw into focus the whole issue of the British countryside and rural life. John Prescott had already established a so-called 'right to roam', forcing landowners to open up footpaths and rights of way. The measure had been greeted with mixed feelings. The government had also placed the countryside and the environment together by creating a new government department – the Department for the Environment, Food and Rural Affairs (**DEFRA**). Now the whole issue of the Common Agricultural Policy (CAP) had to be addressed.

Expenditure on the CAP was becoming excessive. Furthermore British agriculture was not benefiting greatly from it, while it seemed to be of most interest to the French, who were seen as being at the centre of the beef industry's problems over BSE. It was, therefore, decided in 2002 to tie together the two issues of agricultural subsidies and environmental measures in the countryside. Rural Affair Minister Alun Michael announced that some subsidies would be phased out. Under a new EU directive he was free to replace up to 20 per cent of subsidies with government grants to farmers in return for their becoming responsible for environmental protection. Such issues as the conservation of endangered species, river water quality, and maintenance of meadows and hedgerows are to be included in the scheme.

At the same time the new department has additional funds available for the encouragement of organic farming. It is recognised that large-scale industrial farming is unlikely to have a future in the UK. Farmers here cannot compete in an increasingly free world market. Industrial farming is also seen as a danger to the countryside environment.

The issue over which Labour has created most difficulty for itself in this field concerns research into genetically modified (GM) food. In 1998 the government decided to ban its commercial use and brought in regulations (which apply throughout the EU) to force food processors to declare whether GM ingredients have been used. However, Tony Blair himself was committed to the continued approval of research. This angered campaigners, especially Greenpeace and Friends of the Earth, who wanted an outright ban.

The decision by the Labour government in 2006 to back additional international biofuel schemes proved a mistake when the increased use of agricultural output to produce fuel caused a major increase in world food prices. As farmers switched production away from food towards biofuel, they caused shortages in supply. As a result the British and other governments have largely abandoned the pursuit of biofuels as a major initiative.

Carbon emissions

Britain has taken part in the carbon trading scheme which was agreed at Kyoto in 1997. It has not, however, proved to be a major weapon in the war against climate change. The main thrust of policy, adopted by all three main parties in the UK, has involved the reduction in carbon emissions. To some extent the three parties have conducted a contest to see who could produce the toughest targets. Labour's main targets have been as follows (using 1990 as a starting point):

- All 'greenhouse gases' to be reduced by 80 per cent by 2050 (raised from 60 per cent in 2008).
- Carbon dioxide emissions to be reduced by 26 per cent by 2020.
- A series of 'carbon budgets', each one lasting five years, to gradually reduce emissions up to 2022. This will involve budgetary measures to ensure the emissions targets.

There have also been a number of budgetary measures used to reduce the use of forms of energy which create emissions. These include grants for householders to install insulation in their homes and incentives or sanctions to encourage house builders to produce 'zero carbon' houses. Incentives also exist for car owners to buy vehicles with low emissions. These include a differential car duty level, depending on engine capacity, zero tax on electric cars and very low tax on hybrids. Local authorities and private transport providers also enjoy incentives to adopt low emission vehicles. But the main attack on emissions has been a relatively new policy on renewables.

Renewable energy

Britain has adopted some stringent targets on the use of renewable energy sources. Britain was part of an EU agreement in 2007 to increase use of renewables by 2020. Britain's own target is to produce 15 per cent of total energy needs from renewables by 2020 (it was only 1.8 per cent in 2008). This involves largely the development of wind power, and the government has been actively involved in attempting to speed through planning applications for more wind farms. Grants have also been made available for research into wave and tidal power, with the possibility of a Severn River barrier to harness a huge amount of tidal power.

If one includes nuclear power as a 'renewable' source of energy, a key decision was reached in July 2006 when the go-ahead was given for the building of a large number of new nuclear power stations. This key policy initiative is vehemently opposed by most environmentalists, but has since been supported by some ecologists, including James Lovelock, possibly the best known campaigner in this field. In 2009 it was also announced that the government was to subsidise the possible development of new 'carbon capture' coal-fired power stations.

An assessment of New Labour

Despite its rhetoric, the Labour government which came to power in 1997 has a very mixed record on the environment. It has shown considerable global concerns and is widely praised for its attempts to preserve the Rio and Kyoto agreements on climate change. On the other hand its policies on transport have been less coherent. The commitments to reduce road traffic and improve public transport have not been maintained.

The main problems concern the government's difficulties in reconciling competing interests. The conflict between environmentalists and the motorists' lobby is a typical example. So too are those issues which create heated debate between farmers and rural interest groups and, in some cases, within the farming community itself. Its difficulties over what to do about GM foods are a typical example of the latter.

However, it became clear after 2001 that the Labour leadership had become convinced that a robust environmental policy was essential on both a national and a global level. Since then, therefore Labour has led a major shift in the political consensus on environmental matters. The Liberal Democrats and Greens, have, of course, long been campaigning for serious measures to protect the environment, especially to prevent climate change. When Labour added to these campaigns with ambitious targets of its own, it was not long before the Conservatives had to follow suit. This occurred with the elevation of David Cameron to the leadership in 2005.

By 2009, therefore, all three British political parties had shown leadership in adoption of plans to reduce emissions and reduce climate change. The Greens and Liberal Democrats still argue that Labour targets are too modest and too locked into renewables rather than energy-saving. Recently, too, the Conservatives have promised to match or even exceed Labour current targets. The problem any future Conservative government would face is that the party is seen as 'too close' to the industrial and motoring lobbies which have resisted emissions control. Labour has been freer from such constraints, though it has been charged with dragging its feet in the interests of appeasing public opinion, notably over fuel pricing. Ultimately, however, it may well be that Labour's main positive legacy will be in its leadership of the international movement for more effective environmental protection.

THE EUROPEAN UNION AND THE ENVIRONMENT

As we have seen, environmental protection, became an EU concern in 1987. Its jurisdiction lies in the following areas:
- The preservation of fish stocks in the seas around Europe is part of the Common Fisheries Policy (CFP).
- For control over sea pollution, member states must conform to regulations concerning sewage and other potentially harmful releases into the sea.
- There is a scheme in place to encourage clean beaches. Coastal towns which can demonstrate minimum standards of cleanliness receive European awards.
- Under the Common Agricultural Policy, farmers must agree to certain environmental regulations in return for subsidies.
- Emissions controls over industries, notably chemicals and metals, are set by the EU.
- There are European emissions control regulations on cars, lorries and all forms of transport.
- European targets for the cleanliness of rivers have been agreed.
- There are European controls over the hunting of species which are considered to be endangered.

A historic agreement was reached in March 2007 when all members agreed a joint reduction in carbon emissions of 20 per cent from 1990 levels by 2020. At the same time it was agreed that renewable energy production should increase by 20 per cent by 2020. This marked the most concerted effort by the EU to arrest climate change.

SAMPLE QUESTIONS

Short questions

1 Why and in what ways has sustainability become the key environmental issue of today?

2 Explain the key elements of the current debate on emissions control.

3 Why has the Green Party remained marginalised in British politics?

Essay questions

1 To what extent are all the main parties now 'green parties'?

2 'The key issue in the debate on environmental protection now concerns energy production.' Discuss.

3 In what ways, and to what extent, does Britain seek to lead the world in its concern for environmental issues?

BACKGROUND TO THE PROBLEM

How the Northern Ireland problem came about

Until 1921 Ireland was a single political entity under British rule. It elected MPs to parliament in London, but was directly ruled by the British government. Between the 1880s and 1921 there was an ongoing campaign for Northern Irish independence among nationalist Irish politicians, British Liberals and the new Labour Party. At the more extreme end of the nationalist movement Sinn Fein, a political party dedicated to Irish independence, and the Irish Republican Army (IRA, originally the 'Irish Volunteers') were formed to fight for independence.

The momentum for independence gradually built up to something of a climax when there was an IRA-led uprising in 1916 – the so-called 'Easter Rising'. Though the revolt was easily crushed, Britain's new prime minister, David Lloyd George, became convinced that a settlement had to be reached. However, there was a major obstacle to the independence process.

In the north of the island there was a concentration of Protestants who formed a majority in the so-called 'six counties' which comprised most of the ancient province of Ulster (strictly speaking, Ulster and Northern Ireland are not the same thing. Ulster is slightly bigger than what later became Northern Ireland). However, the Protestants were a minority in Ireland as a whole. These Protestants were the descendants of people who had been settled in Ireland since the seventeenth century. They had been given large tracts of land and so, by the twentieth century, they formed a high proportion of the middle classes in the north. In other words they enjoyed considerable economic, political and social power in those northern counties. Most of the Protestants were totally opposed to Irish independence. By the end of the twentieth century, many of their descendants were equally horrified by the prospect of a united country.

The Protestant fear and opposition of a united Ireland are complex emotions, but two main features stand out. The first is that these people, usually known as 'Loyalists', consider themselves culturally British. They are loyal to the monarchy and believe they have more in common with British people than with the Irish. The second issue concerns religion. The religious question in Northern Ireland requires separate consideration and is described fully below. In short, however, the Protestant minority in the north totally opposed absorption into a new Catholic state of Ireland.

It was therefore decided by government and Parliament in London that Ireland would have to be partitioned. Six counties in the north would remain part of the United Kingdom, while the rest of the island was to become a separate state. In 1922, therefore, the 'Irish Free State' and 'Northern Ireland' – a province of Great Britain – came into existence. At first, the Irish Free State remained part of the United Kingdom. It had its own independent parliament and government, but accepted the authority of the British Crown. This fact prevented excessive tension from growing in Northern Ireland. All the Irish people owed allegiance to the Crown, so there was little to fear for the Protestants. But this situation began to change after 1937.

In that year the Irish Free State broke its close links with Britain and became 'Eire', though there was still a weak link with the Crown. More importantly, however, a new constitution was developed under the influence of the Irish president, Eamon de Valera. The new constitution incorporated a number of principles based on the Catholic religion (described below). This created a wide cultural and religious division between Northern Ireland and Eire. In 1949 Ireland became a full republic (known since as the 'Republic of Ireland') with no links to Britain. (It can be noted here that the term 'Republican' which is still applied to modern campaigners for a united Ireland, arises from the movement which had always opposed continuing links with the British Crown.) The schism between the north and the south was now complete.

Religion

The religious divide in Northern Ireland can be understood only in relation to the events of 1688–90. It may seem strange to consider history which is over three hundred years old when explaining a modern political problem, but that is part of the mystery of the province.

In 1688, the Catholic King of England, James II (of the Stuart dynasty), was removed from the throne. He was replaced by the Protestant William III (of the family of Orange). William knew he had to quell the Catholics of Ireland and so sent an army to crush a revolt led by the exiled former King James. At the Battle of the River Boyne in 1690 the Catholic army was defeated and Protestant ascendancy in the north was established. King William's family title, of course, gives its name to the Protestant Orange Order which was founded to celebrate the victory of Protestantism in Ireland. When the Orange Order marches in the north today it is a demonstration of triumphalism which is well understood by both sides of the political divide.

So history continues to play a major role in the troubles. But it is not just an ancient tribal feud. The Protestants in the north fear the domination of the Catholic religion in various aspects of their lives. Education is a prime example of this, but there is also a fear that artistic and cultural life will be suppressed by the dominance of strict Catholic values. Until 1998, indeed, the constitution of the Irish Republic contained principles of law which were effectively religious rules. Divorce, abortion and contraception, for example, were all outlawed in Irish law. On a stricter religious level, some Protestants also fear the authority of the Pope which Catholics accept. This is now a more extreme view, but is held by some such as the Reverend Iain Paisley who leads the extreme loyalist party, the Democratic Unionist Party.

As religious observance has declined, it might be thought that the so-called 'sectarian' divide in Northern Ireland might disappear. This has not been the case. Strict religious belief may be less significant, but religion still represents culture and the conflict is, to a great extent, cultural in nature. There is an old joke in Northern Ireland which illustrates the strange place of religion in the troubles. It runs like this: A Jew was walking along a Belfast street. He was stopped by a threatening group of youths. 'Are you a Protestant or a Catholic?', they demanded. 'Neither,' said the man, 'I'm Jewish'. 'Yes,' said one of the youths, 'but are you a Protestant Jew or a Catholic Jew?' The spiritual side of religion is less important than its cultural and political significance.

To many in Northern Ireland, therefore, being Protestant is synonymous with being 'British', while Catholics are seen as 'Irish'. The religious labels have become convenient ways in which we can identify the political and cultural divide, even though there is nothing intrinsically Protestant about loyalism or Catholic about republicanism.

THE ONSET OF THE MODERN 'TROUBLES'

When the province of Northern Ireland was granted its own devolved government in 1921, it was given political institutions which were, in effect, a smaller version of the Westminster model. A small parliament (known as 'Stormont' after the building where it met) was elected by first-past-the-post after a brief flirtation with proportional representation. From the majority at Stormont an executive government was drawn, with a prime minister and a cabinet. It operated very much like the government in London, though its jurisdiction was limited to domestic affairs. Foreign policy, defence and overall economic management were set in London. There was also a full local government system put in place.

This seems uncontroversial at first sight. However, it came about that all the institutions of government were dominated by the Protestant Unionists. This was reinforced by the practice of 'gerrymandering' where political boundaries were manipulated to favour one political party – the Unionists. Although the Unionists represented about two-thirds of the population of the north, they exerted 100 per cent control over Stormont, the government and most local government. The Catholics felt effectively 'disenfranchised'. But the problem ran deeper than this. It was also the case that Catholics suffered widespread, systematic discrimination at the hands of state institutions.

This discrimination existed in education, housing provision, employment in public service, the granting of official contracts to local firms and, perhaps most seriously, in the law enforcement system. The Northern Ireland police – known as the Royal Ulster Constabulary – was almost exclusively Protestant, and so was much of the judiciary. It was therefore suspected (with varying degrees of justification) that Catholics were also discriminated against in the criminal justice system. As the 1960s wore on, the Catholic minority found it could less and less rely on the forces of law and order. Indeed many actually felt directly threatened by them. This is a key ingredient in the recipe for conflict.

To add to the political and religious strife, Northern Ireland society is also culturally divided. Most schools, sports clubs, pubs, clubs, newspapers and housing estates are associated exclusively with one side of the sectarian divide or the other. The two communities, therefore, rarely mix. The opportunities for mutual understanding and compromise are, thus, limited.

Tension within the Catholic community mounted steadily during the 1960s. A largely middle-class civil rights movement was formed in 1968, a year when protest movements of various kinds had emerged all over Europe and the USA. This began to demonstrate against discrimination against Catholics. It became ultimately allied to a working-class movement in the Catholic housing estates whose grievances were not only economic and political. In hard economic times in the mid-1960s it was clear that the Catholic workers suffered more than their Protestant counterparts. The chemistry between the two movements proved to be explosive.

THE MODERN 'TROUBLES'

The flashpoint for conflict occurred in 1968 when a march by the new Civil Rights Association – a largely Catholic, Republican organisation – was attacked by Loyalists in Londonderry. The Royal Ulster Constabulary restored order, but at the expense of some violence, which antagonised the civil rights campaigners. During 1968 and 1969 there were growing outbursts of conflict between Loyalists and Republicans. Extra British troops were drafted into Belfast to keep the peace. From then on, the British army presence in Northern Ireland steadily grew.

The year 1971 proved to be a critical one. A bomb, planted by the Protestant paramilitary organisation – the Ulster Volunteer Force – killed fifteen Catholics in a Belfast bar. This was in response to what the Protestant community saw as an increasing threat from the IRA. The IRA had mobilised its forces and was recruiting new members rapidly. The response of the British government was to introduce internment.

The process of internment had last been used in the Second World War to remove people of enemy nationality from society by placing them in special camps. In Northern Ireland it was applied to anyone who was *suspected* of being engaged in terrorist activity. No trial was held, though the authorities had to convince a judge that there were grounds for suspicion. Three hundred were interned in the summer of 1971, nearly all Catholics, who were suspected of IRA membership. This angered the civil rights campaigners who saw it as imprisonment without trial. More seriously, it convinced the Catholic, Republican, community that the British government was firmly on the side of the Loyalists.

Demonstrations, sporadic rioting and bombings continued through 1971, culminating in the most serious incident of the troubles to date. In 1972 a relatively peaceful civil rights march in Londonderry was broken up by members of the Parachute Regiment. Thirteen people, some merely bystanders, were shot dead by the troops. The explanation of how this occurred is still not resolved. However, it was seen by the Catholics and Republicans as the clearest sign of British intent – that they would resist political reform at all costs. The British embassy in Dublin was attacked and a bomb was set off at an army barracks in Aldershot. The transfer of violence to the British mainland was a particular shock, as it now became clear that the Northern Ireland problem was about to involve everyone in Britain.

The reaction of the British government was to institute direct rule in Northern Ireland. The devolved institutions in Belfast were suspended. It was clear that the Northern Ireland government had lost its authority in the province and could not maintain order. Furthermore the Unionist-dominated institutions only served to antagonise the Catholic minority. Laws were from now on to be made by the Westminster Parliament and government was to be carried out by the Northern Ireland Office, headed by the Northern Ireland Secretary (the first being William Whitelaw).

Direct rule

The period of direct rule from London lasted from 1972 until 1999 when devolved government took over in the province. For 27 years Northern Ireland suffered from violence, disruption, political initiatives bringing hope followed by disappointments, and renewed sectarian conflict. The story of direct rule is best divided into three themes – the course of sectarian violence, the fragmentation of the party system and the various attempts to find a lasting peace.

Sectarian conflict

Violence continued to dominate life in Northern Ireland through the 1970s. This was characterised by rioting, bombings, attacks on security forces, tit-for-tat killings and punishment beatings. In 1974 the Prevention of Terrorism Act was passed, giving the security forces wide powers to stop and search people, property and vehicles, to ban marches and demonstrations and to detain terrorist suspects for extended periods.

Political assassination was added to the litany of violence in 1979. Lord Mountbatten, a member of the royal family, was killed by an IRA bomb and Airey Neave, Conservative Opposition spokesman on Northern Ireland, was killed in Westminster by the Irish National Liberation Army (INLA). This second death marked the arrival of a new Republican group which was even more committed to violence than the IRA.

By the early 1980s Northern Ireland's main prison, the Maze, was full of terrorist prisoners. Seeking a special 'political' status, the republican prisoners started a campaign to gain privileges normally accorded to such detainees in 1981. Several went on hunger strike and fasted to death. The most celebrated of them was Bobby Sands who actually won a parliamentary by-election while in prison and close to death. Sands entered the mythology of Republicanism and became one of its most revered martyrs. His death brought a new wave of rioting and general violence.

Dramatic bombings continued, the best known of which destroyed part of the Brighton hotel which housed many leading members of the Conservative party who were in town for the party's annual conference in 1984. Prime Minister Thatcher only just escaped, but four others were killed. Eleven people were killed by an IRA bomb at Enniskillen, and 10 Downing Street suffered a mortar attack in 1991.

A climax of violence seemed to have been reached by 1993. There were now a number of groups operating all over Britain, each of which was capable of wreaking havoc. On the Republican side there was the IRA and the INLA. The Loyalist cause was served by the Ulster Defence Association (UDA) and the Ulster Volunteer Force (UDV). The politicians who spoke for these groups were incapable of controlling them. It was at this point, however, that political forces had gathered sufficiently to break the deadlock. An IRA ceasefire was declared in 1994 (following the Downing Street declaration – see below) and the Loyalist paramilitaries followed suit. Apart from the bombing of Canary Wharf in London in 1996, the ceasefire held. Only the INLA and the 'Real IRA' – an extreme breakaway group – continued the campaign of violence.

Party fragmentation

Up to 1970 Northern Ireland politics was completely dominated by the Ulster Unionist Party, which won most of the seats in Stormont and at Westminster. It was opposed by Nationalist parties and Sinn Fein, but these had little or no hope of breaking Unionist control. Everything changed, however, with the onset of the troubles.

A moderate party was formed to represent the Nationalist community. This was the Social Democratic Labour party. Its domestic policies were similar to those of the British Labour Party but it was also committed to the uniting of Ireland by peaceful, political means. This party had no connection with terrorists and did, indeed, shun all forms of violence. A non-sectarian, neutral party, the Alliance, also came into being in 1970. This party gained an immediate following within the Northern Ireland middle classes and hopes were high that it represented the future. After a brief early flurry, however, the Alliance has failed to make a significant impact. Meanwhile, Sinn Fein, which was considered to be the political wing of the IRA, was increasing its support, especially among working-class Republicans.

The Unionists were also not immune from internal dissension. The Unionist Party split almost as soon as violence broke out. The main schism, then and ever since, lies between the more moderate centre of the party and the extremists led by the Reverend Iain Paisley. Paisley is a militant in both the religious and the political senses. His brand of Protestantism is totally opposed to Catholicism (he describes Catholics as 'papists') while, as a Unionist, he is opposed to any compromise with Nationalism. His party became known as the Democratic Unionists (DUP) in 1971.

Since Paisley's defection from the Ulster Unionist Party (UUP), others have followed and there is now a varied collection of Unionist parties including the UK Unionists, Progressive Unionists and the United Unionists Assembly. These groups vary in their attitudes towards the peace process from extreme to moderate. There is also a Women's Coalition party which is dedicated to a peaceful solution and claims to be non-sectarian. The other non-sectarian group – the Alliance Party – has survived but with very little influence.

Party fragmentation has brought with it a number of problems. First, it is extremely difficult to reach general agreement on any new initiatives, so many factions have to be satisfied. The pressure to ensure that all groups are represented in any political system means that complex electoral systems have to be adopted. Some of the groups, furthermore, have their own military wings which they only partially control. Failure to satisfy them all may result in a continuation of violence, even from very small splinter groups. Above all, however, the multi-party nature of Northern Ireland politics means that there is always likely to be a lack of coherence in any of the various movements which jockey each other for influence.

PEACE INITIATIVES

Throughout the 1970s, 1980s and 1990s British governments produced a series of initiatives to try to find a peace formula. The essential details of the most important stages in this process are described below.

Power-sharing and the Sunningdale Agreement 1973–74

With hindsight it may seem naive that the British government should have believed that the political problem of Northern Ireland could be solved simply by creating a system which appeared to give representation to both the loyalist and nationalist communities. But back in 1973 this was perceived to be the main problem. The idea that conflict was more deeply rooted was simply not understood at the time.

So, in 1973, a new assembly was elected and an executive was drawn from it. This 11-person government was comprised of six Unionists, four Nationalists from the SDLP and one 'neutral' member from the Alliance Party. This was a reasonably fair reflection of the divisions in the community, but it still meant that the Unionists held a clear majority. Furthermore, the head of the executive – Brian Faulkner – was soon rejected by his own Unionist Party. Sinn Fein, which now claimed to represent nationalism, was also excluded on the grounds that it was a terrorist organisation.

Despite its problems the government continued to hope for a settlement. The following year the Sunningdale Agreement was signed with the government of the Irish Republic. This allowed for regular consultations between the British and Irish governments over Northern Ireland affairs and a good deal of cross-border co-operation, especially over security. The agreement was seen as a 'sell-out' to the Irish by the Nationalists while the new executive was seen as no more than a continuation of Unionist domination by the Nationalists.

In 1974 a general strike by Nationalist, Catholic workers was called and it was very soon realised that this was a clear demonstration of a withdrawal of popular consent from the new arrangements. The government of Britain conceded defeat and dissolved the new assembly. Direct rule was re-established.

Rolling devolution 1982–86

The Labour government of Harold Wilson had investigated the possibility of a new settlement by calling a **Constitutional Convention** in 1975, but there was still insufficient common ground for meaningful discussion. The convention collapsed after less than one year. Undaunted, a renewed attempt at settlement was begun in 1982. This was a process known as 'rolling devolution' and was introduced by the Conservative Northern Ireland secretary, James Prior.

The idea here was to elect a new assembly, but to give it little power at the beginning. As time went by and the community got used to the idea of having its own government, the powers of the assembly were to be gradually increased until self-government for the province could be established. The SDLP and Sinn Fein boycotted the assembly, so that its early signs were very pessimistic. Some hope for its future were revived by the **Anglo-Irish Agreement** of 1985. By this convention, the government of the Republic of Ireland accepted that Northern Ireland could not be united with the rest of Ireland without the consent of its people. This agreement, it was expected, would allay the fears of the Unionists of a Catholic takeover. But it proved to be insufficient. Unionists wanted a complete surrender by the republic of Ireland and this was not forthcoming. The failure of the Anglo-Irish Agreement contributed to the demise of the rolling devolution process and the assembly was dissolved in 1986.

The Downing Street declaration and the IRA ceasefire 1993–94

The so-called Downing Street declaration – the brainchild of John Major – changed the Northern Ireland situation dramatically and marked the beginning of the modern peace process. The declaration stated that the British government had no 'strategic interest' in Northern Ireland remaining part of the United Kingdom. What this meant – and its significance was not lost on the Nationalist community – was that Britain became a truly neutral player in the game of Irish politics. In the past Britain had always been seen as an ally of the Loyalists. Now it portrayed itself as a neutral arbiter between the two communities.

The following year the IRA called a ceasefire and most of the other paramilitary groups followed suit. An uneasy peace descended and serious talks began. President Clinton of the USA threw his weight behind a settlement and sent Senator George Mitchell as a neutral envoy to try to broker a new political agreement. Sadly for John Major, who had put all his efforts into a permanent peace, he was ousted from office before a new agreement could be reached. It was left to Mo Mowlem, the new Labour Secretary of State, to reach a settlement in 1998. This was the Good Friday Agreement.

Reasons for failure before 1998

Why had all these attempts to find a lasting settlement failed before the Good Friday Agreement? This is a complex question, which must involve considerable speculation. Some of the reasons which have been offered are as follows:
- Political agreement could not be reached until there was some certainty that sectarian violence was over. There was always a fear that if either side could not achieve its aims politically it would simply resort to violence. There was no prospect of a lasting ceasefire until after 1997.
- The British government was treated with suspicion by both sides of the sectarian divide and could therefore never negotiate with both sides on an equal basis.
- The government of the Irish Republic was seen as a malign influence on Northern Ireland affairs by the Loyalists. Until it showed a determination to allow Northern Ireland to command its own destiny, its motives would always be suspected.
- The security forces in Northern Ireland were not seen as even-handed. Ironically, both sides of the sectarian divide believed the British army favoured their opponents. The Royal Ulster Constabulary (RUC) was also viewed as a Protestant force by the Catholic community.

- However sincere attempts to achieve genuine power-sharing were, there was always a suspicion that the majority – i.e. the Protestant Loyalists – would always be in political control.

THE GOOD FRIDAY AGREEMENT

The conditions for peace

Having established the reasons why so many previous attempts at peace-making had failed, we can now examine the circumstances which allowed a convincing agreement to be reached in 1998. Again these must inevitably be speculative, but there is considerable evidence to support them:

- The British government needed to convince both sides that it was a neutral player. The new Labour government was able to achieve this to some extent. In addition the intervention of the United States, President Clinton and Senator Mitchell in particular, went some way to establish trust on both sides.
- The new Secretary of State for Northern Ireland – Mo Mowlem – enjoyed the trust of the Republican community more than any of her predecessors.
- The Unionist Leader, David Trimble, had the necessary respect to carry forward a more moderate Loyalist position. His willingness to negotiate – albeit indirectly – with Sinn Fein was a huge step forward.
- Possibly, the return of some degree of economic prosperity in the second half of the 1990s may have reduced alienation among the working classes.
- The rapid and dramatic growth in prosperity in the Republic of Ireland, together with a distinct loosening of religious influence there, may have allayed some of the fears of Protestants in Northern Ireland.
- The death of 27 people in Omagh (albeit after the Good Friday Agreement was signed) confirmed the community's desire to see an end to violence. Sinn Fein and the IRA, neither of which was responsible for the Omagh bomb (it was the act of the extremist 'Real' IRA), repudiated violence of this kind. The revulsion within Northern Ireland renewed determination to make the agreement work.

The nature of the agreement

The Good Friday Agreement can be divided into five main strands. These are as shown in the box.

Good Friday Agreement

1 There should be a devolved government in Northern Ireland along strict proportional lines with all elements of the community properly represented.
2 There was to be real progress towards the solving of sectarian issues such as the decommissioning of terrorist weapons, reform of the Royal Ulster Constabulary, the gradual withdrawal of British troops and reform of the criminal justice system.
3 There was to be increased co-operation and some power-sharing between the governments of the United Kingdom, the Republic of Ireland and the devolved government of Northern Ireland.
4 All sides in the agreement should renounce the use of violence once and for all.
5 The Republic of Ireland should give up its historic objective of uniting Ireland and should amend its constitution and laws to remove specific terms which were offensive to Protestants.

DEVOLUTION

The electoral system

The devolution process in Northern Ireland had to be very different from its counterparts in Wales and Scotland. In particular, the electoral system to be used had to be such that all minority groups were represented. A form of proportional representation was used in Scotland and Wales, but this was not a radical system and it eliminated the very small parties which might have sought election. In Northern Ireland even very small factions had to have a chance of winning seats in the new assembly. For this reason, the Single Transferable Vote (STV) was introduced. STV allows both small parties and individuals to win seats as it is one of the most proportional forms of electoral system known to politics. The results of the first assembly elections reflect the success of STV in this regard (see Table 5.1). Local government elections were held on the same basis and the results were similar. We can see that Loyalist parties (all the Unionist factions together) won over 50 per cent of the seats, but the political system is so fragmented that no group enjoys a dominant majority. This contrasts with the traditional political system in the province, which was completely controlled by a large, single Unionist Party.

The Assembly

The election result demonstrates that the new Assembly, containing 108 members, represented a multi-party system, very much along the lines of most European systems. In order to pass legislation, coalitions of support have to be built. No single group can bulldoze any measure through the legislature.

Table 5.1 **Northern Ireland Assembly election 1998**

Party	Seats won
Ulster Unionist Party	28
Social Democratic and Labour Party	24
Democratic Unionist Party	20
Sinn Fein	18
Alliance Party	6
Northern Ireland Unionist Party	3
United Unionist Assembly Party	3
Northern Ireland Women's Coalition	2
Progressive Unionist Party	2
Social Democratic and Labour Party	24
Democratic Unionist Party	20

Its powers are extensive. A wide range of primary legislation can be passed. However, such areas as foreign policy, the economy, finance and, above all, security matters cannot be left to the Assembly. Security (mainly policing) and criminal law are the most sensitive of issues in the province (unlike Scotland and Wales where sectarian conflict is not an issue). It also oversees the administration of such services as health, education, housing, transport and agriculture. It is expected that these policy issues, which were formerly run on a sectarian basis, will be conducted in a neutral fashion so that no section of the community will suffer discrimination. A strong committee system, which scrutinises the work of the devolved government, helps to prevent such possibilities from re-emerging.

The idea of cross-community agreements in the Assembly was a key innovation. It is completely different from anything known either in the British political system or in the devolved arrangements in Wales and Northern Ireland. Essentially, the safeguards work as follows:

- All Northern Ireland legislation must conform to the European Convention on Human Rights. This ensures that no sections of the community or individuals may suffer discrimination. Though this provision is in place in Scotland, it does not apply to primary legislation for England and Wales.
- The committees of the Assembly, which consider both proposed legislation and the operation of government, are formed in direct proportion to party strengths in the whole Assembly. Again, this ensures proportionality.
- Legislation must not only command an overall majority of the Assembly but must also be approved by a majority of *both* communities, i.e. Unionists and Nationalists. This unique provision is a vital element in the arrangements. It ensures that a majority cannot govern without the consent of both sides of the sectarian divide. This is, of course, not the case in Westminster, nor does it apply in Scotland and Wales where the nationalists have been excluded from power.

What we see here is a new model for proportional forms of government. It may not work in the long run, but, as a constitutional innovation, it may serve as a blueprint for the settlement of similar conflicts here or elsewhere.

The Executive

This is effectively the government of Northern Ireland. Powers which have not been devolved, such as defence, security, finance, the economy, remain in the hands of the UK government or the Secretary of State for Northern Ireland. It is headed by a first minister. This will be the nomination of the largest party in the Assembly. Accordingly, David Trimble was the first holder of the post, the nomination of the Ulster Unionist Patty. It is assumed that his deputy will be from the biggest party on the other side of the sectarian divide. Thus Seamus Mallon of the SDLP became Trimble's first deputy.

An Executive of ten members works with the first minister. Places on the Executive are awarded in proportion to the strengths of parties in the Assembly. The parties which qualify nominate those whom they wish to serve. Again this ensures that all sections of the community are represented in the government. It was, for example, a radical and dramatic development when Sinn Fein found itself in a position to nominate two members. One of them, indeed, was a former senior member of the IRA, Martin McGuinness, who became education minister. We therefore saw the amazing reality of Unionist politicians sitting down in government with former Republican terrorists. It was an uneasy partnership, but it did take place. Unsurprisingly, the radical anti-Good Friday Agreement party, the Democratic Unionists, led by Iain Paisley, did not take part. As a safeguard, all Northern Ireland ministers must publicly renounce the use of violence to achieve political aims.

Once again the arrangements for the Executive were radically different from those at Westminster, Cardiff or Edinburgh. The Northern Ireland Executive does not feature collective responsibility – each minister is independent and answers directly to the assembly – and it is not controlled by a single party or a partial coalition. Its critics point out that it has a very narrow jurisdiction so that its existence is very much a token of power-sharing. This may be the case, but, if so, it was an important symbol of reconciliation.

EXTERNAL RELATIONS

Northern Ireland had been seen as a British problem within the province. Any attempts at interference from the rest of Ireland were viewed with great suspicion. The agreement, however, accepted for the first time that the Republic did have legitimate interests in the province. Three new institutions were therefore set up.

The north–south ministerial council

This is a regular opportunity for ministers from both sides of the border (i.e. from the Republic and Northern Ireland) to discuss matters of mutual concern. It meets twice a year at the most senior level but more junior ministers may discuss specialised issues at any time. The meeting cannot make binding decisions but is expected to make influential recommendations to member governments. The issues it discusses regularly include security, transport, economic development, agriculture, tourism, fisheries and European affairs.

The British–Irish council

This has also been described as the 'council of the isles'. Representatives from all over the British Isles meet twice a year. Thus, not only are Britain and Ireland represented, but also all their constituent parts – Scotland, Wales, the Isle of Man, Channel Islands and, of course, Northern Ireland. To a large extent this is a token organisation, designed to give equal status to all parts of the British Isles and to express some kind of common heritage and interest. Its range of concerns is inevitably limited. Such matters as drugs enforcement, crime and the environment are discussed in a generalised way.

The British–Irish inter-governmental conference

This involves representatives from the main British and Irish governments, with the intention that heads of government should try to meet twice each year. The issues it is expected to address give us clues as to its purpose. They include, for example, cross-border policing and security, human rights and terrorism.

To some extent in recognition of this open involvement of the Irish government in the affairs of the province, the Republic made a key concession. It had been stated in the Irish constitution of 1937 that an objective of the Irish state was to unite Ireland, i.e. to take possession of the north at some time in the future. This territorial claim was dropped (following a referendum to amend the Irish constitution). Instead, both the British and Irish governments agreed to respect the will of the majority of the people of Northern Ireland. The removal of the Irish 'threat' to the 'Britishness' of the province allayed some of the Protestant fears of a Catholic takeover.

THE RESOLUTION OF REMAINING ISSUES

It was recognised that the creation of political institutions alone could not result in a lasting peace. The other sources of conflict had to be addressed too. The main issues which were reserved for additional negotiation were as follows.

The Royal Ulster Constabulary (RUC)

As we saw above, the RUC was regarded as a major stumbling block to security by the Nationalist community. Most of its members were Protestant (Catholic members were persecuted and even shot by terrorists) and it was seen by Nationalists as a Loyalist force which was not even-handed in its dealings with the community. Even the title 'Royal' suggested to them that it served the British Crown, rather than all the people of the province. Although, by the 1990s, it had been reformed and had become a more neutral body, the Nationalists wished to see the creation of an entirely new police force which could serve both communities equally.

An inquiry was set up under former Conservative minister and governor of Hong Kong, Chris Patten. His proposals, which were presented in 2000, suggested a change of name, completely new recruitment policies, with a minimum quota of Catholics and a new set of safeguards to be introduced. However, they were quickly rejected by the Loyalists, who objected especially to the change of name to the 'Northern Ireland Police Service' or something similar. They insisted on it remaining 'Royal'. They also objected to the enforced membership of large numbers of Catholic officers. The issue of the RUC remains unresolved.

Prisoner releases

The existence of large numbers of terrorists in Northern Ireland prisons remained a potential source of friction on both sides. As an act of good faith by the British government and in recognition of the ceasefire which was holding on both sides of the sectarian conflict, it was agreed that some long-term prisoners should be released early. This was on the understanding that they should renounce violence. In other words they were set free 'on licence'.

Although both Loyalist and Republican paramilitaries benefited from the scheme (which also applied to prisoners in the Irish Republic), many Unionists opposed this part of the agreement, especially when some of the released men committed crimes for which they were re-arrested. The policy was, however, retained as it was seen as an important factor in maintaining a lasting peace.

Demilitarisation

The hard-line Republican movement saw the presence of large numbers of British troops, together with road blocks, watch towers and armed bases, as an occupying army. By 1998, too, the need for such a tight security system, had diminished. There was, therefore, added to the agreement a loose commitment to troop reductions.

In the event, largely symbolic gestures were made towards de-militarisation. A few army bases were closed and troops were less evident on the streets, being confined mainly to barracks in case hostilities broke out. Three years after the agreement was signed, little progress had been made. Indeed, by the summer of 2001, when there was an increase in sectarian violence, the need for the retention of a large British force remained undiminished.

Weapons decommissioning

This issue remained the central feature of the search for a lasting peace. The Good Friday Agreement quoted the following resolution from the talks which preceded it: 'the resolution of the decommissioning issue is an indispensable part of the process of negotiation'. In order to deal with the process a commission was set up (under General John de Chastelaine) which would organise and verify the removal of weapons. In addition the agreement set a deadline for decommissioning at two years after its ratification by referendum. In the event, this date passed without a solution, so the problem rumbled on.

One of the difficulties with decommissioning is that the agreement did not define it precisely. In the months and years which followed, indeed, it became increasingly apparent that the Unionists and the Nationalists defined it in different ways. Unionists wanted to see the final destruction of all weapons held by terrorist organisations. This was to be a clear public gesture that violence was to be renounced for good. The Republican Nationalists, specifically Sinn Fein and the IRA, refused to accept such a tight definition. To them decommissioning meant 'taking weapons out of use'. They were prepared to accept public demonstrations of this concession, but stopped short of actual weapons destruction.

But this dispute was not just a question of words and definitions. Weapons decommissioning had powerful symbolic significance for both sides. To the IRA it potentially meant surrender to the Loyalists and to the British government. Though they were prepared to hold a cease-fire and to demonstrate that weapons were out of use, they were not ready to accept their destruction which would suggest capitulation and would create a permanent situation. The Unionists, on the other hand, wanted a firm assurance that the IRA had renounced violence for good. The mainstream Unionists added that they were not prepared to sit down permanently in government with Sinn Fein, as long as they were backed by a military force. They feared that, if a political conflict were to appear, the Republicans could resort to violence again if the weapons were still in existence. The hard-line Unionists, such as Paisley's DUP, went further, seeing decommissioning as a sign of defeat, ironically, the same view as that of the IRA.

In August 2001, as the deadline for decommissioning was running out, the IRA and the de Chastelaine commission announced an agreement to put weapons out of use once and for all (still stopping short of full destruction). However, in the absence of details and a timetable of action, the Unionists rejected the plan, and the decommissioning process was back almost at square one. Sinn Fein continued to protest that it did not control the IRA and could therefore not be blamed for slow progress on the issue. But this was not enough for the Unionists, who remained cautious and suspicious.

Standing, as it does, at the centre of Unionist concerns, decommissioning remains the main stumbling block to final agreement. It cannot guarantee peace as there will always be extreme splinter groups of both Loyalists and Republicans, but a successful agreement would lead to the opportunity for a lasting political settlement. Sinn Fein would no longer be seen as a front for terrorists and the withdrawal of a large British military presence may become a possibility. Peaceful politics might take centre stage at last.

WHY THE GOOD FRIDAY AGREEMENT WAS POSSIBLE

If we wish to answer this question we need first to consider why previous attempts at a settlement failed. The following problems may be included.

- Previous attempts were seen as a token attempt at power-sharing, but they were also perceived as little more than devices to give the Catholic community some representation, but not equal status. The power-sharing assemblies and executives which had existed before 1998 still allowed the Unionists to dominate the political system.
- There was a lack of trust, mostly among Republicans, of the motives of the British government. Most negotiations had taken place in secret so that suspicions were inevitably aroused that private deals had been made by ministers and other officials.
- There had never been sufficient political will among Northern Ireland politicians to reach a long-term agreement. The cumulative effect of

atrocities played its part as the population, weary of continual grief and disruption, put pressure on elected representatives to end the violence.

- The motives of the government of the Irish Republic were suspected by the Loyalist community. Interference by the Republic was always seen as an attempt to persuade Britain to give up the province to them.
- Perhaps above all, previous attempts at settlement had taken place within the context of continued violence. Politicians on both sides of the divide felt that any political progress was likely to be undermined by the terrorists. Furthermore, whenever there was a political deadlock, the paramilitary wings of the parties simply chose to commit acts of violence in pursuit of their aims.

The preparation for the Good Friday Agreement was designed to overcome most of these problems. The key elements were as follows:

- The Downing Street declaration, which stated that Britain was neutral in its attitude to Northern Ireland sovereignty, allayed the suspicions of the Republicans.
- The ceasefire meant that negotiations could take place in good faith and without pressure from terrorists.
- The intervention of representatives of the USA was important. The involvement of President Clinton and Senator George Mitchell both inspired the people of the province to search for peace and provided genuinely neutral go-betweens who could move the peace process forward. Senator Mitchell, indeed, was the key figure in bringing Republican and Unionist politicians together.
- The declaration that Sinn Fein was willing to renounce the use of violence was a key development.
- The statesmanship of leading politicians, notably David Trimble for the Unionists, John Hume for the SDLP and Gerry Adams of Sinn Fein, must receive credit. These men showed a willingness to make some concessions and so find common ground. In the past, sectarian politicians had sought outright victory, but Trimble, Hume and Adams understood that any final settlement would need a consensus. Similarly, British ministers, such as Patrick Mayhew, Mo Mowlem and Peter Mandelson, showed greater vision than in the past in understanding the difficulties of Republican and Unionist politicians.

HOW SUCCESSFUL WAS THE GOOD FRIDAY AGREEMENT?

As we shall see, the effects of the Good Friday Agreement were mixed.

Successes

The assembly and the executive survived for longer than any of their pre-decessors since 1972. This was, in itself, an achievement. The longer political institutions can survive, the more chance there is of a lasting peace. Apart from sporadic outbreaks of rioting and some atrocities by extreme groups who do not support the agreement, the ceasefire has also held.

The institutions of devolved government also seem to have worked well. It was certainly a triumph that the foot and mouth epidemic which seriously affected farming in the rest of Britain was dealt with decisively in the province. The committees of the assembly have made a great deal of progress in making the Civil Service more accountable and in creating more open government. There are also signs that the health and education services are being sensitively run. The education service, already felt to be stronger than its English counterpart, abolished school league tables and is moving further towards independence. In general, therefore, the ideal that devolved government should create a 'real' and independent sense of regional government may be succeeding.

Public support for the institutions was also high. Opinion polls showed a good deal of confidence being expressed on a non-sectarian basis. The fact that Unionists and Republican politicians, once implacable enemies, had been able to sit together in the Assembly and the executive did inspire confidence and may help to reduce tension.

Finally, and perhaps most importantly, devolved government provided lasting protection of human rights and the maintenance of equality. The agreement itself built into Northern Irish politics safeguards which ensured that executive action could never be seen to be sectarian in nature. The Assembly cannot pass sectarian legislation and the cross-party committees keep a careful watch over institutions to ensure that they do not fall into the pre-1968 situation when they were unionist dominated.

Problems

The Agreement certainly did not remove the threat of sectarian violence. There were regular outbreaks of rioting, the worst example of which were the attacks on young Catholic children being taken to school in the Ardoyne district of Belfast in 2001. There were also been punishment beatings by paramilitaries, a few sectarian assassinations and attacks on security forces.

By the autumn of 2001 the problem of decommissioning had still not been solved. Clearly the IRA did not have sufficient faith in the long-term success of the political process to give up weapons permanently. Until the issue of armed terrorism is solved it seems unlikely that the Good Friday Agreement, or any other such settlement, will succeed in the long run.

Though the agreement saw politicians from across the sectarian divide finally meeting openly, its real test was whether it could start to bring the communities together and prevent the polarisation of politics which had occurred in recent decades. By 2001 there was little sign of this. As we have seen, a constant level of violence remained. The Orange Order marches in the summers of 2000 and 2001 also continued to cause tension. More worryingly, and in 2001 however, the 2001 general election saw advances made by the two main extremist parties, the Democratic Unionists (who are still refusing to take part in the Northern Ireland executive) and Sinn Fein. Both Parties won more votes and seats at Westminster than in 1997, an indication that voters were losing faith in the moderate, pro-agreement parties such as the UUP and the SDLP. Hopes that progress could be made in such areas as reform of the Royal Ulster Constabulary and reduction of troop levels had been dashed and looked remote, with the two communities seeming to move further apart.

THE ASSEMBLY SUSPENSION 2002–7

The failure of trust 2002–6

In November 2001 the Assembly was reconvened with high hopes for the future. Attempts to restart devolved government had consistently failed as the Unionists would not accept that Sinn Fein had ceased its terrorist operations. When three IRA members were arrested in Colombia in August 2001 charged with training guerrillas there, a further attempt to reconvene the Assembly was abandoned. The 11 September 2001 attacks on the World Trade Center in New York caused a further delay. However, in October 2001 the Sinn Fein leader, Gerry Adams, publicly requested that the IRA should finally and clearly decommission its weapons. The IRA responded by stating that it had put its weapons 'beyond use'. The following month, the Ulster Unionist Party rejoined the Executive and the Assembly was re-formed.

All seemed well in early 2002, especially when the IRA publicly decommissioned a large quantity of weapons. Disaster struck, however, when four IRA members were arrested and accused of spying on the Northern Ireland government. Both the UUP and the DUP withdrew from the Executive and the British government was left with no alternative but to suspend the Assembly and Executive again and transfer power to London again. This time the suspension was to last for five years.

In 2003 elections were held for the suspended Assembly, even though it was not in power. Considerable advances were made by the two extremist parties, Sinn Fein and the DUP and, even though this was only a 'shadow' Assembly which was not conducting business, the peace process appeared to have been put into reverse.

Through 2004–5 discontent rumbled on with the two unionist parties making it clear that they would not return to government until the IRA had finally announced a final peace and disbanded itself. In December 2004 a major bank robbery in Belfast was ascribed to the IRA, as was the death of Robert McCartney in a bar brawl early in 2005. In the following year the International Monitoring Commission on Decommissioning declared that the IRA was indeed putting its weapons out of use. Meanwhile the IRA itself ordered all its members to pursue their goals by 'exclusively peaceful means'.

The St Andrews Agreement

In October 2006 Tony Blair and the Irish Prime Minister, Bertie Ahern, met with Northern Ireland party leaders in Scotland and reached a final agreement known as the *St Andrews Agreement*. Serious negotiations followed over the next few months. The key element was the commitment by Sinn Fein to support the Northern Ireland Police Service even though it was still dominated by Protestant officers. In return there were additional guarantees offered to the nationalists on the protection of human rights. March 2007 was established as a deadline for the agreement. As the province held its breath, Iain Paisley, the DUP leader, finally sat down with Gerry Adams and Martin McGuinness of Sinn Fein and signed the final accord with a promise to restore power sharing. On 8 May 2007, Iain Paisley was sworn in as First Minister and Martin McGuinness as his deputy. The elections to the new Assembly had already been held with the results shown in Table 5.2.

Table 5.2   **Northern Ireland Assembly elections 2007**

Party	Votes (%)	Seats
DUP	30.1	36
Sinn Fein	26.2	28
UUP	14.9	18
SDLP	15.2	16
Alliance	5.2	7
Others	8.1	3

Why the St Andrews Agreement was successful

After five years of deadlock the breakthrough was relatively sudden and un-expected. A number of reasons for success can be identified. These included the following.

- There is no doubt that economic aid offered to the province by both the British government and the European Union was a major factor. This additional aid of over £1 billion was promised on the strict condition that an agreement was reached. Aid was also promised by the USA. A threat to raise the costs of water supply to the province was also used to bring the parties into line.
- It is also clear that a relatively good relationship emerged between the former implacable enemies, Paisley and McGuinness.
- The commitment to reform the Northern Ireland Police Service was one of the keys to Sinn Fein co-operation.
- The declaration by the IRA that it would cease all operations gave some reassurance to the Unionist side.
- A concession by the British government to transfer powers over policing to Belfast by 2008 (this had actually not occurred by the start of 2009) encouraged both sides to refuse to allow security problems to prevent final settlement.

SUMMARY: THE FUTURE OF NORTHERN IRELAND

By the end of 2008 the peace and the power-sharing arrangements had survived. A number of terrorist acts during 2008 by dissident members of the former IRA (either the Real IRA or the Continuity IRA) have failed to deflect politicians from retaining devolved government. Similarly, sporadic outbursts of violence among young people from both sides of the sectarian divide have not shaken the new-found co-operation in Belfast. The retirement of Iain Paisley as leader of the DUP and his replacement by the more hard-line Peter Robinson has also not affected good relations. All parties remain committed to the reconstruction of the Northern Ireland economy and to the breaking down of entrenched sectarian communities. However, challenges remain. These include the following.

- There is a continuing need to reform the police service so that the Catholic community can have some confidence that its officers will act in a non-sectarian manner.
- Education in the province remains largely divided on religious grounds with the vast majority of children attending single-faith schools. This threatens the long-term path to breaking down religious barriers.
- There is still a great deal of discrimination in employment on both sides of the sectarian divide.
- The economic recession of 2008–9 has put reconstruction on hold and the resultant unemployment may well act as a recruiting ground for the remaining terrorist organisations.

- Many parts of the province, notably Belfast, Armagh and Londonderry, remain as 'patchworks' of communities divided on religious grounds. There remains a good deal of tension between these communities which always threatens to break out into open violence
- Though power-sharing has been successful in recent years, with some progress on housing, policing and education issues, it remains a fragile political structure.

SAMPLE QUESTIONS

Short questions

1 In what ways has terrorist activity now ceased in Northern Ireland?

2 Explain the operation of power sharing in Northern Ireland.

3 In what ways has devolution made a difference in Northern Ireland?

4 What are the remaining obstacles to a lasting peace in Northern Ireland?

Essay questions

1 Why did lasting peace become a possibility in Northern Ireland after 1998?

2 What are the remaining sectarian issues in Northern Ireland?

3 Is extremism in Northern Ireland now a thing of the past?

Issues concerning women

BACKGROUND

Women's emancipation

Although the cause of improvement in the status of women can be traced back into the nineteenth century, the effective story must begin with the time when women achieved the right to vote after a sustained campaign of civil disobedience and parliamentary campaigning. Women over 30 years old were allowed to vote in 1918 and 21-year-olds (the age of male suffrage) followed in 1928.

But women's suffrage was not the breakthrough which it might at first appear. It had been hoped, and even assumed, that once women were given a political voice many other benefits would automatically follow. With politicians now accountable to women and seeking their votes, surely they would begin to listen to demands for further concessions. Furthermore, the movement had been almost exclusively middle-class in character. There was little interest in the plight of women in working-class families such as lack of education, poor career prospects and the common burden of large families in poor circumstances of health and housing.

The truth was that, in the first half of the twentieth century, the problems of women, their rights and status, were too deeply rooted to be solved merely by access to the political system. The political parties did not, as had been expected, place women's issues on their political agenda, there was no avalanche of women entering the House of Commons and the extra-parliamentary movement seemed to wither after it achieved its primary goal.

Sandwiched between the two stages in the enfranchisement of women came an Act which had almost as much potential significance. This was the Sex Disqualification (Removal) Act of 1919. This legislation opened up both the universities and the professions to women. There had previously been a range of prohibitions on women's ability to pursue advanced careers. In the event, relatively few women entered politics for many years to come, but the opening up of higher education and the professions had a more immediate impact.

Nevertheless, progress in the early part of the twentieth century remained slow. Between 1928 and the 1960s, therefore, the women's movement retreated into the background of British politics. When it re-emerged in the 1960s, the impetus came from the USA.

Radical feminism and the New Left

A crucial event in the development of the modern women's movement was the publication of an American book – *The Feminine Mystique* – written by Betty Friedan in 1963. Friedan's work was a devastating criticism of a culture which had come to be completely dominated by men. She demonstrated that 'patriarchy' was in fact a complete system of oppression of women. Women not only suffered discrimination in fields such as employment, education and the arts, they were also being denied opportunities to realise their full potential. From the moment of birth, she complained, gender stereotypes are encouraged which suggest that men are superior. This went much further than the women's movement had ever gone before, representing a radical analysis of a male-dominated society and implying similarly radical measures to combat patriarchy.

In the early 1960s the infant women's movement was part of a broader phenomenon which came to be known as the 'New Left'. This essentially left-wing political philosophy saw society as polarising into two large groups. The first contained those who were enjoying all the benefits of the prosperous consumer society. They were in the mainstream of a mass culture which was the result of fully developed capitalism. The other was a collection of groups who had become alienated from the mass culture. They were denied many of its benefits and made to feel outsiders. The principal examples of alienated cultures were ethnic minorities, poor people, disaffected youth, gay people and, of course, women. In each case radical, often revolutionary, movements grew up in the 1960s.

The women's movement, inspired by Friedan's work, spread into Europe. Its key figures were Kate Millet and Shulamith Firestone in the USA, Germaine

Greer in Britain and Simone de Beauvoir in France. In varying degrees these campaigners recommended militant measures to liberate women from the control of the men. They suggested that women should separate themselves entirely by forming their own communes or should engage in subversive activities to undermine patriarchy very much as the suffragettes had done fifty years before. These radical feminists, as they came to be known, argued that legislation to grant women equal opportunities and higher status would not be adequate. The problem of women's status would require a radical transformation of society.

During the 1970s the radical feminist movement began to weaken and become dissipated. This was, to some extent, part of a general decline in the strength of the New Left. However, it was also overtaken by the fact that a wide range of concessions were appearing. These were designed to meet some of the clearer demands of the women's movement, but also had the effect of splitting the women's movement. In the 1970s it was a new liberal kind of feminism which was gaining the ascendancy.

Liberal feminism

Liberal, as opposed to radical, feminists were not revolutionaries. They wished to see reform, but did not challenge the fundamental order. In other words they believed it would be possible to achieve equal status and liberation for women through changes within the *existing* social order. Three important developments in Britain (all of which were also supported by the militant feminists) occurred in the 1960s and 1970 to give a boost to the liberal movement and set it on the way to further successes.

The *birth control pill* became widely available after 1967. This heralded a period of sexual liberation for women, which became the centrepiece of a more general youth liberation movement (the so-called 'hippy' or 'flower power' era). It resulted in two developments. The first was that married women were able to take control *themselves* of family planning and so rely less on men. This meant that women were better able to control the size of their family and/or delay childbirth, thus enabling them to pursue a career. The second was that un-married women were more sexually liberated as they could protect themselves easily from fear of pregnancy. Of course, for many this was an undesirable result, but it was welcomed wholeheartedly by all feminists.

Also in 1967 the **Abortion Act** was passed. For the first time abortion became legal in Britain (England and Wales only at first). This had an immediate effect on the illegal abortion industry which resulted in many health problems and even deaths for young women. More importantly here, however, abortion became the flagship issue for women. In practical terms it stood alongside the birth control pill as a liberating force. But it was much more than that. Abortion became symbolic of women taking control of their own bodies and health. Feminists saw the prohibition on abortion as a feature of a male-dominated society. Put simply, it was men deciding what was best for women on their behalf. So the legality of abortion became a vital gesture of liberation.

The **Divorce Law Reform Act** of 1970 made it much easier for women (incidentally as well as men) to obtain a divorce. It established that there was only one ground for divorce which was the irretrievable breakdown of the marriage. The Act established that a two-year separation (five years if the divorce was contested) constituted a breakdown. Not only did this liberate many women who were trapped in unhappy and unfulfilling marriages, it also helped to take away the social stigma which used to surround divorced women. Like the other two reforms described above, easier divorce had its opponents who saw it as a retrograde step in terms of morality and social stability. But, also like the other two, feminists welcomed the liberalisation of the divorce laws as a key step forward for women.

In the same year the **Matrimonial Proceedings and Property Act** gave courts the power to grant property to divorcing women and to force husbands to make financial provision for ex-wives and their children. So, not only was it easier for women to obtain a divorce but the financial consequences would also be less severe.

The scene was now set for even more important battles to be fought by the feminist movement. These were the issues of equal pay and the outlawing of sex discrimination in a wide variety of fields.

EQUAL PAY

By 1970 there had developed a crescendo of women's protests against unequal treatment of women in the workplace. There were significant differences in the pay of women compared with men. The **Equal Pay Act** of 1970 attempted to correct this situation. At first sight it seemed to have solved the problem, but it turned out to be a flawed measure.

The Act stated that women should be paid the same wage as men if they were doing the same job. However employers were able to avoid the legislation simply by giving women different job titles or by slightly altering the nature of their work. In this way it could be claimed that men and women were not doing the *same job* in the strict sense of the word. Two more Acts were needed to tidy up the equal pay legislation.

The **Sex Discrimination Act** of 1975, which is described more fully below, established that if a woman's work was effectively the same as that done by a man then she was entitled to equal pay. In 1984 the **Equal Pay (Amendment) Act** was a final attempt to close up all the loopholes. It was passed to bring Britain into line with European Union legislation (which was to be binding in the UK). This introduced a new test for equal pay. Provided work is *of equal value,* even if it is different in nature, women should be paid the same as men (and vice versa, of course). The 1984 Act was the most radical of all the measures on pay as it was an attempt to establish total equality for women in the workplace

But equal pay was only one of the issues concerning the status of women. It was seen as a symbol of wider discrimination which was taking place, but on its own it was inadequate. A broader, all-embracing measure was needed. This arrived in 1975.

The Sex Discrimination Act

The new Labour government which came to power in 1974 was determined to complete the radical reforms concerning equal opportunities which had been started in the 1960s. It therefore passed the landmark Sex Discrimination Act as a priority. The Act contained two main elements as shown in the box.

Sex Discrimination Act 1975:

1 Outlawed discrimination on the grounds of sex (i.e. for either men or women, but not covering sexual orientation) in a wide variety of activities.

2 Established the Equal Opportunities Commission whose role was both to administer the existing legislation and to further the issue of sexual equality into the future. Since 1975 many cases have been brought by individuals and by the Equal Opportunities Commission which have 'filled out' the basic laws. This body of 'case law' has established some of the following principles:

- Even when an employer is not discriminating *directly* against women, (s)he may be accused of engaging in practices which *have the effect of discriminating*. For example if an employer will not employ people who are lone parents, this will have the effect of tending to discriminate against women. It is also not permitted to refuse to employ a woman on the grounds that she is likely to become pregnant and so take too much time off work.

- If a woman can prove that she has equal qualifications to men and yet is continually passed over for promotion, a case may be made that the employer is discriminating.

- If women are doing the same work as men, but have a different job title, they must not be discriminated against in terms of pay.

- In the provision of services such as insurance, bank loans, mortgages and rental agreements, women must be treated on an equal basis to men.

These cases are a sample of the way in which the sex discrimination laws work. They are also reinforced by the European Court of Justice and by the European Court of Rights, which ensures that women are given equal treatment at work, in terms of working conditions and in welfare benefits. The passage of the Human Rights Act in 1998 made it easier for women to claim discrimination under the European Convention on Human Rights. They may, since then, bring a case in the British courts. This saves both time and money.

REMAINING ISSUES

The battles for equal treatment for women in most aspects of life have been won. However, there remain a number of areas, which are often less clear, where women do not feel they have achieved equality or justice. The main examples are described below.

Sexism

The term 'sexism' refers to a cultural attitude towards women which implies that they are inferior or that they have a limited role to play in modern society. Sexist attitudes, claim campaigners, are carried in such institutions as schools, TV and radio, the press, sport and entertainment. It is further argued that, as long as sexist attitudes persist, real, concrete examples of discrimination will follow. Furthermore, the more extreme examples of sexism may lead to the degradation of women.

Pornography, hard and soft, and the gratuitous display of women in sexual poses to advertise goods are seen as particularly undesirable examples of sexism. Promoted by former Cabinet Minister Clare Short, women's groups have sought stricter laws against pornography and so-called 'page three girls'.

The problem with sexism is that it is difficult to tackle it with legislation. All that can be done is that women's groups, including the Equal Opportunities Commission, raise awareness of the problem and seek to combat it through education and public campaigning. Moreover, the anti-sexism movement has had to face accusations of 'political correctness' by Conservatives and liberals who see it as a form of cultural coercion.

Domestic violence

Until the 1970s the existence of widespread violence by men against their female partners was scarcely recognised. It was almost impossible for women to persuade the police to prosecute in such cases. Furthermore, it was recognised that many women were suffering systematic violence but were trapped by circumstances – usually poverty and responsibility for children – and so could not escape.

These problems were attacked on two fronts. The first was to force the police to accept that domestic violence is a serious crime and to begin prosecutions. This campaign has yielded results and all police forces now have special domestic violence units. The second problem – women being trapped in a cycle of violence – was tackled by the opening of a network of refuges. In these 'safe' houses women and their children were able to escape from violent partners, their location being kept secret. Social and voluntary workers who are attached to these refuges are also able to attempt to find long-term solutions for the women.

Rape

Legislative action is not required to strengthen protection against rape. The problem has been that too few cases have reached successful prosecution. The reasons for this are that:
- Women are constrained from reporting rape because they have feared they will not be treated sympathetically by the police.
- It is difficult to prove a charge of rape, especially when the defence is that the woman consented.
- Also in cases where consent is the main issue, women may find cross-examination in a trial a gruelling experience.
- In cases where the alleged rapist is a close friend, perhaps boyfriend (so-called 'date rape'), it is especially difficult to secure a conviction.
- Wives have long claimed that it is possible to be raped by one's own husband. Until recently courts did not accept this.

Considerable progress has been made. Many police forces now have special rape units and officers trained to deal with women. In court women receive some protection by judges when giving evidence, especially when they may be cross-examined by the alleged rapist. The importance of date rape has now been recognised and it has become possible for husbands to be convicted of rape.

Nevertheless, women's campaigners continue to argue that rape is not taken as seriously as other crimes by either the police or the courts. This involves a change in attitudes, rather than any change in the law. In particular, it is argued that the past life of a woman should not be taken into consideration when she has accused a man of rape.

Positive discrimination

Women are still considered to be suffering from discrimination. This occurs especially in employment. The law says that discrimination must not occur, but it is happening in subtle ways which avoid prosecution. The main concern is the so-called **glass ceiling** which is said to exist in many occupations, mainly the professions. The glass ceiling theory says that there is a level of promotion above which women find it very difficult to rise. The main culprits are said to be law, medicine, teaching, business and government.

The more extreme campaigners suggest that the answer to the glass ceiling is positive discrimination. Such a scheme requires that quotas should be established, so that a minimum proportion of women should be promoted to higher levels. This is, of course, a highly controversial proposal as it is suggested that some 'inferior' women may be promoted simply to fulfil a quota. Supporters, on the other hand, claim that positive discrimination will change the 'culture' in many organisations. With better opportunities, more able women will enter such professions so that the quotas will be filled by able people.

PARLIAMENT AND POLITICS

Just as it was assumed by the suffragettes that obtaining votes for women would lead to further examples of emancipation, modern campaigners see increased participation of women in politics as vital for the movement. The election of Margaret Thatcher as Conservative leader in 1975, and then as Prime Minister in 1979, may have been a key development. However, women's groups tended to disown her, partly because she was extremely unpopular in some sections of the community and partly because she refused to champion any women's causes.

Attention since has centred on having more women elected to Parliament. Aided by a Labour Party policy of insisting on more women candidates in winnable seats, a breakthrough seemed to have been made in 1997. A total of 120 women were elected, 101 of them from the Labour Party. More women were also seen in the cabinet and by 2001 there were seven and many more in junior ministerial posts. In 2001 fewer women were elected, but the number remains high. Women do play a key role in politics – far more than previously. The story continued in 2005 when progress on more women in Parliament remained slow.

There remain some issues in politics. In particular the rules and procedures of Parliament are considered unsympathetic to women MPs. Long hours, a lack of childcare facilities and the sheer nature of the job, which involves much travelling, does not lend itself to motherhood. It was hoped that proposed reforms to the House of Commons in 2002 would address some of these concerns. However, the reforms were largely cosmetic and there was a slight fall in the number of women MPs after the 2005 election, an indication that the role of MP was not becoming more attractive to women.

There is also lack of a specific cabinet post which deals with women's issues. There is a junior minister in charge of policy for women, but the fact that it is a junior post indicates how low it is on the political agenda.

POSTFEMINISM

In the twenty-first century many commentators have observed that we have entered a post-feminist era. This suggests that all the major objectives of the women's movement have been met in the UK and the rest of the developed world. Equal rights for women are now enshrined in law and there are strong safeguards against discrimination in both British and EU law. While women are still heavily underrepresented in the fields of politics and business, much progress has been made in the media, education, medicine and law. Nevertheless a number of issues remain. Among them are the following.

- Among many immigrant cultures women are seen as discriminated against at best and ill treated at worst. Such issues as forced and teenage marriage, domestic violence and educational discrimination for girls and women in some cultures are opposed by women's groups.
- Equal pay remains a major problem. Although there is equal pay legislation, it remains true that, in many professions and occupations, women are consistently paid less than men.
- Domestic violence against women is still common and, many argue, it is not treated seriously enough by law enforcement agencies.
- Convictions remain very low, at less than 5 per cent of all reported incidents of rape.

The 'post-feminist' era has also seen something of a reaction against radical forms of feminism. Many women are now arguing that they should have a free choice to take up the traditional roles of home-maker and mother, roles which had been downgraded by feminists. Indeed, some Conservatives who are concerned with the decline of the family point a finger at feminism as one of the main influences.

The Equality Bill

In 2007 the Labour Government granted representation for women's issues in Cabinet and the Deputy Leader of the party, Harriet Harman, was appointed Minister responsible for women and equality. Partly as a result of this appointment, the Equality Bill was produced in April 2009. As far as women are concerned, the main provisions of the legislation, which is expected to become law in the Autumn of 2010, are:

- Wages paid by firms will have to be public knowledge so that women will be able to see if they have been discriminated against.
- Public sector employers will have to publicise any pay inequalities between men and women.
- Employers may positively discriminate in favour of any specific group, including women, without being prosecuted under anti-discrimination laws.
- The Equality and Human Rights Commission will carry out investigations into industries (such as finance and construction) where there are large gender pay gaps.
- Where government contracts are being awarded, consideration will be given to whether firms offer women equal pay and conditions.

So, after many years where reality has lagged behind the intentions of legislation, another attempt is being made to create genuine equality for women, especially in the workplace.

SAMPLE QUESTIONS

Short questions

1 Why has equal pay not been achieved for women in the UK?

2 What is meant by the term 'glass ceiling' and how does it operate?

3 How does legislation seek to remove discrimination against women?

Essay questions

1 Has feminism succeeded in its main aims in Britain?

2 To what extent have women achieved genuine equality in Britain?

3 Why is 'women in politics' such a key issue for campaigners for women's rights?

European integration

7

- ➤ Postwar Europe
- ➤ Towards the European Community (EC)
- ➤ The Maastricht Treaty 1992
- ➤ The Amsterdam Agreement 1997
- ➤ The Nice Treaty 2003
- ➤ The proposals for a constitutional treaty
- ➤ Theories of integration
- ➤ Subsidiarity

POSTWAR EUROPE

After two world wars, both of which devastated European industry and threatened permanently to sour relations between its states, Europe woke up to the belief that a lasting solution to continental conflict had to be found. The interwar League of Nations had failed and the United Nations was to be a worldwide organisation which would not solve Europe's problems. Therefore an entirely new kind of arrangement had to be found.

It soon became apparent that there were two rival plans for European integration. One was essentially a cultural, legal and political union. This was promoted by Britain, in particular by Winston Churchill, who had been prime minister from 1940 to 1945. The other was based on the concept of an economic union which would serve a dual purpose in making the states of Europe more interdependent, while at the same time speeding the economic recovery of the continent. This was essentially a French plan, led by one of its most prominent civil servants, Jean Monnet.

These two proposals had the same objective – to remove the fundamental conditions for conflict – but suggested completely different ways of achieving them. Political integration, underpinned by cultural convergence and a unified legal system, would provide institutions within which future disputes could be settled. The cultural dimension would also go some way to preventing extremist movements, notably fascism and communism, from emerging again in Western Europe. The economic plan, on the other hand, would result in the great European powers having such a strong vested interest in peace that war would become unthinkable. Put another way, once there was economic interdependence, the benefits of peace would always outweigh gains to be made through war.

The debates over Europe's future have to be seen in the light also of the geopolitics of the time. First, there was an overwhelming desire to prevent a resurgence of German power. Furthermore, any future arrangements would need to ensure that Germany, which was likely to become the strongest economic power after it had recovered from the immediate devastation of war, should not be able to dominate the new Europe. Second, the important continental European states – notably France, Germany and Italy – were extremely wary of any British attempt to dominate a future settlement. Third, it was clear that Europe would have to rely on American aid for many years to come. A new European community could not be allowed to threaten United States' interests in the region. Therefore, the idea of a military alliance in Europe which did not include the United States was unthinkable.

It is also worth considering at this stage some of the reasons why Britain became detached from the European 'project' even at its early stages. The distancing of Britain from Europe was to affect continental relations to the end of the twentieth century.

One issue was undoubtedly Britain's 'special relationship' with the United States. Certainly, Winston Churchill saw this as an opportunity for Britain to play a pivotal role in the post war world. If Britain was able to position itself as a bridgehead between America and Europe, with close institutional links with both, Britain would be able to dominate the future of Europe. Interestingly, this same idea seems to have occurred to Tony Blair after 1997. However, the large European states were suspicious of British motives and were not prepared to consider any plans which would result in excessive American influence.

A second important factor in the estrangement of Britain and Europe was the strong influence of socialism on the early project. Many of the 'pioneers' of a European community were socialists or social democrats. They saw integration as a means to introduce greater equality and social justice throughout the continent. Although Britain had a quasi-socialist Labour government from 1945 to 1951, it was Conservative-led by the time a more integrated Europe began to emerge in the 1950s. Naturally enough, the Conservative Party was less than enthusiastic in supporting what it saw as a socialist enterprise.

Finally, we should remind ourselves that Britain was still an imperial power. Apart from the difficulties of reconciling Britain's special relationship with its colonies with membership of a European economic union, this led the other

Europeans to be suspicious of British motives. Could Britain be a truly European partner while its attention lay firmly in the wider world outside Europe? As we have seen above, this feeling also applied to the UK–United States axis.

For these reasons Western Europe in the period after the Second World War was very much prepared to 'go it alone' at least in the economic sense. It was ready to accept American aid for reconstruction (the 'Marshall Plan') and to join NATO for collective security after the onset of the Cold War, but the economic situation was different. There was to be no permanent economic union with the United States as the latter would be too dominant. If an integrated political union was proposed, other countries feared it would be British-dominated.

So the development of a European Community was, therefore, very much a West European affair, with Britain and the United States kept at arm's length. Nevertheless, it is useful to consider the less successful of the two plans – the Council of Europe.

The Council of Europe

In 1948 Winston Churchill, then leader of the Opposition in Britain, delivered a speech to European leaders at the Hague in the Netherlands. When one considers how Euro-sceptic the bulk of the Conservative party had become by the end of the 1990s, this speech was breathtaking in its radical tone. Churchill not only proposed a new pan-European organisation but also suggested that each state should be prepared to give up some of its national sovereignty.

> **national sovereignty**
> Sovereignty refers to ultimate power and the ultimate source of political authority. National sovereignty therefore means the ability of each state (i.e. nation) to maintain ultimate control of its own affairs. EU membership clearly threatens national sovereignty.

Most of the states of Europe had recently fought two wars in order to preserve or regain their status as independent nation states. The concept, therefore, that they should be prepared to surrender some of that independence was optimistic to say the least. In the event, it was indeed unrealistic. Inevitably, the full plan was rejected. In its place, a watered-down version of the Churchill plan was adopted. The Council of Europe came formally into existence in 1949 with an initial sixteen member states.

The general idea of the Council was to create a new 'European culture'. It was to emphasise what Europeans have in common and so eliminate its differences. This common culture included such features as:
- Emphasis on the importance of the arts and 'high culture'.
- A respect for fundamental human rights.
- An attachment to democracy and the rule of law.
- Stress on the importance of education.

In the event, the Council has proved to be a great disappointment to those who have hoped for cultural integration. The Assembly of the Council, which contains delegates nominated from member states, does little more than discuss matters of mutual interest. No decisions are binding and no controversial issues are ever adopted by members.

That said, the Council did enjoy one major success. This was the development of the European Convention on Human Rights and the Court which adjudicates on disputes under the Convention. The Convention, which was signed in 1950, has had a profound impact on the status of rights in Europe. Virtually all the members have adopted the Convention, either in its entirety, or as part of their own rights legislation. The last significant member to resist adopting the Convention was Britain. It was not until 1998 that the terms of the Convention were included in the Human Rights Act.

The European Court of Human Rights (which is *not* an institution of the European Union) hears appeals from European citizens who believe their rights have been abused. Britain has been especially affected by the powers of the court, having lost over fifty cases since the 1960s. These have included issues such as the treatment of prisoners in Northern Ireland, press censorship, the method of trial for juveniles and night flights over Heathrow which deprive residents of sleep.

Apart from the important activities of the Convention and the Court, the Council has had a limited role. It does arrange cultural exchanges, organises educational programmes to improve European understanding and discusses such concerns as crime, drugs, terrorism and the media, but these are of little political significance. The narrowness of the Council's role demonstrates that, as an experiment in political integration, it is a failure.

The development of the European Union

While the Council of Europe was proving a disappointment to its supporters, the alternative institution – an essentially economic union – moved from one level of integration to the next with relative ease. Most of its members shared a common goal and enjoyed a great degree of unity in achieving it.

Two Frenchmen – Jean Monnet and Robert Schuman – believed that the most effective way of creating an integrated Europe was to pursue an economic union. There is no doubt that they both foresaw a wider political union in the future, but understood that a single economic market would be the first step towards such an objective. The first stage was a relatively modest arrangement and can be seen as something of a prototype for the European Community which was to follow.

The European Coal and Steel Community (ECSC)

In 1951 the Treaty of Paris brought together six countries – France, West Germany, Italy, Belgium, the Netherlands and Luxembourg (the last three named known collectively as *Benelux*) in a single industrial enterprise.

In itself the ECSC was a limited system. It provided for a single market in coal and steel among the member countries. Fair trade was established between them and a common external tariff established against these goods coming in from abroad. In this way it was hoped that the industries would flourish, encouraged by free competition within the community and some protection from the outside. The Paris Treaty also provided for a central body to regulate production among the member states.

At first sight this innovation – known as the Schuman Plan – seemed to be a modest one. With the benefit of hindsight, however, we can see how revolutionary it was. The radical measures which brought about the ECSC included the following vital principles.

Each member state was prepared to give up some of its national sovereignty to the Community. This idea, of 'pooled' or 'shared' sovereignty in specific functional areas, was the first of its kind in the world. It set the tone for all future developments towards the creation of the European Union. All previous supranational bodies (such as the Council of Europe or the League of Nations) had allowed member states to retain their national sovereignty. This meant that they could choose whether to adopt any agreed measures or to ignore them. The ECSC, on the other hand, insisted that, to be a member, all states had to agree to conform to all decisions. It was this insistence on shared functional sovereignty that kept Britain out of the community. The Labour government of the day, which had recently nationalised both industries (coal and steel), was not willing to give up one ounce of British independence. This was to set a pattern for the British attitude to Europe for nearly two decades to come.

The three branches of national governments – the legislature, the executive and the judiciary – were to be replicated, in an amended form, within the new set-up. Thus there were created the following bodies:
- *The High Authority*: a kind of senior Civil Service which was to develop policy and organise the implementation of decisions.
- *The Council of Ministers*: ministerial representatives from the member countries which would make all important decisions.
- *The Assembly*: nominated members from the six states which were to give general advice to the High Authority and the Council of Ministers.
- *The Court of Justice*: to deal with disputes between member states. The judges were nominated from the different states and were to be independent.

The economic integration which was established in the ECSC was, it was clearly stated, to be the prelude to an even closer political union in the future. Although the structure of the ECSC was essentially experimental – nothing like this had been attempted before – it proved to be so acceptable that, when the more ambitious successors of the ECSC, leading to the European Union itself, were formed, they followed much the same blueprint.

The 'Common Market' (EEC)

Encouraged by the success of the ECSC, and determined to take integration further, negotiations began among the six members to extend the scope of the market. During 1956 the creation of the 'Common Market' (European Economic Community: EEC) was discussed and the following year, 1957, the **Treaty of Rome** was signed. This was effectively the founding document of European integration. An additional treaty, for the pooling of nuclear energy resources, was also signed. This was known as Euratom.

Britain did not take part in these early discussions. Both prime ministers of the period – Anthony Eden (who resigned in 1957) and Harold Macmillan (who took over from Eden) – made it clear that political and trade links with the Empire and Commonwealth were more important to Britain than a European system. It was also true that, following the humiliation of the failed Suez episode in 1956, Britain was licking its wounds and certainly not in a position to take part in the great experiment. The other potential members around the fringes of the central six were also less than enthusiastic. Spain and Portugal were still ruled by fascist dictators (Franco and Salazar respectively) and their intense nationalism did not allow them to consider integration. The Scandinavian countries, with their tradition of neutrality, were also far from interested. So it was to be a small exclusive club. The Treaty of Rome contained five main agreements (see Box).

Treaty of Rome: main agreements

- The abolition of tariffs among member countries.
- The establishment of a common external tariff – i.e. all members would charge the same tariffs on goods and services imported from outside the Common Market.
- The removal of all barriers to free competition among all members states.
- The intention to create the free movement of all goods, services, capital (i.e. finance) and labour between member states by 1970.
- A more general intention to establish a Common Agricultural Policy. This was part of France's price for joining.

The Treaty of Rome also established the institutions of the Common Market, very much along the lines of what we see today and modelled on the set-up of the ECSC. The functions of these bodies is described and discussed below. Put simply at this stage, however, they were:

- **The Commission**: an unelected bureaucracy to develop policies designed to implement the Treaty of Rome.
- **The Council of Ministers**: elected ministers from the member states who would effectively ratify the laws and regulations of the Common Market and discuss future policy.
- **The Assembly or Parliament**: to advise the Commission and Council on policy, but unable to make or amend European law.
- **The Court of Justice**: to handle disputes between members and to deliver interpretations of European law.

We can see how similar this arrangement was to that of the ECSC.

So, in 1957 the great European project was under way. Only six original members had signed up and success was far from assured. By 2008 it had grown to 27 members with several others queuing up to join. A single market had been established and twelve of the members were using a single currency. At first sight this seems an impressive achievement in a relatively short time, and so it was in many ways. However, a glimpse at the institutions which were established in Rome tells us that the economic development of Europe has not been matched by political progress.

TOWARDS THE EUROPEAN COMMUNITY (EC)

By 1962 plans for the Common Agricultural Policy (CAP) were complete. The CAP is a complex system described more fully later in this book.

CAP: basic principles

- All agricultural products were to be traded freely within the community. There were to be no tariffs and any regulations, such as health or content standards, would be common to all members.
- There would be protection from outside competition in the form of tariffs and subsidies for producers within the community who found it difficult to compete with the outside world.
- Producers of a wide range of goods would receive guaranteed minimum prices.
- A system was established whereby the Community would buy up surpluses of goods in order to keep prices up. These surpluses could be used if there were serious shortages in the future, but could be destroyed if necessary.

The CAP was more than merely a free-trade system. It was also a device for protecting key industries and reaping the benefits of specialisation. As such it represented an important step in the further integration of Europe.

The Common Fisheries Policy (CFP), which had similar aims to the CAP and was also designed to preserve fish stocks, was signed much later, in 1983. It proved as controversial as the CAP, not least because the issue of territorial waters is one where national interest tends to clash with European integration. In some ways, therefore, its establishment was an even greater achievement. The first phase of integration – the establishment of a tariff and regulation-free zone with free movement of goods, labour and finance – had been effectively established by 1968, ahead of schedule. Three years earlier, in 1965, the three European institutions – Euratom, the ECSC and the Common Market – had been joined by the Merger Treaty. It was therefore time to consider the next phase of development.

In the meantime the Community was expanding at last. Three countries joined in 1973. These were Britain, Ireland and Denmark.

The Single European Act 1985–87

By 1985 the Community was ready to take a further step forward. This was movement towards the creation of a single market. This involved three main provisions.

First, there was to be completely free movement of goods, capital and people between member states. There was already such a provision *in theory*. However, in practice there were still various forms of restriction. For example members were still preventing some people from moving from one country to another. This inhibited the idea of a free labour market. There were still various forms of restrictions and concessions on the movement of goods through borders. Duty-free concessions were an example, as were variable health and safety regulations. Banking practices also varied so that there was not a truly free capital market.

Second, each member state was to incorporate the Single European Act into its own laws. This meant that it would be *illegal* in terms of each country's own *domestic laws* to discriminate against any goods, labour or capital being exchanged within the EC. Each member was thus fully committed to the single market and would no longer be able to obstruct progress.

Third, a target date of 1992 was set for the final completion of the single market. The Single European Act (SEA) was finalised in 1985, ratified at the Council of Ministers in 1986 and had been incorporated into the law of every member state by 1987. It is, of course, an irony that the SEA was fully supported by

Britain's Prime Minister of the day, Margaret Thatcher. Possibly the most important step in the development of European integration (perhaps with the exception of the single currency) was therefore backed by the leader who was later to become one of the most implacable opponents of the extension of the European union.

The SEA also gave the European Parliament some additional powers, notably to veto the introduction of new members. More importantly, however, the SEA extended the scope of qualified majority voting. At this stage it may be useful to discuss the issue of qualified voting.

Qualified majority voting (QMV)

When European integration began, and especially when there were only six members, it was assumed that all decisions would require the agreement of *all* the members. This effectively meant that each member would have a veto over all decisions. The importance of this principle cannot be overemphasised.

If a member state can veto decisions it means that it has not sacrificed its own national sovereignty to Europe. It also means that each state had an equal status since everyone's veto was worth the same. Little Luxembourg could obstruct a decision as easily as Germany, the biggest member. This is all very well in terms of sovereignty. However, it makes decision making extremely difficult. In order to make progress, therefore, the Community had to introduce majority voting.

A straightforward majority vote system, as applies in domestic parliaments is not, however, desirable. This would take away the power of states to an unacceptable extent. Conversely, it would mean that an alliance of the smaller states could thwart the will of the larger members. For example, when there were six members, the four smallest states would have been able to outvote France and Germany together! Clearly a compromise was needed. A system was required which would take account of the differing size of member states, but would also protect the small states from being 'bullied' by the larger ones. The answer was qualified majority voting. Each state is given a differential voting power, according to size. With 27 members the voting powers were as shown in Table 7.1.

qualified majority voting

A system of voting in the EU Council of ministers, the ultimate law making body of the EU. Most decisions today require only qualified majority approval. A qualified majority refers to more than 50 per cent, but less than unanimity. The precise percentage of a qualified majority varies depending on the membership size of the EU, but it is just above 70 per cent. The precise nature of qualified majority voting (QMV) is described in the text.

national veto

Key EU decisions require the unanimous approval of all member states. Examples of such decisions are taxation and the admission of new members. Such a requirement means that any one member state can prevent agreement by voting against. This is effectively a national veto.

Table 7.1   European Union members' voting strengths 2009

Country	Votes	Country	Votes
Germany	29	Bulgaria	10
France	29	Denmark	7
Italy	29	Slovakia	7
UK	29	Finland	7
Spain	27	Ireland	7
Poland	27	Lithuania	7
Romania	14	Latvia	4
Netherlands	13	Slovenia	4
Portugal	12	Estonia	4
Greece	12	Cyprus	4
Belgium	12	Luxembourg	4
Czech Republic	12	Malta	3
Hungary	12	Total	345
Sweden	10	Qualified majority	
Austria	10	(68 per cent)	232

In order for a measure to achieve a qualified majority to be approved it requires three criteria:

- It must be passed by a majority of countries (i.e. at least 14 members). This requirement is increased to two-thirds when the council is considering a proposal which has not been proposed by the Commission.
- It needs to achieve 74 per cent of the votes (i.e. 72 votes or more)
- The approving countries must account for at least 62 per cent of the total population of the EU.

Especially since the expansion of the EU to 27 members, the qualified majority voting system has favoured the smaller countries. Their voting strengths are not proportional to their population. Thus tiny Luxembourg and Malta, given four and three votes respectively, are clearly overrepresented when compared to the 29 votes given to the four biggest members.

Jacques Delors 1985–94

Jacques Delors, a French socialist, became President of the Commission and thus the most senior permanent policy maker in 1985, the year the Single European Act was developed. His election (by the Council of Ministers) marked a new direction for Europe. He wanted to see progress in two areas.

First, Delors recognised that there would eventually have to be monetary union if Europe were to move towards a genuinely single market. His idea was a four-part plan.

1 Prospective members of a single currency system would be required to adhere strictly to the Exchange Rate Mechanism (ERM) which already

existed. He understood that this system of fixed exchange rates to bring the economies of Europe closer together had to be supported.

2 The economies of member states would have to 'converge'. Convergence meant that key economic variables such as inflation, interest rates, government borrowing and unemployment would have to become similar in all the member states. This would reduce the potentially disruptive effects of adopting a single currency.

3 There would be an interim phase during which the currencies would be absolutely fixed against one another and interest rates would be set for all members by the European Central Bank. This would prevent disturbances in the finance markets of Europe. It would also enable countries to adopt the single currency smoothly in a short period.

4 There would be a rapid changeover to the single currency by all member countries at the same time.

In the event the Delors plan was adopted and came to fruition on 1 January 2002.

Second, Delors wanted to see progress towards closer political union. It was this intention which infuriated Margaret Thatcher. During the negotiations for the Single European Act she had accepted what was seen as an inevitable development. After the SEA, however, Delors wanted to see further progress as quickly as possible. His determination led to Thatcher's speech at a European conference in Bruges in 1988 in which she repudiated the idea of a closer union. This marked a clear watershed in Britain's relationship with Europe. The Conservative Party moved decisively towards a Euro-sceptic position. Even so Britain did join the Exchange Rate Mechanism (a decision which Thatcher agreed to with great reluctance). In theory, therefore, Britain could have entered the single currency system up to the point when it was forced out of the ERM in September 1992.

Delors was undaunted by Thatcher's opposition and moved steadily towards the ratification of his plan. He was finally successful at Maastricht in 1992.

THE MAASTRICHT TREATY 1992

Formally known as the **Treaty of European Union**, Maastricht marked a significant step forward. The name of the organisation changed to the European Union. This change was more than cosmetic. The term 'Union' suggested that members intended to form a closer, more permanent institution.

Maastricht had a number of facets, making it not only one of the biggest steps forward, but also one of the most extensive. Its main provisions were as follows:

- The future *political* development of the Union was to be based on the principle of **subsidiarity**. This established that government institutions should be as decentralised as possible. The concept of subsidiarity is discussed in more detail below.

> **subsidiarity**
> A principle established by the 1992 Maastricht Treaty. It proposes that decision making in the EU should, as far as possible, be pushed down to the lowest possible level. In practice it can be seen as an attack on the power of nation states and support for regionalism in its place.

- The Single European Act was incorporated into the Treaty of Rome. In effect this gave the European Union a 'constitution' for the first time.

- A number of further decision making areas were to become the subject of qualified majority voting rather than unanimity. The significance of this has been described above. By removing national vetoes over a number of functions, national sovereignty was further eroded. It was this measure which caused the British Prime Minister John Major so many problems with his own party.

- A commitment was made to establish in the future a European Defence force and to move towards a common set of foreign policies.

- There was a final commitment to move towards a single European currency. The year 2002 was agreed as the target date. Three countries, including the UK, were allowed to opt out of this aspect of the Treaty.

- In order to facilitate and maintain the single currency, the principle of **convergence** was developed. It was recognised that it was essential, if the Euro was to work, for all members of the system to adopt economic policies which would prevent major disruption of monetary union. Thus, for example, it was recognised that member countries would have to keep control over inflation, public borrowing and unemployment according to fixed targets. In this way a single interest rate, set by the European Central Bank, could be applicable to all the European economies.

- It was agreed that there would be movement towards the idea of 'European citizenship'. This implied completely free movement of people between member countries (a process which had already begun as a result of the **Schengen Agreement of 1985**), equal citizenship rights throughout the Union and some progress towards common policing for international crimes. In the longer term there was an intention to create a 'European Bill of Rights' which would be binding on all members.

- An attempt was made to reduce the democratic deficit in the Union's political institutions. In particular, the Parliament was given greater powers of legislative amendment and veto. There were also increased powers given to the Court of Auditors which would better enable them to investigate cases of corruption.

- The **Social Chapter** was negotiated. This established a wide range of rights for workers such as the 'working hour directive' to prevent excessively long hours of work and short holidays, rights for women workers with or without children, equal treatment for part-time workers and stronger safeguards against unjustified job losses. As with the single currency issue, Britain negotiated an opt-out from the Social Chapter based on demands from the Conservative Party. It was felt that the protections offered would make the labour market considerably less flexible and make Britain uncompetitive. In the event, the Labour Party made a commitment to sign the Social Chapter and did so as one of its first acts when it won power in 1997.

The first four clauses of article B of the treaty are worth reproducing in full as they summarise clearly the direction the Union is to take (see Box).

Treaty of European Union 1992: Article B

The Union shall set itself the following objectives:
- To promote economic and social progress which is balanced and sustainable in particular through the creation of an area without internal frontiers, through the strengthening of economic and social cohesion and through the establishment of economic and monetary union, ultimately including a single currency in accordance with the provisions of this Treaty.
- To assert its identity on the international scene, in particular through the implementation of a common foreign and security policy including the eventual framing of a common defence policy, which might in time lead to a common defence.
- To strengthen the protection of the rights and interests of the nationals of its member states through the introduction of a citizenship of the Union.
- To develop close co-operation on justice and home affairs.

So the European Union became wider and deeper. Maastricht was very much the creation of Commission President Jacques Delors and proved to be his greatest achievement. This is not to say that it was an unqualified success for the supporters of European integration. We can assess the significance of the Treaty by comparing its successes and failures.

Successes

- At least twelve of the members did commit themselves to closer union. Indeed the outcome of Maastricht was entitled 'Ever Closer Union'.
- All signatories to the single currency accepted that they would have to accept economic disciplines in order to maintain stability under the convergence criteria.
- The Social Chapter represented a major step forward for the rights of workers and for establishing a genuinely open labour market throughout the continent.

- The single currency issue was resolved and, as we now know, the timetable towards union proved to be realistic and achievable.
- By insisting on the concept of subsidiarity the European Union made some progress towards allaying fears that it was becoming little more than a centralised bureaucracy.

Partial failures

- The treaty failed to establish a firm principle of citizenship. Although there was an intention to move towards common rights and responsibilities, no specific measures were taken.
- Despite members committing themselves to the idea of common defence and foreign policies there was little progress in determining how this might be achieved.
- Schengen had begun the process of establishing free movement but Maastricht failed to persuade all members, notably the UK, that they should abandon border restrictions.

Failures

- Clearly the fact that the UK remained determined to opt out of key elements – mainly the single currency and Social Chapter – can be seen as a failure to persuade John Major to stand up to the rebels in his own party. In the event this proved to be a disaster for the Conservatives. Britain's uncertain position at Maastricht split the Conservative Party and contributed to its heavy defeat in the 1997 election.
- Attempts to democratise the political institutions were feeble and did little to reduce claims that the Union was not really interested in democracy.

So we can see that Maastricht enjoyed limited success. It is likely that the movement towards a single currency will prove in the future to have been its principal achievement.

THE AMSTERDAM AGREEMENT 1997

Negotiated between 1995 and 1997, the Treaty came into force in 1999. If Maastricht had been a series of intentions, Amsterdam was a confirmation of those policies, converting them into commitments. It was also designed to establish and modernise many of the Union's institutions. This was for three purposes. First, the various bodies needed the necessary powers to carry forward the plans which had been agreed at Maastricht. Second, the changes were intended to make the institutions more democratic. Finally, the agreement anticipated the enlargement of the EU. The areas covered were:

- The establishment of common rights for all, completely free movement of people, common policies on asylum and immigration. This to include a common system of freedom of information for all citizens.
- Common standards in the fields of the environment, consumer protection and public health standards.
- A more precise commitment to common defence and foreign policies. A 'High Representative' to express common foreign policy and represent the Union as a whole was to be appointed (in the event Javier Solana was the first holder of this post).
- The voting allocations in the Council agreed to take account of the next group of new members.
- A series of proposals to democratise the institutions of the Union before they were to be enlarged by the addition of new members.

It was especially recognised that future new members might have extremely variable standards of human rights, treatment of immigrants, health and consumer protection arrangements. By establishing these standards new members would be left in no doubt as to what was expected of them. Potentially, however, it was the institutional changes which are likely to have the most profound results. These are described in more detail in Chapter 8.

transitional states
These are states that were formerly part of the Soviet communist bloc, such as Hungary and Poland. They are said to be in transition from a centrally planned economy to a market-based capitalist economy.

accession states
States that have recently joined the EU and are still adjusting their economic and political systems to membership.

THE NICE TREATY 2003

This was agreed in 2001 and came into force in 2003. It was largely concerned with the problem of how to make the institutions of the EU workable when it expanded towards 27 members. To achieve better decision making it made the following reforms:

- The qualified majority system was revised to take account of new members. In order to prevent any major problems from those new members, the QMV system was further weighted in the advantage of small states (see Table 7.1 above).
- A number of issues, mostly concerned with the appointment of officials, were transferred from unanimous voting to QMV. There were no significant transfers of sovereignty over *functions* and *powers* as a result of Nice.
- The size of the Commission was reduced. It was to become 26 when there were 27 members. This meant that every member could not expect to be

represented by a Commissioner. The smaller states had to accept a rota system determining who would have a Commissioner in place.

- The size of Parliament was to be increased, but not to the extent of the increase in population. The target for the size of the Parliament was 732.

But it was in the area of Common Foreign and Security Policy (CFSP) that it was hoped that Nice would become significant. In particular Nice introduced *enhanced co-operation*, a principle which introduced closer integration in the foreign policy aspects of the EU. While military integration remained something of a distant dream, Nice did confirm that members were now committed to a genuinely supranational approach to foreign policy.

THE PROPOSALS FOR A CONSTITUTIONAL TREATY

After Nice policy makers turned their attention to a major reform of the EU, taking it a stage further towards full integration. The opening shots were fired at the Laeken Council of Ministers in late 2001.

The Laeken Declaration

The Declaration was really a series of questions about the future of the European Union. Among the most important of these were the following

- With the movement towards a fully enlarged Union, perhaps up to 30 members, what institutional reforms were needed to create a permanent set of arrangements?
- In particular, how could decision making in the EU be made more efficient and transparent, especially within the context of enlargement?
- How could the democratic deficit be addressed?
- How could the citizens of Europe become more connected through its institutions?
- Was this the time for a movement to a sense of European citizenship and a European convention on civil rights?
- What is the appropriate and permanent division of functions and powers between the EU and the member states' own governments?

In order to consider these questions and, hopefully, provide some answers a Convention on the Future of Europe was set up under the chairmanship of Valéry Giscard d'Estaing, a former French President.

The Convention on the Future of Europe 2002–3

This met between 2002 and 2003 and, despite a great deal of scepticism and disagreement among its members, to nearly everyone's surprise it produced a draft constitutional treaty in late 2003. The Italian presidency of the EU was given the task of producing a new treaty ready for ratification. The members immediately fell into disagreement, with Spain leading the way and Poland representing the many concerns of the newer member states. The Italians were unable to resolve the issues and the proposals were seen as a failure.

However, by the time the EU presidency had passed to Ireland in 2004, both Spain and Poland had relented and serious negotiations began. Despite many problems, approximately 90 per cent of the convention's proposals were ultimately adopted. A Treaty Establishing a Constitution for Europe was approved in Brussels in June 2004 and was signed by the member states in October 2004 in Rome. It was heralded as a 'second Treaty of Rome'. However, this was only the start of the treaty's problems. It now had to be ratified unanimously by all 25 member states whose representatives had signed it.

What the Constitution Treaty proposed

This was a long and complex document, but its principal proposals can be summarized thus.

1 **Consolidation**. The first task of the Treaty was to make sense of the all the various treaties which had been signed by members states since 1957. All the terms of these treaties were therefore to be consolidated into a single Treaty. In this sense it was largely a 'tidying up exercise'.

2 **Democracy**. This was to be enhanced by increasing the role of the European Parliament, allowing it to consider proposals coming from groups of citizens from outside the political establishment. It would also give powers to the parliaments of member states to monitor EU policies. The role of both parties and pressure groups was to be enhanced by granting them greater access to decision making institutions.

3 **Competence**. One of the more controversial aspects of Treaty. This divided areas of government 'competence' into three types. *Exclusive competence* concerns powers which are exercised only by the EU. The main examples are trade, competition and monetary policy (for those in the eurozone). *Shared competence* relates, as the name suggests, to powers to be shared between the EU and member states. The main examples are social policy, environment, justice and security. *Complementary competence* refers to powers retained by member states which could in future be shared with the EU. These included social policy, economic management, crime and policing

and energy. Here again this was largely a clarification of a situation which most believed already existed under past treaties. However, it would clarify once and for all the relationship between the EU and its members.

4 **Rights**. There was to be a new **Charter of Fundamental Rights** which would be enjoyed by all citizens of the EU and binding on all the member states.

5 **Institutions**. A permanent set of institutional arrangements was to be established. The most controversial aspect, however, was the creation of a permanent Chair of the Council of Ministers. This figure was seen by many as a *de facto* 'President of Europe'.

Not unexpectedly the Treaty was highly controversial, not last because it was capable of various different interpretations. Fundamentally these divided into two main camps.

Supporters argued that:
- It was a limited set of reforms.
- It was largely confirming realities and principles which were already agreed.
- It would extend the scope of citizens' rights.
- It would improve the *demos* of the EU and help to reconnect citizens with European governance.
- It would *clarify* rather than change the relationship between the EU and its members.
- It would make future reform easier to implement, but did not actively reform the EU fundamentally.
- There were adequate safeguards in place, preventing further reform without wide consensus.

Opponents argued that:
- If supporters were right and it was limited in its aims and effect, it was not necessary.
- It did represent a major shift of sovereignty away from member states towards the EU.
- It would reduce, not increase, the safeguards against 'creeping' process of integration.
- The rights of citizens should be the responsibility of member states.

The failure of the Constitution Treaty

During 2006 the process of ratification of the proposals progressed, at first in an encouraging way. The parliaments of Germany, France, Spain and Austria, among others, all approved ratification without serious opposition. Potential problems in the UK were predicted, but, with a comfortable majority, it was expected that the government would be able to force it through. All the optimism came to an abrupt end on 29 May 2006.

In France ratification required more than a parliamentary majority. There was also to be a referendum. The French voted 54 per cent to 44 per cent **against** ratification. France, a country renowned for its enthusiasm for European integration, had clearly changed its attitude towards the future of the EU. A few days later the Dutch people confirmed the demise of the Treaty by voting even more decisively against it, by 61 per cent to 38 per cent.

A European Commission survey revealed that many people had voted against the treaty mainly on the grounds that they did not understand it. The second most popular reason was the potential loss of national sovereignty. The French objections, however, were more fundamental. They were less concerned with any loss of French sovereignty and more concerned with the impact the treaty would have on the economy.

The French have traditionally supported what is known as the *'social model'* of the Union. In this context this model concerns the way in which the EU interacts with national economies. It is fundamentally an economic structure in which the state is expected to play an active, interventionist role. This can involve such initiatives as guaranteeing economic rights for workers, supporting industries in maintaining employment levels, maintaining a large public sector workforce with very favourable pay and working conditions and constant state management of economic variables. The social model also gives less scope for the operation of free markets, preferring substantial government regulation. It also involves less competition policy and accepts that some industries should be artificially protected even this may result in 'uneven' competition.

The French voters, influenced by much propaganda from conservative and other right-wing politicians, saw the proposed treaty as a kind of 'Trojan Horse', a secret device for introducing a less social model in Europe, to be replaced by a so-called *'Anglo-Saxon' model*. This model is based on the belief that free markets and competition should be allowed to thrive. Furthermore the intervention of the state in the economy and social policy is almost always seen as counterproductive, stifling enterprise and creating a 'dependency culture'. Fundamentally it is based on the neo-liberal model adopted by both the USA and the UK in the 1980s. It is clear that the social model and the Anglo-Saxon model are not compatible. It was assumed by many in France that the treaty would result in a European union which was considerably more committed to free markets, competition policy and withdrawal of states from economic and social management.

The UK did not vote on the treaty as it was already considered to be dead before the public debate got fully under way. Nevertheless there was much controversy. The British concern, expressed most forcefully by the Conservative Party and the UK Independence Party (UKIP), was mainly that the treaty would result in large shifts of sovereignty from national governments to the EU. The Labour Party arguments, that it was largely an administrative device to make the EU more efficient and democratic and that it would actually *prevent* any further losses of national sovereignty, made little progress.

The failure of the treaty gave European leaders a major problem – where to proceed from this apparently hopeless position. All were agreed that the enlargement of the EU made reform essential, but agreement seemed a distant dream. Nevertheless negotiations continued among the larger member states and by the end of 2007 a replacement treaty was ready. This was the **Reform Treaty**, later known as the Lisbon Treaty.

The Lisbon (Reform) Treaty

The new treaty was very much a copy of the old Constitution Treaty. Indeed, some of the changes were merely cosmetic. However, a number of the concerns expressed by the UK, Poland and France were met. The Treaty was, therefore, fundamentally the same as the Treaty on the Constitution but including the following changes:

- It dropped the name 'Constitution Treaty' to meet the objections of those who claimed it was a 'European Constitution' which would effectively establish a 'federal' Europe.
- There was to be a statement of fundamental human rights, but countries would have the ability to opt out of certain clauses for special national reasons.
- Important opt-outs were to be allowed for countries who did not wish to take part in certain common foreign policy positions (a Polish and UK demand).
- A number of other national 'opt-outs' were added in some areas of legislation.

> **Euro-federalism**
>
> The transfer of various types of jurisdiction to EU institutions away from member states is often described as a process of Euro-federalism. It is not true federalism as member states can restore their national sovereignty while in a federal system this is not possible. In practice the sharing of sovereignty between member states and supranational instituitons can be described as a form of federalism.

Nevertheless, this was fundamentally the same settlement as the Constitution Treaty. It was ratified during 2007 and all the heads of government signed in December in Lisbon (hence the term 'Lisbon Treaty'), though Gordon Brown significantly delayed his signature, indicating some reticence from the British government.

There was more optimism that the new treaty would be ratified by all member states. These hopes were, however, dashed when the Irish people voted against ratification in a referendum in June 2008, by a majority of 53 per cent to 47 per cent. The unanimity rule was therefore broken and ratification had failed again. By the summer of 2009 no way out of the deadlock had been found. The most common solution proposed was to hold a second Irish referendum in the hope of a 'yes' vote. However, this did not take account of the possibility that the UK Parliament might not approve the new treaty despite the government's majority. A number of conclusions can be drawn from the problems of passing a reform treaty:

- Although there is a broad European consensus on the future direction of the EU, there are important reservations including the fear of loss of national sovereignty, notably in the UK and Poland, the loss of the French social model and difficulties over the voting system in the Council of Ministers.
- The rule that requires unanimous approval for a new treaty is a very high hurdle to jump, especially since the EU has grown to 27 members. The fact that Ireland, one of the EU's smallest members, could block a major reform was a major shock.
- Although there is a general recognition that reform, democratization and improved efficiency in decision making are vital to the future of Europe, enthusiasm for movement towards a more 'federal' Europe remains lukewarm.

In the event, the Lisbon Treaty was eventually ratified in late 2009. A second Irish reformation was indeed held and voted decisively in favour. The Final Treaty was quickly signed and the debate over its desirability was effectively ended.

THEORIES OF INTEGRATION

Now that we have reviewed the various stages by which European Union has evolved and integration has matured, we can examine the various theories of integration which have guided the process and which are likely to inform the debate about future developments.

International co-operation

This is the weakest form of integration. It means that groups of nations may meet regularly to discuss matters of mutual concern. However, if they are unwilling to give up national sovereignty, action can be taken only if they succeed in reaching agreement among themselves. Countries may be legally bound by the resulting agreement if a treaty is signed, but nobody needs to feel coerced.

In such a scenario, each issue must be negotiated in its own right. There is a general commitment by countries to try to reach agreement, but this may not prove possible. If there is no supranational body to which they have given up sovereignty, the organisation need not be threatened if agreement cannot be reached. The North Atlantic Treaty Organisation (NATO) has always operated largely on the basis of such co-operation. Members sacrificed no national sovereignty to NATO, but have agreed from time to time to engage in mutual action, sometimes even committing their own troops to military action under 'foreign' commanders. But in every case the member countries have been free to withdraw co-operation without losing their membership of NATO. The British Commonwealth is a further example of this kind of organisation. It acts only if members can agree (for example to adopt sanctions against the apartheid regime in South Africa in the 1970s and 1980s). The Commonwealth, like NATO, has never been able to act independently of its own membership.

Had the European Community adopted this form of integration, there can be little doubt that it would have made little progress towards a single market and might not, indeed, have survived at all. The steps needed to create a single market and monetary union were so radical that they required members to accept that they had to cede some sovereignty to the Community.

Neo-functionalism

When the European Coal and Steel Community was created there began a process by which European countries began to transfer national sovereignty to a supranational body. In these early stages it was clear that the way forward was for various government *functions* to be given over by member states. At first it was control over the trade in coal, iron and steel. When the European Community itself was formed, controls over trade in general were transferred. As we have seen in the review

> **functionalism**
> This refers to the process whereby an increasing number of functions – such as control over trade, environment, agriculture, fisheries etc. – are transferred to the European Union away from member states. It has been described as 'creeping federalism'.

which is described above, more and more functions have moved over to Brussels. Policy and law on agriculture, fisheries, environmental control, consumer issues, working conditions and many others followed trade as functions which member governments were willing to give up.

This approach to integration can be described as neo-functionalism. It is a gradualist approach which is attractive to those of a more conservative disposition. Countries do not have to give up control over a function if they do not wish to. The European Community has always allowed members a veto over any change in functional responsibility. Thus Britain was able to negotiate opt-outs from the single currency and the Social Chapter when Conservative governments felt they were a step too far, functions which they were not willing to give up. By the same token, functionalism means that a consensus is always needed if further integration is to take place.

The alternative to functionalism is to transfer political sovereignty to the supranational body and then allow that body to decide which functions it wishes to take over. The end result may appear similar, but the *process* of transference in functionalism is more cautious and remains in the control of individual members. It is this latter principle which has always governed the way in which European integration has proceeded.

Pooled sovereignty

Opponents of European integration have always stressed the fact that national sovereignty has to be sacrificed if progress is to be made. In other words the transfer of sovereignty is seen as a *negative* development. In some ways this is a valid argument. It is undeniably true that members of the European Union have had to give up some of the independent functions of their national governments.

pooled sovereignty
Some regard the transfer of sovereignty to the EU as the loss of sovereignty by member states. Others, however, see this as a process of sharing or pooling sovereignty. Thus, nation states may lose some national sovereignty, but also gain sovereignty over the EU as a whole. The term pooled sovereignty tends to be used by those who support European integration.

A less sceptical view can, however, be considered. This suggests that members are not giving up sovereignty but simply sharing it with others or 'pooling' it. The losses of national sovereignty are, in this way, compensated for by *gains* in sovereignty over *other* states in the Union. Thus, for example, when Britain finally signed the Social Chapter in 1997 it lost some national sovereignty over the regulations concerning conditions in the work/place. On the other hand, any future developments in this field have to be negotiated and Britain will have some say in future on working conditions in Germany, Greece, Spain and every other member state.

There are also functions which are, by their very nature, supranational. This certainly applies to environmental protection (pollution, for example, does not recognise national borders). Similarly, as an increasing proportion of output is accounted for by multinational companies, national governments become unable to control their operations. Policy on competition (i.e. opposing monopoly power) must, therefore, be carried out at supranational level. In such cases sovereignty has to be pooled.

This notion of pooled sovereignty will not do for its opponents. They have argued that national sovereignty is of a much higher order than shared sovereignty.

The domestic government has much more interest in managing its own affairs – after all national governments are elected primarily to do that – than in interfering in the affairs of others.

Multi-level governance (MLG)

This concept is closely associated with related movements such as subsidiarity and a 'Europe of the Regions'. It challenges the widely accepted perception that power in Europe is gradually drifting upwards towards Brussels. MLG accepts that there is a gradual drift away from *national* sovereignty, but insists that the power has not all drifted upwards. Instead it sees Europe's future in terms of various *layers* of governance. These layers include supranational, national, regional and local levels.

The model concerns the ways in which policy making is carried out. Thus there are some policy decisions which are increasingly being made locally, others that have become regional, some which remain national and finally those that have been devolved upwards to the EU. However, it is not merely subsidiary in practice. If we consider regional government, this can become clear. Subsidiarity suggests that regional governments make autonomous decisions *independently*. Thus Scotland, Catalonia and Saxony, all semi-autonomous regions, increasingly involve themselves in 'overarching' institutions which pull them together into a single policy-making community. In other words there are now institutions which deal with the *common* problems of all these regions (in this case the Committee of the Regions).

The regional aspects of MLG are already quite well developed, but there are supporters of plans to extend the system to localities and to smaller regions. Its main attraction is that it can prevent the EU becoming a huge, monolithic centre of power and can, instead, disperse power more widely. It is basically a liberal ideal in that it proposes a pluralistic future for Europe.

Federalism

This model of integration has been a common way in which groups of sovereign states have come together to form a larger union. Perhaps the most celebrated example of a federal settlement was the creation of the United States of America in 1787. Germany is another prominent example, as are Nigeria, Russia and India.

Federalism is the consequence of a tension which exists between two opposing forces. One is an overwhelming desire to create a new state. The Americans felt that they could not survive in a hostile world as thirteen separate countries. In Germany the driving force for union was partly economic, partly cultural, a need to unite the Germanic peoples and restore national pride. The other is the determination of the states which are to be absorbed by the new union to retain some of their own sovereignty.

The result of such a conflict is a federal settlement. All the uniting states agree to give up sovereignty over certain government responsibilities. Furthermore, their decision is permanent. They do not expect ever to repossess these sovereign powers. At the same time the participants identify which powers they wish to retain for themselves. Here it is understood that the central, or federal, authority will never be able to take over these 'reserved' sovereign powers without the permission of the separate states.

At first sight, federalism seems an attractive blueprint for the constitutional future of the European Union. Member countries would retain their own sovereignty and there would be no way that Brussels would be able to get its hands on them in the future. But there remain problems, the main examples of which are shown in the box.

Problems with federalism

- A European federal state would be a new state which would stand above the member states. In other words, national governments would be downgraded and seen as inferior. This is certainly the experience of other federal states.
- Federalism also implies permanence. Under existing arrangements member states feel they have the opportunity to change their relationship with the centre through negotiation. This is not the case with a federal settlement which would be 'entrenched'.
- There is a fear that there would be a tendency for the federal authority to gather more and more powers to itself. Until President Reagan began to reverse the process in the 1980s, it was certainly true that the federal government of the United States gained power over the individual states.
- In all other federal arrangements, the most important powers have been given to the centre. These include economic and monetary control, defence, foreign affairs and internal security. The individual states have, by contrast, been confined to less fundamental activities such as social policy, transport and planning.

Nevertheless federalism is seen by some as the way forward for Europe. Sadly for its supporters, federalism has received several setbacks as repeated attempts to adopt a new quasi-federal reform, or constitutional, treaty have failed.

European government

Opponents of complete political integration tend to refer to this vision as the European *super-state*. Supporters see such a development as possibly inevitable and certainly desirable. The latter view is both radical and genuinely internationalist. It is based on the proposition that the independent nation state has had its day. They believe that its survival will hinder progress and argue further that the nation state has been a historical phenomenon which is not appropriate in the modern age of globalisation and interdependence.

Ironically, it was a great Conservative politician, Winston Churchill, who was one of the first postwar statesmen to dare to suggest the idea of a European government. He suggested that a single sovereign government for Europe would be the only way to prevent conflict between the nations of the continent. To those who feared that such a government would destroy cultural diversity, Churchilll replied that culture was a European phenomenon in itself, more important than national cultures.

In the event Churchill's ideas were far too radical for most British politicians. Meanwhile, on continental Europe, they were rejected as an attempt to sponsor British domination. There remain a few supporters to this day, but the idea of sacrificing all national sovereignty to a European state is unlikely to find widespread favour in the foreseeable future.

SUBSIDIARITY

This principle was adopted for the European Union at Maastricht in 1992. It is fundamentally a liberal idea, but has also been shared by many socialists and even some conservatives throughout the continent.

To understand it we should be aware that government in Europe can be carried out at four different levels. These are: supranational (Europe), national, regional, local.

We can now consider what functions of government can and should be carried out at each level. Clearly there are some functions which should be divided between two or more levels, but the principle of subsidiarity suggests that there is normally a rational division of powers. The box demonstrates a likely scheme of subsidiarity.

There are two striking features of such a scheme. The first is that a large number of key functions are shown at supranational level. This may appear alarming to defenders of national interests. However, it should be pointed out these are issues which do not impact on the everyday lives of citizens so that European government may not bear down on citizens quite as heavily as may be feared.

The second feature is that most functions in this scheme are *not* placed at national level. To some extent this is a natural process. It is becoming increasingly

---

A scheme of subsidiarity

- **Supranational**. International trade; environmental protection; defence; foreign affairs; long-distance transport; finance; some indirect taxation; energy planning; competition control; consumer protection; workers' protection; agriculture and fishing.
- **National**. Health care; criminal law; direct taxation; micro-economic development; arts and culture; personal taxation; national transport; welfare benefits; environment; higher education.
- **Regional**. Regional transport; environment; urban planning and regeneration; rural affairs; economic development; some indirect taxation.
- **Local**. Education; personal social services; local planning; local transport; local environment; crime prevention and detection; provision for elderly people; mental health provision; local taxation.

---

impractical for nation states to be able to control many issues. Some examples can illustrate this second point.

- **Defence**. Traditional wars of invasion and defence are over. Conflicts are increasingly international and highly technical and can only be dealt with through international action. Problems in the Balkans, the Gulf and with terrorism after 2001 are clear examples.
- **Foreign policy**. Individual countries have insufficient influence to be able to shape international events. As Europe becomes a single economic bloc, issues concerning trade and economic issues must be conducted collectively.
- **Environment**. Environmental problems such as global warming, emissions control, energy depletion, conservation issues do not recognise national boundaries.
- **Competition**. Since most large corporations are now multinational, control of monopoly power must also be carried out on a supranational basis. At the same time the process of European integration itself has taken functions away from nation states. Again some examples are shown below:
  - *Monetary union*. Control over finance, interest rates and money supply is now European-based.
  - *Single labour market*. Uniform regulations concerning working conditions etc. are needed.
  - *Single product markets*. Consumer protection and trade regulations are controlled in Europe.

SAMPLE QUESTIONS

Short questions

1 Explain and assess the importance of qualified majority voting.

2 Why was the Lisbon Treaty so contentious?

3 Distinguish between supranationalism and intergovernmentalism.

Essay questions

1 To what extent is the EU now effectively a 'superstate'?

2 What are the main obstacles to further European integration?

3 'Germany and France have a fundamentally different attitude to European integration than most other member states.' Explain and discuss.

Institutions of the European Union 8

PROBLEMS FOR STUDY

One of the errors which is often made in studying the institutions of the European Union is to attempt a comparison with national political systems. This carries a number of difficulties. The EU is *not* like a national state (though it may be ever closer to becoming one). There are crucial distinctions which must be borne in mind. These include the following.

The EU remains an organisation of nations rather than a full-scale *supranational* body. The members are not yet prepared to abandon national interests completely. Instead, they have shown a willingness to reach a series of agreements with other states. This may involve compromises, deals and accommodations to the interests of others, but it does not mean that national distinctions can be put aside. This affects very deeply the nature of the EU's

supranationalism

A description of a circumstance or institution where national interests are put aside and replaced by the interests of the European Union as a whole. Thus, decisions are said to transcend national interest. Examples of supranational bodies are the European Commission and the European Court of Justice. Examples of supranational policy issues are the Common Agricultural Policy and Environmental protection.

institutions. They have to have functions and methods of operation different from these of national governments. The latter do not have the problem of attempting to reconcile national differences (though divergent regional interests are often a problem). This is not the case with the EU.

Partly because of its international nature, and partly because of the great variations between member states, the EU lacks political *coherence*. This means it is difficult to find common purposes in the way that individual states do. Britain in the years following 1997, for example, has had a clear need and desire to improve public services. Germany has had to overcome the problems of reunification since 1991. Poorer countries like Portugal, Ireland and Greece have naturally been concerned with the need for economic development. France worries about the future of its agricultural base. The EU has had one overwhelming goal – to achieve the single market and monetary union – but thereafter its purposes are less clear. Also less coherent are the main political *issues* and *conflicts*. This is what makes the party system meaningful and gives the electorate a clear picture of what government is doing and how it is performing. Conflicts within the EU tend to be national in nature, rather than about political issues. We tend to think about political institutions in terms of parties, policies, manifestos and mandates. This does not work so well with the EU.

Each member state has its own distinctive political system. Furthermore, political control of each country may change at any time. As we have seen above, the EU is very much about negotiation between member states, so problems are bound to arise when the political situations within member states are liable to change at any time. For example, when the issues surrounding the single currency and the Social Chapter were being resolved, Britain was governed by a party which was fundamentally split on these concerns and eventually decided to opt out. After 1997, however, the British position changed, particularly in the case of the Social Chapter. Thus the landscape of discussion has altered. Similarly, we may consider the practice of Denmark and Ireland to put important constitutional changes to a referendum. Thus Denmark voted against the Maastricht Treaty (on deeper economic and monetary union) and Ireland against the Nice Treaty (on enlargement). Both events caused consternation and delay within the EU. The European Union does not operate in a vacuum. Its institutions, therefore, must take account of the fact that it is at the mercy of political currents within member states. After enlargement this problem is likely to grow more serious.

We must also be careful, when considering the institutions, not to assume that they carry out the same functions as their apparent 'counterparts' in national governments. The European Parliament, for example, cannot be described accurately as a 'legislature', even though that is its title. Its functions are certainly different in most respects from that of Westminster. Similarly, we may think of the Council of Ministers and the Commission as the Union's government and bureaucracy respectively. This would be a mistake. The Commission, as we shall see, carries out some functions normally assigned to government. The Council, meanwhile, is, to a large extent, the main legislative body. The Court of Justice does interpret law as national judiciaries do, but the main judicial role is played by national courts.

USEFUL APPROACHES FOR STUDY

If it is dangerous to think of institutions purely in terms of functions and processes, how can we usefully study them? An answer may be to apply a variety of political *concepts* to them. In this way we can judge how well they perform and where there are weaknesses which need to be addressed. Some examples of this approach are shown below.

Democracy

If we use the term democracy in its broadest sense, i.e. government being open to the influence of popular opinion and ensuring its decisions are based on popular will, every institution can be usefully interrogated. Does the European Union respond meaningfully to European opinion? Is it possible to have influence over the institutions? Do decision makers take opinion into account? Do parties and pressure groups reflect opinion effectively through the institutions? These are all important questions about European democracy.

Representation

Political institutions have a primary duty to represent the people and the various groups which make up civil society. All the EU institutions seek to do this. They have a special difficulty in that they must be nationally representative as well as seeking to reflect the many political ideas and interests which flourish throughout Europe. All the four main institutions – Parliament, Commission, Council and Court of Justice – have arrangements to try to make them representative. How well these arrangements serve the people, however, is another matter which we will consider below.

Accountability

This is a special problem in so large a political community as the EU. It is also difficult as only one body – Parliament – is directly elected. The ministers who meet regularly to make key decisions are accountable to their *own* people and parliaments, but not to the people of Europe as a whole. If you are a British citizen, some decisions which will affect you are made by ministers from Italy, Belgium, Portugal and the rest. But these ministers cannot be made responsible to that British citizen.

Authority and legitimacy

Political power should be exercised only in a democracy where there is proper authority for that power. Only with such authority can an institution be said to be legitimate. European Union institutions draw their authority from less secure sources than do national bodies. Parliament is elected, of course, which helps a great deal. However, turnouts to these elections vary and it is rarely clear how well or otherwise an MEP (member of the European Parliament) has performed his or her duties. They also represent huge electorates who cannot be expected to know where they stand on many issues. The leading Commissioners are appointed by the European Council, which gives them a high form of authority, but we are used to members of the government needing a more direct form of authority. The Council of Ministers carry the authority *as individuals* of their own governments. However, as a collective body they have much weaker authority, especially as we may not know how individual ministers have reached their own decisions.

Limited government

It is a basic principle of liberal democracy that government should have strict legal limitations placed on its powers. There should also be instruments in place to ensure that it does not overstep these limits. We may usefully ask, therefore, whether strong enough safeguards do exist and, if so, how well they are enforced. Students of European government and politics may well consider other democratic concepts in the same way. For example such issues as human rights, the separation of powers, the rule of law and open government may be treated in the same way.

THE EUROPEAN COMMISSION

Role

It is difficult to sum up the role of the Commission in one single word. In some ways it is like a cabinet which discusses policy and sets agendas, it is a bureaucracy which administers the operation of the EU and it is also a policy-making machine. The term **executive** is possibly the best single term if we are to insist on one, but even this is not wholly satisfactory. One thing the Commission is certainly *not* is a decision-making body. It has no democratic legitimacy and no popular mandate to be able to make decisions.

The main thrust of the Commission has been to drive forward the strategic development of the Union. In particular this has involved the creation of the single market and, since 1992, the achievement of monetary union. The Commission has developed the timetable and procedures for such change and has recommended the measures needed to realise the aims of greater union. At each stage towards closer union the Commission has produced initiatives which provide the Council of Ministers (which is the Union's regular decision-making body) and the European Council (which makes strategic decisions) with the framework for progress. In effect the Commission therefore produces draft treaties and amendments to existing ones or draft legislation and regulations for discussion by the Council of Ministers or European Council.

It also administers the existing systems of the European Union, such as the Common Agriculture and Fisheries Policy, environmental protection, regional policy, transport projects, competition policy and the Social Chapter. Working with member governments the Commission is occupied with the task of ensuring that all these programmes operate effectively. In cases where it feels that a country may be in breach of laws and regulations it will report the matter to the European Court of Justice for possible legal enforcement. Part of this wider task is to produce an annual budget for the Union. This means setting the level of contributions from member states (according to agreed formulas) and determining how the finances should be distributed through the programmes referred to above. The budget must be approved by the European Parliament so there may be a period of prolonged negotiation before it is settled.

Particularly after 2000, the Commission has a special role to play in the enlargement of the Union. It must make the plans for the admission of new members. This may involve special transitional arrangements, adjustments to existing policies and major reform of budgetary arrangements. As new applicants have emerged, the Commission have conducted negotiations and research into the prospective member's suitability.

Finally it should be emphasized that, to an increasing extent, the EU conducts foreign policy collectively, i.e. *as if* it were a single state. To this end there are over 130 Commission offices in non-member states. The EU also negotiates as a single body in such organisations as the United Nations and the World Trade Organisation. The Commission must, therefore, seek to develop common positions which have the agreement of members states when carrying out such functions. The most dramatic example of this occurred during the various international meetings which took place during the economic crisis of 2008–9. Since concerted action was required to respond to the crisis (in terms, for example, of interest rate policy, fiscal stimulus, bank bail-outs and monetary policy) the Commission had to play a leading role, along with the European central Bank, in developing EU-wide policies.

The European Union, as a single political entity, must deal with other states and organisations. This may involve trade disputes and agreements, transport arrangements, environmental protection, diplomatic problems, issues of international crime and the like. Though the heads of government may often capture the headlines at international conferences, it is the Commission which deals with day-to-day international relations. We may now summarise the Commission's functions as follows:

- Developing policies to realise full economic and monetary union.
- Managing existing European Union programmes.
- Developing the Union's annual budget.
- Making the necessary arrangements for enlargement.
- Managing the union's external relations.

Structure

The Commission is headed by its **President**. He or she is the most visible symbol of European unity and can therefore be seen at the outset as a figurehead. As we shall see, the Commission is divided into nineteen functional sections, but the President is able to represent the Commission *as a whole*. It is the President who represents the strategic policies coming out of the Commission. He or she has the authority to deal with members' most senior ministers up to head of government level, and can also deal personally with other states and international organisations outside the Union. The best-known President was, arguably, Jacques Delors (1985–94), whose vision and drive led to the development of full economic and monetary union. His successor, Jacques Santer (1994–99), was charged with the realisation of monetary union. Romano Prodi (1999–2004) was very much concerned with issues surrounding enlargement and a common defence and foreign policy.

The current (2009) President, José Manuel Barroso (2004–) from Portugal has had perhaps the fullest role in modern times. He has had to preside over the largest ever enlargement of the EU (ten new states joined in 2004), has dealt with many major foreign policy issues (Iraq, Afghanistan, the credit crunch and economic recession) and, above all, has attempted to see the adoption of a new Reform Treaty. In summary he has taken on the task of attempting to forge a common EU position on a number of extremely complex issues. It is perhaps fair to say that in economic affairs he has enjoyed a good deal of success, not least because the Euro has gradually strengthened as a currency and appeared to be relatively robust in the face of economic recession. Though he has failed to secure passage of a Reform Treaty he can be credited with preventing the project dying in the face of its many obstacles. It has been in foreign policy, however, where Barroso has most conspicuously failed. There is little or no European unanimity over the war on terrorism, the wars in Iraq and Afghanistan, the Arab–Israeli conflict, over the remaining problems in the Balkans and over relations with Russia. It is in such policy areas that the limitations in the role of the President can be most clearly seen.

The President is nominated by the European Council on the retirement of the existing holder. This nomination must be approved by the European Parliament. Naturally, it is a crucial decision and the subject of extensive political activity. Three main issues arise: the nationality of the candidate, their political stance in domestic politics and their more general position on the future of Europe.

A word of caution is needed at this stage. The term 'President', like so many in the Union, may be misleading. Normally a political President is a country's head of state. He or she becomes the representative of a whole people who takes the lead in international affairs, crises and emergencies. Presidents also involve themselves in the business of government formation, often nominating heads of government and other ministers for parliamentary approval. This does not describe the EU President.

There is no European state (yet!) so there can be no head of state. The President does not have the legitimacy of national presidents because he or she is not elected by the people and so has no popular mandate. There is also no European 'government' in the normal sense of the word so he or she has no role in that direction. The use of the word 'President' simply refers to the fact that he or she is head of the Commission.

European Commission

Presidency	Development and Humanitarian Aid
Vice Presidency (Administrative Reform)	Enlargement
Vice Presidency (Transport and Energy)	External Relations
Agriculture	Trade
Competition Policy	Health and Consumer Protection
Internal Market	Regional policy
Research	Education and Culture
Enterprise and Information	Budget
Economic and Monetary Affairs	Environment
Employment and Social Affairs	Justice and Home Affairs

The rest of the Commission is divided into nineteen sections, each one headed by a Commissioner. This list also demonstrates the range of activities which are the current concerns of the European Union.

Commissioners are appointed by the relevant Council of Ministers. Their nomination must be approved by the European Parliament and they can be removed by the Parliament. They are required to be politicians who have held a 'prominent' position in their own countries before entering the Commission. Some of Britain's commissioners illustrate this principle. Chris Patten was Conservative Party Chairman, cabinet minister and the last British Governor of Hong Kong, Leon Brittan had been Home Secretary and Neil Kinnock was a former leader of the Labour party. Each operates with a small 'cabinet' (not to be confused with the British-style cabinet) who are close advisers. Below them comes a small army of European civil servants, who make up the European Union bureaucracy. They number 15,000 approximately. This is, in fact, a very small figure. It would, for example, represent the same size as a single small government department in Britain. The limited size of the Commission reflects, first, the fact that its role is limited and, second, that much of the administrative work of Europe is carried out by member countries themselves.

Each Commissioner must work closely with their own Council of Ministers (see below). They must also forge close links with relevant ministers in all the member countries. Their role is, therefore, political in the sense that they must attempt to resolve conflicts and seek compromises or consensus. They are not, however, political in that they are expected to be politically neutral and not to favour any single member state.

As a group the Commissioners sit as the Court of Commissioners – the nearest the European has to a cabinet, though it does not finalise any decisions. They are presided over by the Commission President. The court co-ordinates the policies of all the sections and discusses and recommends future policy for the Union as a whole.

Operation and processes

Each section of the Commission is expected to formulate policies which will carry forward the aims of the Union in their own particular area of jurisdiction. These policy suggestions are known as **initiatives**. They are often confused by the media with decisions. Initiatives are not decisions. They are merely proposals for discussion by the Council of Ministers or the European Council.

In developing policy the Commission consults very widely. Apart from the governments and other politicians from member states, pressure groups centre a great deal of their activities on the Commission. Political groupings in the Parliament may send delegations, as may parties from individual states. Much of the process also involves senior members of the bureaucracies of member states. Indeed each state has a permanent Civil Service establishment in Brussels whose role is to liaise with Commissioners.

Initiatives are sent both to the European Parliament and to the Council. A number of outcomes may result. They may simply be rejected outright. They may be amended by Parliament or the Council and referred back to the Commission. The Commission may accept amendments, but, if there can be no agreement, they may insist that amended proposals are passed by a unanimous decision of the Council, rather than just a majority. In some cases the initiative will be accepted unaltered.

When a policy has been adopted the Commission is charged with the task of implementing the decision. As we have already said, this may involve making arrangements with member governments. In such cases they will oversee the operation of the policy. In some cases the Commission itself will implement the policy.

Commissioners must appear regularly before the European Parliament and its committees. On these occasions they must account for what their section is doing and may be asked to explain their policy initiatives. The budget which the Commission produces annually is also the subject of parliamentary scrutiny. Often the Commission is forced to reconsider the budget after it has been rejected by the Parliament. In extreme circumstances the Parliament can also dismiss the whole Commission or an individual commissioner. The best known example of such an event occurred in 1999 when the entire Commission was forced to resign amid charges of corruption and nepotism against some of its members. Since then the European Parliament has conducted much closer scrutiny over commissioners.

Problems and issues

Many of the arguments concerning the 'democratic deficit' in Europe have centred on the Commission. This is because it has not been accountable enough for its activities. However, its legitimacy can also be questioned as can its credentials as a representative body.

Before 1999 the Commission was usually seen as a law unto itself, exposing itself to the minimum of accountability. In its defence the Commission could always claim that it was not the decision-making body of the Union and control was therefore exercised by the Council of Ministers. This has certainly been true. However, its strategic position means that it has had a huge amount of influence over the development of the EU. As such, it has always needed to be accountable. Since 1999, when the whole Commission was forced to resign by parliamentary action, commissioners have been forced to report to Parliament on a regular basis. Corruption of any kind can mean instant dismissal.

Parliament also now reserves the right of veto over major appointments. So, to some extent, the problem has been addressed.

Representation has become a problem as the EU has expanded. The old principle that each members state should have one commissioner can no longer be sustained. A compromise solution is that all larger members are guaranteed one commissioner while a rota system operates for representatives from the smaller states. This is largely a cosmetic device as commissioners are required to put aside any national leanings they may have. It should, therefore, not be necessary for them to be drawn from a representative sample of member countries. Despite this there remains a problem. As an unelected body the Commission cannot be said to be truly representative. It has no elective mandate and the peoples of member states have no say in appointments. It may be that, in the future, there will be demands for at least the senior commissioners to be elected.

The Commission draws its authority, and therefore its legitimacy, from the Council of Ministers. This is a partially democratic process, but the appointment of commissioners remains shrouded in some mystery and may lie very much in the hands of the larger countries. A greater involvement for Parliament may improve the situation, but popular participation in the formation of the Commission, which would enhance its authority most effectively, looks to be impractical. It is true that the **College of Commissioners**, the collective face of the Commission, is in effect a **cabinet**, but it is a cabinet without a normal democratic source of authority. It does, however, have a mandate granted by the Council of Ministers and by the terms of the various treaties that have been signed since 1957. Ultimately, however, its greatest democratic weakness is that it has no mandate from the peoples of Europe. As we shall see below, there is now some room for the European Parliament to grant authority, but this remains indirect and problematic.

The final major issue for the Commission concerns enlargement. With more members it may be that there will have to be a larger Commission simply to ensure that each country is properly represented. On the other hand, increased size may have the beneficial effect of diluting the influence of larger countries in both appointments and policy making.

THE EUROPEAN PARLIAMENT

Role

Despite its name and the fact that it is directly elected, the Parliament is not the legislative body of the European Union. It does not make law, or legitimise it, nor does it act as the source of authority for the executive branch. It is not required that a proposal receives parliamentary approval to be enforceable. It is also not in a position to develop and propose legislation of its own. The government of the EU is shared between the Commission and the Council of Ministers or European Council. None of these bodies is drawn from the Parliament. In other words the European Parliament does not perform three of the most important functions of most national parliaments. Having established what it is not, we must ask what the European Parliament actually does. Its main role is a consultative one. It would be false to suggest that the Parliament has the power to veto a proposal outright. The role of the Parliament in legislation is a complex one and it is not the intention here to describe it in full. To simplify the system, which was mostly established at Maastricht in 1992, we can identify a number of activities:

- It can attempt to reject a proposal. However, if the Commission and Council are determined enough, they can force most measures through. However, Parliament can insist that some proposals require the unanimous approval of the Council.
- It can suggest amendments. This is more powerful than the veto, but in most cases an amendment need not be accepted by the Council of Ministers.
- It can refer proposals back to the Commission and the Council for further consideration, i.e. a delaying power.
- It can approve proposals and so give them greater legitimacy.

As we have seen above, Parliament also has some of the functions we would expect of a representative assembly. It can:

- Oversee and veto the appointment of senior commissioners.
- Insist on the dismissal of commissioners who may be corrupt or incompetent.
- Question commissioners on Union policy and administration.
- Examine the annual budget, reject it and seek amendments to it.
- Request the Commission to consider new policy initiatives.
- Represent and publicise during debates the views of important interest groups in the Union.
- Approve or veto an application for membership from a new country.

Structure

The membership of the Parliament is very complex. It is divided on both national and political lines. This means that each member (MEP) represents a nation, a region within that nation and a political position. At different times and on different issues an MEP might adopt a variable stance. Green Party representatives, for example, are likely to see environmental issues on a Europe-wide basis and therefore not consider national and regional interests. Typical Conservatives, on the other hand, will tend to be more interested in their own nation's interests. A Liberal might be European-oriented on human rights issues, but protective of regional interests where economic development is concerned. Table 8.1 shows the representation of the Parliament in terms of nations and of party groupings. The European Peoples' party groups are essentially conservative parties.

All these MEPs are elected directly and represent areas which are roughly similar in size. The party groupings are inevitably loose. However, they do attempt to act in a unified way wherever possible and where a political issue is clear cut. However, this is often not possible because of the contrasting regional, national and political allegiances which MEPs have.

As with most representative assemblies a great deal of the work of the European Parliament is done by committees of MEPs. These are mainly **standing committees**, but there are also special committees convened to deal with

Table 8.1 **National and party representation in the European Parliament 2009**

National representation		Party groups	
Germany	99	European Peoples	265
France	72	Socialists	184
UK	72	Liberal Democrats	84
Italy	72	Greens and radicals	55
Spain	50	Left-wing coalition	35
Poland	50	Nationalists	54
Romania	33	Ultra nationalists	32
Netherlands	25	Others	27
Belgium	22		
Czech Republic	22		
Greece	22		
Hungary	22		
Portugal	22		
Sweden	18		
Austria	17		
Bulgaria	17		
Finland	13		
Denmark	13		
Slovakia	13		
Ireland	12		
Lithuania	12		
Latvia	8		
Slovenia	7		
Cyprus	6		
Estonia	6		
Luxembourg	6		
Malta	5		
Total	**736**		

special temporary circumstances. These approximately 'shadow' the main sections of the Commission. Indeed there has developed a growing relationship between commissioners and their cabinets and the relevant parliamentary committee. It is through committees also that the accountability of the Commission can be achieved. The committees also act as focus of attention for the many pressure and interest groups which now operate at the European level. The following committees were in place in 2009:

Foreign Affairs	Development	Trade
Budgets	Budgetary Control	Employment
Economic/Monetary Policy	Environment and Food	Industry and Research
Internal Market	Transport/Tourism	Regional Development
Agriculture	Fisheries	Culture and Education
Legal Affairs	Civil Liberties and Justice	Constitutional Affairs
Women's Rights/Equality	Petitions	

This long list demonstrates the extent of the jurisdiction of the European Union in general and the Parliament in particular. All MEPs take part in committee work and it therefore accounts for a high proportion of their work. For the same reason many MEPs now tend to specialise in one area of the EU's work.

Operation and processes

Since the Maastricht Treaty was ratified in 1994 the main legislative work of the Parliament has been known as **codecision**. This suggests that, in a variety of policy areas, the Parliament has equal power with the Council of Ministers to approve new laws and developments. The following subjects are subject to codecision procedure:

codecision

A process related to the European Parliament which was established at Maastricht in 1992. It refers to a system where the European Parliament must be consulted on some kinds of legislation and effectively has a veto or can refer the proposals back to the Commission for reconsideration. Effectively it gives almost equal powers to the Council and the Parliament over some legislation.

- consumer protection
- culture
- customs co-operation
- education
- employment
- environment
- equal opportunities and equal treatment
- free movement of labour
- health
- implementing decisions regarding the European Regional Development Fund
- implementing decisions regarding the European Social Fund
- Internal market
- non-discrimination on the basis of nationality
- preventing and combating fraud

- research
- setting up a data protection advisory body
- social equality
- statistics

This list may appear to be quite impressive, until one appreciates what is left off. Policy areas such as the common agricultural and fisheries policy, taxation, defence and foreign affairs, new treaties and regional policy are not yet the subject of codecision. In other words, Parliament can only pass an opinion on such issues, a process known as **co-operation**.

For codecision procedures a proposal is normally considered by a senior committee member, known as a **rapporteur**, who summarises the proposals and sets up the discussions. Committees consider proposals, taking evidence from commissioners and interested groups along the way. They then make recommendations for amendments or overall approval to the Parliament as a whole. This is not unlike the legislative system which operates in the Congress of the USA.

Parliament in plenary session (i.e. all members meeting) normally considers proposals in two readings. One reading considers amendments, the other looks at the complete proposal. The decision of Parliament is communicated to the Council of Ministers, which may accept or reject the decisions of the Parliament. Where a dispute arises, a special committee is formed to try to make compromises and reach a consensus. Where the Parliament has only co-operative powers, the decisions are also made known to the Council of Ministers, but the Council does not have to accept them.

In addition to its legislative powers the Parliament, as a whole, or as individual members, may take up the grievances of groups of citizens or even individuals. This will involve calling commissioners to account for their decisions. A system of **petitions** exists whereby large groups from the Union can request special consideration from Parliament.

Special procedures exist for the other functions of Parliament, including the admission of new members, consideration of the annual budget, questioning of commissioners and disciplinary hearings.

Problems and issues

Alongside the Commission the European Parliament stands at the centre of the issue of the Union's democratic deficit. This is understandable. When considering any political system, it is natural to fix our attention on such matters

democratic deficit

A description of a number of problems which are considered to exist within the EU political system. It relates to the belief that there is insufficient democratic spirit within the EU. Specifically it relates to such problems as the lack of accountability of institutions, the lack of effective representation and an inability to engage citizens in EU politics in any active way.

as elections, representation, legislation and accountability. These issues always revolve around the legislature. The striking feature of the Parliament at first view is its weakness, and this is the best place to begin a critique.

Why is the European Parliament so weak?

It is a very large, unwieldy body. Even before the post-2002 enlargements it contained 785 members, and members are divided, as we have seen, along political, national and regional lines. Parliaments need a degree of coherence to be able to act decisively. The European assembly lacks this. The coherence may be in the form of a party majority, as normally occurs in the United Kingdom, or a logical coalition of parties, such as a Conservative group of the type which often dominates the French system. There is certainly no sense of 'government and opposition' which can reduce issues to clear alternatives.

The executive sections of the Union – the Council and Commission – are not drawn from the Parliament. Indeed the two branches of the political system are completely separated. This has two effects. On the one hand, it prevents the executive branch from dominating Parliament. There is no patronage system to keep MEPs in line, nor are there strong, unified party groupings. This prevents coherence of the type described above from developing. On the other hand, the decision makers in the Union do not rely on the support of the Parliament. Most important decisions can be forced through the Council if it is determined and united enough. Using the American model, therefore, the Parliament does not act as a 'check' or 'balance' to the power of the executive. They do not rely on each other so Parliament does not occupy a powerful central position.

MEPs have no clear political mandates. When they are elected it is on the basis of their *national* rather than *European* political allegiance. Most voters in Europe have limited knowledge of EU issues. This prevents them from granting any clear authority to those whom they elect. When it comes to European decisions, therefore, MEPs cannot claim to have the authority of their electorates. European ministers understand this and are not prepared to submit themselves to the weak authority of Parliament. Indeed it can be argued that the popular authority of national ministers in the council is stronger than the uncertain authority of MEPs. This greater claim to authority is inevitably translated into political power. It is therefore more appropriate to think of Parliament as having influence, rather than power. As a representative body it can reflect the fluctuating interests and views of the European people, but its legitimacy actually to make laws is very shaky.

The power of legislatures is often based on their ability to call government to account. The European Parliament does have this power over the Commission and it has, indeed, been strengthened in recent years. However, **power in reality lies with the European Council and the Council of Ministers**. These bodies are not accountable to Parliament. In fact, individual national ministers are accountable only to their own parliaments.

Many EU decisions are extremely complex in two senses. First, they are difficult to understand in terms of their consequences. Second, they are difficult to agree and implement because each decision must be applied to 27 separate countries. Policies which tax the experience and expertise of full-time administrators in the Commission are often impenetrable for MEPs who are rarely experts in the field. The technicalities of the Common Agricultural Policy, the effects of environmental schemes or the implications for European labour markets of new regulations for part-time workers, for example, may be simply too complicated for MEPs to consider in a meaningful way. Where there are clear party groupings and political mandates, such issues may be reduced by leaders to their bare essentials. It is unusual for this to happen in the European Parliament.

Parliament has a President who presides over their deliberations, but in general it has no leaders of its own. Without leaders who can act as figureheads and unifying forces the Parliament finds it difficult to deal *as a body* with external organisations. This has been especially noticeable in relations with the developing world. Many MEPs favour stronger European initiatives in the Third World but have difficulty in presenting a coherent case. With its own powerful leaders, this kind of parliamentary initiative might have a better chance of success.

How is the Parliament becoming stronger?

For supporters of parliamentary power the picture is not totally gloomy. After the Maastricht and Amsterdam treaties the European Parliament became considerably more powerful. The codecision procedure gave it almost equal legislative powers with the Council of Ministers over an admittedly limited range of jurisdiction.

It is also true that the Commission and individual commissioners are more accountable to Parliament than before. The events of 1999, when the whole Commission was removed, demonstrated to parliamentarians the true extent of their potential. In future the nomination of new officials, not least the President of the Commission himself, will have to take careful account of parliamentary opinion.

The party groupings have, correspondingly, become more meaningful. The Socialist grouping, for example, has acted together very effectively in the field of workers' rights, while the Conservative Peoples' Parties grouping tends to take a special interest in agricultural affairs. As one would expect, the Green alliance is extremely active in its own special field of interest.

The Commission has responded by strengthening its links with the Parliament. Their initiatives are now subjected to closer scrutiny by standing committees so they must take more account of how MEPs are likely to react. With the d'Estaing Commission (see below) established in the spring of 2002, more reform was promised. In the event, the Lisbon Treaty, finally ratified in 2008–9, left the position of the European Parliament largely unchanged.

Three recent developments demonstrate the growing importance of the Parliament.

First was the rejection of a Commission nominee, Rocco Buttiglione, in 2004. Buttiglione was proposed as Commissioner for Justice, Freedom and Security. However he had a reputation as an illiberal homophobe. Most of the Parliament disliked him and so he was rejected. This was the first time such a nomination had been rejected by Parliament. Encouraged by their new status, MEPs then rejected a number of further nominations presented by the new resident, José Barroso.

The second was the battle to ratify the Directive on a Single Services Market (the Bolkestein Directive). This Commission proposal extended the principles of the single market to services in 2006. Up to then there was only a single market in goods. The Parliament held up ratification by forcing through several hundred amendments. Effectively, therefore, the legislation introducing a single services market was the product of the Parliament rather than the Commission.

Finally Parliament has increasingly used its power to report annually on the state of human rights in both member and non-member states, and this has had a major influence on the debates on further enlargement. Its report on Turkey, for example, has provoked a major debate as to whether that country should be allowed to join. It has also had the effect of forcing improvements in human rights in Turkey and in other aspiring members.

THE EUROPEAN COUNCIL

Although this body has a grand title and appears to be of great importance, given the fact that it is made up of heads of government, we need not spend too much time in discussing it. This is partly because it normally meets only twice a year and partly because its business is largely only the confirmation of decisions which have been made elsewhere. Nevertheless, it is the EU body which has received perhaps the most media attention. We must also be careful not to confuse it with the similarly named Council of Ministers, which is discussed below.

The European Council is the name given to the normally twice a year meeting of the heads of government of the member states. They meet under the 'presidency' of one of the members. Each country takes a turn at the presidency for six months. This means that a member will be president of the Council every seven and a half years (less often after any further enlargement, of course). Being president is largely symbolic and carries with it the now considerable expense of organising an international conference. The only other advantage of the presidency is that the holder may be able to add a few minor items on the meeting's agenda which are of special interest to that country.

The Council exists to ratify key strategic decisions. These proposals will have been negotiated by ministers and officials for months before the actual meetings. It is at the European Council that the principles of new treaties are agreed. It also maps out the immediate future of the Union. The heads of government have the opportunity to settle any final matters which are in dispute and to find out where each of their fellow members stand on important issues.

Nevertheless European Council meetings (also known as heads of government summits) have marked important stages in the development of the European Union. Some recent notable meetings have included the following.

- **December 2002**. The final decision was made to admit ten new members in 2004.
- **June 2006**. A decision to press ahead with the attempted ratification of a Constitutional Treaty (a process which ultimately failed).
- **March 2007**. EU leaders agreed new targets to reduce emissions and control climate change. It was agreed that there should be an overall EU increase in the use of renewable energy by 2020. Carbon emissions, meanwhile, are to be 20 per cent lower than 1990 levels by 2020. This was the first EU-wide environmental agreement to be reached at heads of government level.
- **October 2008**. A rare unanimous condemnation of Russia's 'invasion' of South Ossetia.
- **December 2008**. The agreement of a common European 'rescue package' to halt the banking and economic crisis.

THE COUNCIL(S) OF MINISTERS

Membership

There is not one Council of Ministers but several. In fact, the term refers to all meetings at ministerial level on every subject which comes under EU jurisdiction. Thus there are meetings of all ministers in charge of their own countries' financial affairs, agriculture, transport, trade, defence, foreign relations etc. There are normally over a hundred meetings of the various councils in a year.

The various functions of the different councils are as follows:
- General Affairs and External Relations (considered the senior council)
- Economic and Financial Affairs (also known as ECOFIN)
- Justice and Home Affairs
- Employment, Social Policy, Health and Consumer Affairs
- Competitiveness
- Transport, Telecommunications and Energy
- Agriculture and Fisheries
- Education, Youth and Culture

When ministers meet it is to settle the remaining issues which need to be resolved. In other words they do not confront each new proposal from scratch. During the course of the year, a body known as the **Committee of Permanent Representatives (COREPER)** prepares the way for ministerial meetings. These bodies contain civil servants (i.e. not politicians) from member states who have the permanent role of representing their own countries in the consideration of policies. COREPER is, in many ways, one arm of the senior Civil Service of the European, the other being senior members of the Commission.

Role and procedure

Before considering the work of the Council itself, we should consider further the position of COREPER, the permanent form of the Councils. COREPER is effectively the point at which the interests of the EU as a whole, represented by the Commission, meets the interests of the various member states – represented by their permanent officials. It is here, from day to day, that the supranational nature of the EU is played out and confirmed. Some national interests have to be sacrificed for the sake of progress and agreement. Others cannot be given up and so create problems which may have to be referred to the full Council of Ministers. Few people outside politics are aware of the existence of COREPER, but in many ways it is one of the key institutions of Europe.

When the ministers themselves meet, they form the sovereign body of the EU. Their approval is needed for any proposal to become European law. In some cases, as we have seen above, a codecision is needed with Parliament, but on the whole it is the Council which is the ultimate source of authority. The Council has a number of alternative courses of action when faced by proposals and initiatives. It can:

- Reject them outright.
- Refer them back to the Commission for amendment.
- Amend them on the spot and then accept the amended version.
- Where there is a difference of opinion with the Parliament, may refer them to a special committee for a compromise to be reached.
- May accept proposals as they stand.

These procedures are relatively formal as this is effectively a law-making exercise. The system of voting is described in Chapter 7. Most decisions, as described there, require a qualified majority, which means that a minority of states can be outvoted. Where a unanimous decision is needed – that is, in all key decision-making areas – each member of the Council has a veto.

Law-making is not the only function of the Council. General debates on policy also take place and the Council may decide that an issue should be referred to the Commission for detailed policy to be established. They may also issue instructions to EU officials where negotiations with foreign powers and organisations are needed.

There are essentially six different types of action which the Councils can make. They are interesting in that they demonstrate the different *layers* of decision making in the EU. They are as follows:

- **Regulations**. These are binding on all member states.
- **Directives**. These are also binding on members though there is some discretion as to how they may be implemented in different countries.
- **Decisions** are again binding but only upon those countries or organisations to which they are directed.
- **Recommendations**, as the name suggests, are not binding but are expected to be carried out.
- **Joint Actions** concern decisions which affect the whole EU and where the EU is expected to act as a single body (for example in relations with non-member states or international organisations).
- **Common Positions** are similar to joint actions except that they merely express the EU's attitude to an international issue or problem.

As we can see, although the Council is effectively one half of a European legislature (the Commission being the other half), its output bears only a partial relationship to 'normal' laws. This is because the extent of the jurisdiction of the EU varies from one issue to another.

Problems and issues

The Councils remain one of the more democratic institutions of the EU. Ministers are certainly accountable to their own parliaments and share some of their powers with the elected Parliament. However there are still a number of key issues which have to be faced if there is to be future reform.

Meetings take place largely in secret. Since the Councils are effectively making law, this seems remarkably undemocratic. We now expect the proceedings of Parliament to be fully public; why not the Council? There remains at present the suspicion that deals and agreements are being reached by ministers without popular knowledge or approval. In particular it is difficult or even impossible for citizens and groups in Europe to find out whether decisions have been made on a supranational or an intergovernmental basis.

> **intergovernmentalism**
> This exists in contrast to supranationalism. It is a situation or institution where it is expected that there will be a conflict of various national interests and it is necessary to reach compromises and a consensus. Thus the Council of Ministers is, by nature, an intergovernmental body.

Although the balance of power between the Councils and the Parliament has swung recently in the latter's favour, it can still be argued that the *unelected* Councils should not be superior to the *elected* Parliament. As things stand, this is not the case. Democratic politics normally insists that the law-making body should be fully accountable to the people. The line of both authority and accountability between the Councils and the people is indirect.

Ministers attend the Council meetings without clear mandates. True, they are delegated from their national governments and must report back to them, but there is no *popular* mandate. It is difficult for electorates to judge how their representatives have performed when most decisions are not openly reached. Of course it is said, understandably, that it is impossible to mandate ministers strictly as it is expected that they make compromises and accommodations with their counterparts from other countries. Nevertheless, the freedom of action of ministers may be too great to satisfy democratic principles.

It remains controversial which decisions should be the subject of unanimous votes and which require only a qualified majority. This question prompts another: what issues concern *vital* national interests and therefore need a national veto, and which could be the subject of compromise and so only need a majority?

THE EUROPEAN COURT OF JUSTICE

Role and membership

First, it is necessary to emphasise what the European Court of Justice (ECJ) does *not* do. It does not prosecute individuals who may have breached EU law. This is the task of the courts of member countries themselves. They may hear appeals, but not cases of 'first instance'. They perform in the following circumstances:

- The Court may consider a dispute over the meaning of one of the EU treaties.
- An individual or organisation (usually the latter) may appeal to the Court on the grounds that a Commission decision, or a decision by a member government, may have breached Union law or may be contrary to natural justice.
- The Court may consider a dispute concerning the meaning and operation of a Union regulation or directive.
- If an individual or organisation believes that an interpretation of Union law by a court within the member country was wrong, they may ask for a final judgement.
- States which are members of the Union may be brought before the Court for breaches of Union laws and regulations.
- Disputes *between* member states over the meaning of the laws and treaties may be brought to the Court.

The judges in the court number fifteen and are drawn from all member states. Each judge sits for six years. As with virtually all democratic states, judges cannot be removed on the basis of the decisions which they reach. Judges will not normally sit in judgement in cases involving their own country of origin. They are all highly experienced lawyers who have specialised knowledge of European law.

A flavour of the Court's work can be gained by reviewing the most common subjects of cases. In 2007–8, for example, the following subjects accounted for the majority of the Court's time:
- agriculture (the Common Agricultural Policy)
- fisheries (the Common Fisheries Policy)
- foreign policy
- competition policy
- environment
- freedom of services
- freedom of movement of workers
- social issues (e.g. pensions, working conditions)
- defence

It is also interesting to review the record of individual countries in the Court. If we look at cases brought against countries in the same year for not complying with Union law (brought either by other states or by the Commission), we can see who are the most common offenders:
- France: 25
- Italy: 22
- Greece: 18
- Germany: 12
- Netherlands: 12

It is interesting to consider that the UK, thought to be one of the more Euro-sceptic of members, recorded only four cases in that year! Only Sweden seemed to be more conformist.

Issues

The ECJ is perhaps the most respected of European Union institutions. It conforms to the key democratic principle – that the judiciary should be independent of government. The judges are placed under no political pressure and have no vested interest in favouring any single party. It is fully representative in that judges are drawn from all over the Union. There can be no suggestion that the larger, richer countries might be favoured.

This is not to say, however, that the Court is uncontroversial. In some ways it is symbolic of the degree to which member countries have given up sovereignty to the EU. Domestic courts can be overruled by the ECJ. Furthermore, laws which have been passed by the parliaments of member states may be set aside if the Court decides that they do not conform to EU law or one of the treaties. On the other hand many individuals and organisations have cause to be grateful to the Court for the establishment of their rights. In some of its most celebrated cases the Court has, thus, confirmed the right of professional footballers to move freely from one club to another when out of contract (the famous 'Bosman' ruling), equalising the pension rights of men and women, granting part-time workers the same protections as full-timers and forcing car makers to treat consumers equally in all countries. A selection of important ECJ cases illustrate the breadth of its work.

1990 Factortame. This famous ruling decreed that the UK's Merchant Shipping Act of 1988, which prevented foreign fishing fleets from operating in British waters, conflicted with EU rules and could not be enforced. This sent shockwaves through the British legal and political establishment as it demonstrated the loss of sovereignty which the UK was experiencing.

2001 European Commission versus Republic of France. The French government had banned the import of British beef because of the outbreak of BSE ('mad cow disease'). The European ban was lifted but the French government refused to comply. The ECJ ordered the French to restore imports (a ruling it ignored).

2005 Foreign workers' rights ruling. This case was brought in the UK to clarify EU law. The court ruled that workers brought into a country from another country should enjoy the same employment rights and protections as those enjoyed by workers in the country where they were working.

2006 Richards versus UK Secretary of State for Work and Pensions. Richards, a transsexual woman, was treated as a man for the purposes of pensions and so was denied a pension at 60. The court ruled that Richards should be treated as a woman and so receive a pension at 60 even though she was born a man.

So the Court is seen both as restrictive to individual countries and as the guardian of equal rights for all within Europe. In the cases shown above and indeed in all cases, the rulings of the court are binding precedents and must be obeyed by all members states. There are some who resent the fact that 'foreign' judges can interfere in domestic affairs, but there are others who value the role of the Court in preserving freedom and equality.

OTHER EUROPEAN UNION BODIES

The Committee of the Regions

In recent years the concept of a 'Europe of the regions' has grown in importance. This embraces the idea that, as nation states become less important, regional identities will take over. As economic integration gathers pace, the significance of national borders will diminish. Rather, economic issues will affect regions. It is therefore natural that this body has become more prominent. Created under the Maastricht Treaty and meeting first in 1994 it has steadily gained in status.

Although its members (317 in number) are nominated from regional bodies within member states, its role can be seen as quasi-legislative and Britain has seen it as a potential second chamber for the Parliament based on regionally elected representatives.

Its role is to ensure that regions are properly represented in decision-making processes. In this sense it further undermines the claim of the Parliament to be an effective body. The Commission, Parliament and Council of Ministers are now required to consult with the Committee in case there are regional implications of any new proposals. They are also charged with the task of ensuring that Union funds destined for regional projects are shared out fairly.

Above all, however, the Committee is taking a proactive role in promoting the interests of the poorer regions of Europe such as Greece, southern Italy, Northern Ireland, south-west England and parts of Spain. Since the 2004 enlargements its role has had to expand as so many new poor regions had entered the EU. Large parts of Slovakia, Slovenia, Romania and Bulgaria are notable examples. It fights for an increased share of the EU budget and presses for more regional programmes in such fields as the environment, transport infrastructure, urban regeneration, rural protection and local employment.

The Court of Auditors

This 27-member body, drawn from all members, has the task of protecting the interests of European taxpayers who finance the Union. It has two main functions, both of which were strengthened after major inefficiency and widespread corruption had been revealed during the 1990s.

First, it examines the efficiency of the work of the Commission and the other agencies of the EU. It highlights examples of waste and recommends action to put matters right. Second, it investigates possible corruption. This can occur within member states, in organisations which are in receipt of EU funding (such as farmers or local government bodies) or within the Commission itself. It is important particularly because the European Parliament is so weak in this field.

The Economic and Social Committee

This is a parallel organisation to the Committee of the Regions. It is the same size and its membership is also nominated from member states. If the Committee of the Regions represents regional interests, the Economic and Social Committee represents the great variety of interest groups which flourish in Europe.

The various decision-making bodies are obliged to consult the committee on issues such as consumer rights, workers' rights, welfare provisions, citizenship rights, free movement of labour and trade union law.

It does not have the same high status as the Committee of the Regions, since many member states see it as a threat to their independence. Its role appears to be to speed the process of integration in many new areas. The Committee of the Regions, on the other hand represents a decentralising force which can bring benefits directly to people. However, if the EU is to maintain any claim to be a pluralist body it needs to ensure that group interests are properly represented.

The European Ombudsman

This individual, who is backed by a large body of investigators, is an agent of the Parliament. He or she hears complaints from European citizens who believe they have been the victims of unfair treatment or maladministration by a Union body.

Although the department of the Ombudsman is busy, hearing several cases a year, it is largely a cosmetic exercise. Few cases are upheld and the more serious claims tend to appear in the Parliament or the Court of Justice. The European Union has an ombudsman mainly because it has become an essential feature of any democratic organisation.

The European Central Bank

The European Central Bank (ECB) came into existence in 1998 and resides in Frankfurt, Germany's financial centre. It was needed during the preparations for the introduction of a single currency in 2002 and became a key body when the Euro came into full use. Some basic economic principles must be understood in order to grasp why this body is so essential. Three ideas summarise the position.

First, with a single currency there must be control over the total money supply in the Union. This used to be the responsibility of each member country, but, with one currency, it must be done centrally. Control of total money supply is essential to maintain confidence in the currency and to prevent inflation.

Second, a single currency means a single financial market. Banks and other financial institutions will have to operate in full competition with each other. As such, they must all operate within similar interest rate levels. It is therefore essential, in order to maintain stable financial markets, to set a single European interest rate.

Third, the fiscal policies of each country are likely to affect the total supply of money. When governments borrow money to finance their expenditure, most of the borrowing is raised from the banking system. In order to finance government borrowing, banks are allowed to create new money. Thus, if one country decides to borrow significant amounts of finance, it will have the effect of increasing total money supply. Before the single currency this affected only the country in question. With a single currency, however, the actions of one country may affect the money supply of all. Therefore, countries must be subject to fiscal disciplines, i.e. must keep borrowing down to a reasonable level. This principle has been enshrined in the so-called 'stability pact' among member states. Its importance is shown by the fact that even Germany, the Union's biggest economy, received a warning over its high borrowing levels early in 2002.

The ECB is charged with the task of maintaining the three principles described above. It does this by controlling money supply, by setting an interest rate for the eurozone and by ensuring that members keep within set borrowing levels.

Although the Bank is non-political, its role can be politically controversial. Its problem is that the same interest rate does not necessarily suit all countries at the same time. Those who are suffering slow growth and unemployment want low interest rates to stimulate borrowing, investment, spending and therefore production levels. At the same time, countries enjoying a strong economy do not want low interest rates as this might over-stimulate their economy and lead to inflation. The ECB must, therefore, balance the contrasting interests of different countries when setting rates. Similarly, it may be forced to exercise control over borrowing when individual governments may feel they have very good reason to borrow heavily. They may argue that the expenditure is needed to stimulate employment and growth or to promote better public services. In such cases the bank is liable to find itself in conflict with some member governments.

In order to prevent any charges that it might be put under political pressure, the ECB is an entirely independent body. However, the fact that its directors are not accountable to any democratic bodies has led to criticism that there is no adequate control over how it operates.

The bank became a prominent player in the economic crisis which unfolded in 2008. It was not directly involved with the measures to salvage various European banks – that was left to the member states. However, when the economic recession followed the credit crunch, the bank, under intense pressure, recognised the need for substantial reductions in the eurozone interest rate. At the same time it became clear that the tight fiscal rules which the bank imposed on member states (in particular controlling government borrowing) had to be relaxed to allow for a dramatic stimulus to the European economy. Thus, though the bank is independent of politics, it remains a political body in that its members understand the need to take account of overwhelming political contingencies.

OVERVIEW

The institutions of the European Union have tended to grow and expand without any coherent plan. Extra bodies have been added as new issues and problems have emerged. The existing bodies have also evolved to meet new circumstances. Since the Treaty of Rome, however, no serious attempt at overall constitutional reform has been made. This situation changed, however, in 2009 when the Lisbon Treaty was ratified.

The prospects for further reform are considered in Chapter 9 as one of the issues facing the European Union in the new era of economic and monetary union.

SAMPLE QUESTIONS

Short questions

1 Explain the importance of the European Commission.

2 In what ways has the European Parliament become more important since 1992?

3 Explain the relationship between the European Commission and the Council of Ministers.

4 Explain the role and importance of the European Court of Justice.

5 Assess the importance of the President of the European Commission.

Essay questions

1 Assess the extent of the democratic deficit in the EU.

2 What are the main disputes about institutional reform in the EU?

3 In what ways and to what extent has enlargement caused institutional problems in the EU?

European Union issues

➤ The democratic deficit and institutional reform

➤ The Common Agricultural Policy (CAP)

➤ Enlargement and the political institutions

➤ A common defence, security and foreign policy for Europe

➤ European rights and citizenship

➤ The single currency

THE DEMOCRATIC DEFICIT AND INSTITUTIONAL REFORM

The nature of the democratic deficit

The issues concerning individual institutions of the European Union are described in Chapter 8. However, a number of general remarks can be made at this stage. The main concerns which politicians from member countries and commentators have include the following:

- It is generally felt that the institutions of the European Union are not accountable enough.
- There is too much secrecy in the EU and too much of its proceedings is carried out behind closed doors. This is connected with the lack of accountability, as it is clear that, if the public and their elected representatives are not provided with information, they will be unable to make judgements about the performance of the institutions.
- Representation in much of the EU is indirect. The Parliament is elected, but no other bodies are (unless we accept that the Council of Ministers is indirectly elected).
- No decision-making bodies have a clear mandate. The public of Europe cannot, therefore, judge how well their political leaders are responding to their demands.
- There is no European constitution. The political system of the EU has been formed though the various treaties which have been negotiated since

1957. This means that the relationships between the institutions are not clear.

- There is a lack of a system of 'checks and balances' within the system. For example, the Parliament is a single chamber, without an upper house to check its power, Parliament itself has limited powers over the executive branch (i.e. the Commission and Council of Ministers combined). The European Court of Justice does provide some degree of control, but the absence of a constitution means they have little documentary evidence on which to base their decisions.
- Some member countries such as the UK and Denmark have argued that there cannot be any further political integration until the democratic deficit is addressed. Others, such as Germany and Italy, on the other hand, have suggested that, if Europe can move towards a federal system, many of these problems will be automatically resolved. Meanwhile the continuing process of enlargement of the Union makes the need for democratic reforms more pressing. The new members will want their interests safeguarded and will be unwilling to accept the general lack of accountability. The democratic problem is particularly acute for those countries, such as Poland and the Czech Republic, who have quite recently escaped from the yoke of totalitarian communist regimes.

Some solutions

In recognition of these problems the European Union set up the Constitutional Convention in the spring of 2002 under the chairmanship of Valéry Giscard d'Estaing, a former French president. With over a hundred delegates from both existing and prospective members, it was given eighteen months to report back on political and constitutional reform. If the Convention had failed, the future progress of the EU would have been seriously impeded.

The d'Estaing Convention prosed the following:
- The Parliament should be reformed to make it more representative, accountable and effective.
- The nature of the Commission should be changed, probably making it more accountable, possibly making arrangements for more control over appointments by the Parliament. It also recommended popular elections to the Commission. The way in which the Commission works should also be made more transparent.
- The relationships between the Commission, Council of Ministers and Parliament should be reviewed to make decision making clearer and more efficient.
- The problem of the lack of political leadership for the EU should be addressed, with a proposal for an elected President for the Union.
- A British idea is that there should be a bicameral legislature. Some kind of second parliamentary chamber is certainly on the cards.

- There are proposals for a European 'Bill of Rights' which would, once and for all, establish the basis of citizenship and rights for all members of the EU, including its millions of new citizens to come.
- After d'Estaing reported, it was up to the heads of government to make key decisions in this area.

The fact that the resultant Treaty on the Constitution and its successor the Lisbon Treaty both ran into difficulties was a serious threat to the future of European democracy. However, the ratification in 2009 of the Lisbon Treaty (effectively a watered-down version of d'Estaing's proposals) meant that the process of institutional reform could continue.

THE COMMON AGRICULTURAL POLICY (CAP)

The Common Agricultural Policy (CAP) was created in 1960, a time when there were only six members of the Community. Its founders can, therefore, be forgiven for not foreseeing the many problems which would arise when new members were admitted. It has to be said that it was France which was the prime mover in the CAP and it was seen as a price which had to paid for France's continued membership. It had a number of objectives.

- It aimed to guarantee the incomes of farmers (and wine growers) even in markets which are extremely volatile.
- It aimed to prevent agricultural prices from rising too much when there was an unexpected supply shortage. In this way consumers could be protected.
- To ensure that European agriculture could survive in the face of world competition, a system of price supports and subsidies provided protection.
- Ultimately it was hoped that the Community could become self-sufficient in food. To some extent this was the result of memories of the post-Second World War period, when there were severe food shortages. This aim had been achieved by 1973.

The ways in which these objectives have been pursued constitute a wide range of systems of intervention. The main measures are:

- *Subsidies* try to ensure that some agricultural sectors can survive despite low market prices and to maintain high output levels.
- A *price support* and *levy system* protect some sectors from external competition. If prices fall below a certain level which will not give farmers sufficient income, tariffs are placed on imports to hold up the price.
- *Quota systems* have been put in place in those sectors where there is long-term over-production with the danger that prices will fall too low to sustain farm incomes. Each country, region and individual farm may be given

a maximum quota or production limit. In this way the total production of the EU is controlled. Milk, for example, is produced under this system.

- *Stock intervention* is also used in some sectors. This is a scheme which prevents prices rising too much by releasing stockpiled goods on to the market and so keeping the price down. More often, however, it is a system of buying up stocks in order to hold up the price. This is the most controversial aspect of the CAP as it works against the interests of consumers by keeping prices artificially high. It has also resulted in huge wasteful stocks of goods building up and sometimes having to be destroyed. There have, in the past, been infamous 'wine lakes' and beef or butter 'mountains'.
- *Over-production* is a major problem in the CAP. In the 1990s, therefore, a system known as 'set-aside' was developed. This was a device where farmers were actually paid to take land out of production altogether.

Problems and reform

An attempt to reform the system in 1965 had failed when France exercised its veto. The consequent deadlock was broken in 1966 by the so-called 'Luxembourg Compromise'. This plan meant that the Council of Ministers would retain control over the CAP and that each member would be able to retain a veto over key decisions. The EU was saved, but has been saddled ever since with the problem that reform of the CAP has been made difficult by the power of each country to block change.

Ever since then, the CAP has proved to be one of the most unpopular aspects of the EU and certainly the most difficult to reform. Indeed, the CAP illustrates one of the most important problems for the EU as a whole. National interests show themselves to be at their most powerful when agriculture is at stake. Member governments are reluctant to alienate their own agricultural interests and so fight tenaciously to protect them when agriculture meetings are held. The idea of a 'supranational' body controlling agriculture seems out of the question for many years to come.

The most frustrating aspect of the CAP for those who do not have an interest in agriculture is this difficulty in instituting reform. Indeed, for most members of the European public, complete abolition of the CAP seems the best option. The CAP is unpopular for a number of reasons.

- It eats up a huge portion of the EU budget. It is the taxpayers who pick up this bill. In 2008 a total of €43 billion was spent on the CAP plus a further €8 billion on rural development programmes. This represents 34 per cent of the total EU budget in the period 2007–13. It should be pointed out that, though huge, this marks a fall in the proportion of toal expenditure from a one-time high point of 70 per cent.

- It is seen to be supporting farmers, irrespective of whether they deserve this support. It provides few incentives for farmers to make themselves more efficient. It is argued that pure, free competition with no intervention is the best way to promote efficiency through competition.
- It is a system of trade protection. This raises food prices in Europe and discriminates against Third World producers. Campaigners argue that the system keeps Third World farmers poor, while European farmers grow rich.
- The huge quantities of unused intervention stocks are viewed as obscene when large parts of the world are on or over the verge of starvation. Here again, however, the volume of these stocks has fallen dramatically since 2005.
- Those countries which do not have large agricultural sectors, the UK being a prime example, resent the fact that it favours countries which do rely more on their own agricultural industries. The proportion of CAP expenditure to various countries in 2007 is certainly instructive:

France	20%	UK	9%
Spain	13%	Greece	3%
Germany	13%	Ireland	3%
Italy	11%		

It is therefore clear that expenditure on agricultural support bears no relationship to the size of each recipient country. Germany and the UK have particular cause for a sense of injustice. The reason is, of course, that the larger recipients have bigger agricultural sectors, but this does little to reduce resentment from those countries which have larger manufacturing or service sectors, neither of which receive support.

With the many problems which the CAP throws up, it is hardly surprising that frequent attempts at reform have been made. Several stages of reform can be identified.

McSharry. The first was in 1992 when the set-aside system was introduced and began to slow down over-production and so reduced the need for inter-ventions in the market. These were known as the McSharry reforms after the Irish trade commissioner who promoted them. Over-production of cereals and oils was partly tackled in this way.

Agenda 2000. The second tranche of reforms came in 1999/2000 when some subsidies, for example on cereals and beef, began to be progressively reduced (not least because the World Trade Organisation has been working towards a progressive reduction in protective tariffs and subsidies). To some extent countries were also allowed to apply to divert former subsidies into environ-mental projects. Britain was the most enthusiastic supporter of this new innovation and has a target of converting 20 per cent of agricultural subsidies into environment schemes. This new system effectively paid farmers to reduce their output and become guardians of the environment instead.

The new initiatives also encouraged rural development with grants made available for producer co-operatives to be set up to improve efficiency. Such grants and subsidies were tied to conditions that environmental protection should be promoted.

Decoupling. In 2003 a further major reform was announced, coming into force in 2005. This was known as decoupling. Rather than giving subsidies to specific products such as wheat or vegetables, block grants were given based on the size of farms. These were known as **Single Farm Payments (SFPs)**. In this way agriculture was supported without distorting the markets for individual commodities. It was criticised for favouring large industrial farms and estates, but also praised for restoring a degree of free markets in agricultural output. Above all, however, it was designed to create more social justice in the system of subsidies. The granting of subsidies based on the size of farms will produce more equality between those whose land is less productive or who are unable to access funds of investment, and the super-eficient 'factory farms'.

Decoupling and SFPs were seen as essential if the CAP was to cope with enlargement. The subsidies were inevitably spread more thinly as ten new members joined in 2004 and a further two in 2007, but the less efficient farmers in the new member states receive subsidies more in line with those received by the more established agricultural regions of Western Europe.

Doha. The 'Doha Round' of international trade talks began in 2001 and by 2009 had still not been concluded. Its main aims are to create a free trade system for world agriculture, to boost the position of agriculture in developing countries and to open up access to EU markets from the rest of the world. The central issue is that the EU would like to exchange better access to European markets to agricultural commodities from the developing world for access to manufactured goods in the developing world. It remains to be seen whether such a deal can be reached. The main obstacle is the belief among developing countries that the EU generally and the CAP in particular are fundamentally protectionist. Britain has attempted to lead the way in creating a free trade environment, but has been unsuccessful in persuading most fellow members.

The 2007–13 proposals. The Commission produced a plan to reform the CAP during the six-year period 2007–13. The main reform proposals are as follows.

- Subsidies will be gradually reduced, to be replaced by rural development grants and support for environmental schemes.
- Milk quotas will be gradually phased out.
- Farmers will be obliged to spend at least 10 per cent of any subsidy they receive on environmental protection.

- The 'set-aside' schemes will be phased out. Set-aside was a scheme to allow farmers to leave land totally unproductive in return for subsidy. This was to reduce over-production.

In summary, therefore, the main thrust of reforms since 2000 have been these:
- To reduce overall expenditure on the CAP.
- To attempt to make the CAP compatible with a freer world trade environment.
- To make the CAP compatible with improvements in the environment.
- To make the CAP a fairer system and to reduce fraud.
- To support farmers who are on lower incomes, especially those in the poorer new member states of the EU.

Enlargement

The increases in the size of the EU up to the end of the twentieth century created relatively few problems (see Table 9.1). The countries which joined late were already economically well developed and, by and large, had fully democratic political systems. There were, therefore, relatively few problems over their ability to make contributions and the demands which might have been placed on the Union budget. Fears that the membership of Greece and Portugal – the two poorest of the first fifteen members – might be disruptive were largely unfounded. The entries of 2004 and after, however, were to be of a very different character.

Table 9.1 Stages of European Union enlargement 1957–2007

Year	Entrants
1957	France, Germany, Italy, Belgium, Netherlands, Luxembourg
1973	UK, Ireland, Denmark
1981	Greece
1986	Spain, Portugal
1995	Sweden, Finland, Austria
2004	Czech Republic, Estonia, Hungary, Latvia, Lithuania, Poland, Slovakia, Slovenia, Malta, Cyprus
2007	Bulgaria, Romania

Conditions of entry

States which wish to enter the EU must conform to a number of conditions according to the original Treaty of Rome and the Copenhagen criteria which were established in 1993:
1 They must accept all existing EU legislation.
2 They must be members of NATO (to avoid any conflict of interest over foreign and defence policy).

3 They must have adequate safeguards for human rights.

4 They must have democratic political systems.

5 Their economies should be basically capitalist. This does not prevent some public ownership of industry and public services, but, essentially, free markets must be allowed to operate. Otherwise, Europe would no longer be a truly single market.

6 They must be experiencing reasonable healthy rates of economic growth. This does not mean that they have to be particularly wealthy, but that at least they are moving forward economically.

7 Since the original conditions were set, it has also been added that new entrants have to adopt the Euro as their currency (after a suitable transition period).

These conditions are mainly there to protect the interests of the existing members. However, they proved to be an incentive for the group of former communist states which joined in 2004 and after. The criteria for entry had encouraged them to introduce free markets, to develop democratic institutions and to improve human rights. Ultimately the Commission took the view that sufficient progress had been made to recommend the entry of these states. This was particularly true of Romania which joined in 2007 despite its dismal human rights record as well as its difficulty in reforming both its political system, which was riddled with corruption, and its weak economy, which was severely short of investment.

The benefits of enlargement

Although there remain a number of fears about enlargement (shown below), there has been a considerable amount of enthusiasm for admitting new entrants. Indeed, it was Margaret Thatcher who had first pushed this agenda forward in the 1980s. Her motivation was a belief that a larger community would also be diluted. She feared closer political integration and believed that, the more members there were, the more difficult it would be to achieve it. In the 1980s in general, there was a broad debate between the idea of 'widening' and 'deepening'. In the end, the larger members, such as France and Germany, came to the conclusion that both could be managed at the same time, much to the chagrin of a sceptical Conservative Party. Apart from Thatcher's hopes, there are a considerable number of other perceived benefits:

Enlargement into Eastern and Central Europe has finally confirmed the end of the Cold War divide. In other words Europe will feel more permanently secure as a result of integration.

- It is speeding up the process of democratisation and improving human rights throughout Europe.
- The size of the market has grown considerably. This widens the opportunities for European companies to exploit larger markets.

- As the European single economy grows, there will be new opportunities for greater specialisation and the benefits which that brings. Economists understand that the larger market, the greater specialisation with free exchange, the growing size of industrial or commercial enterprises and increased competition will all promote growth and efficiency.
- The increased size of the eurozone will create a bigger and more stable world currency – indeed it will become *the* dominant world currency, replacing the dollar in that position. This was demonstrated vividly when, during the economic crisis of 2008–9, the Euro remained relatively robust while markets in general were falling alarmingly.
- In terms of geopolitics, Europe is becoming a major world power (provided it succeeds in being able to develop a common position on foreign policy). This may bring benefits in terms of trade and stability.

Problems of enlargement

The effects of enlargement are not all one-sided. It is recognised that many problems will emerge. Most European politicians believe that the balance of evidence favours admitting new countries, but this does not mean that the perils can be ignored. Some of the expected difficulties are as follows.

It has placed a considerable strain on the finances of the EU, notably the structural (regional) fund and the CAP. The larger countries have accepted the fact that expenditure has to be reduced on established members in favour of the 'transitional economies'.

Staying with agriculture, two more problems have emerged from the creation of a much bigger single market. The first is the danger that farm units are becoming much bigger as levels of competition increase. The development of huge industrial farms, especially in Europe's so-called central 'breadbasket' in Poland and Hungary, would have serious adverse environmental effects (memories of the great American 'dustbowl', which was created in the 1930s, spring to mind). Second, an even more powerful agricultural bloc would damage further the interests of the Third World. If an enlarged European agricultural system is to continue with protective policies, there might be even fewer opportunities for poor farmers from the 'south' to penetrate the market.

The entrants of 2004 and after are considerably poorer than the older ones. This places a strain on the regional development programme of the EU. It is recognised that subsidies for the poorer parts of Europe will have *long-term* benefits for all – larger markets, greater competition etc. – but in the *short* and *medium* terms, this will be a huge burden on the Community budget. It may be difficult to persuade taxpayers that some sacrifices now, which hit them hard, will lead to benefits later which will be much less tangible.

Many, on both the political left and right, have become concerned by the extensive migrations of labour that have occurred since 2004. First, trade unions have noted that migration from the east increases the supply of labour in Western Europe, a development which has inevitably led to lower wages in many industries. Second, there has also been some evidence of unemployment rising where migrant labour has appeared to compete with domestic workers. Third, migration has placed a strain on the education and welfare systems of Western Europe, especially as migrants often send much of their earnings home rather than spending them in the countries here they work (which would generate tax revenues). Finally, many on the right have been concerned that large influxes of foreign workers may lead to social conflict.

Apart from these main problems, there is a collection of concerns which are more contentious. Some, for example, fear the import of organised crime from Eastern Europe. Similarly there is a suspicion that the way will be more open for the infiltration of illegal drugs. Business groups have also expressed fears that they will find it difficult to deal with their counterparts in the new members as their normal practices are so different from those in Western Europe.

ENLARGEMENT AND THE POLITICAL INSTITUTIONS

One final set of problems can be treated separately. These concern the stresses that have been placed on the political institutions of Europe by enlargement.

Parliament

With many new MEPs (785 by 2009) the Parliament has become simply too big. It therefore seems likely that existing representatives will have to cope with much larger constituencies. A British suggestion is that a second chamber will be needed in order to represent the regions of Europe as existing MEPs will find it difficult to do so. We have already alluded to the fragmentation of the Parliament in Chapter 8. With perhaps over 30 members in the future, the range of national groupings increases again. Lessons may have to be learned from the experience of the USA, where the Senate return two members from each state, no matter its size, while the House of Representatives returns members from large constituencies and is expected to reflect their *regional* concerns.

The Commission

As things stood in 2002 each member state was entitled to one of the twenty commissioner posts. The largest five were allowed two each. The purpose of this device was to ensure that each state at least *felt* represented at senior level. With further enlargement, it has not been possible for every member to send a commissioner to Brussels. It is accepted, therefore, that some countries in the future will not be able to have a commissioner. In effect the smaller states have to operate a 'rota' system for representation on the Commission.

The Council of Ministers

Enlargement does not present a problem in terms of numbers. However, a much larger Council does create difficulties with decision making. On those issues where a unanimous decision is required it has become increasingly difficult to reach a conclusion. In order to get round this problem, it is expected that even more decisions will have to become subject to qualified majority voting in the future. This is all very well and will make decision making more effective. However, the larger states are likely to become concerned that they may be outvoted by a large coalition of smaller states. The new voting strengths in the Council, which were negotiated at Nice in 2000, have gone some way to prevent this, but it remains a future concern. Furthermore the final settlement over the distribution of votes for qualified majority voting has not yet been reached. It is in the fields of defence and foreign policy that this issue is likely to be most acute.

The attempts at institutional reform

The Constitutional Treaty, which failed in 2007, and its successor, the Lisbon Treaty which was ratified in 2009, included attempts to reform decision making to take account of the increased size of the Union. This involved less unanimous voting (notably over defence and foreign policy) and an extension of qualified majority decisions. The fact that there remains a deadlock over such reform has meant that enlargement has created enormous problems. These became especially acute when the Union needed to adopt common financial and economic policies to deal with the economic crisis which began in 2008. Clearly the interests of the various states which were at different stages of decline, inevitably varied a great deal.

An evaluation of enlargement

We can now summarise the benefits and disbenefits arising out of enlargement since 2004 (Table 9.2).

Turkey and beyond

The greatest enlargement issue facing Europe in the future is likely to be the application to join by Turkey. Not least among the problems, the larger

Table 9.2 Benefits and problems of enlargement

Benefits	Problems
• A larger market promotes competition and efficiency. • Free movement of labour reduces wage costs and so keeps prices low. • The Euro will become a larger and therefore stronger world currency. • Enlargement further unifies Europe and reduces the prospect of conflict. • The European Union becomes an increasingly large and influential force in world affairs. • The poorer parts of Europe are offered the prospect of greater prosperity.	• Enlargement places stresses on the EU's political institutions, making decision making cumbersome. • Cheap labour from Eastern Europe threatens the wages and employment of Western European workers. • There are increasing demands on structural funds and the CAP. • The introduction of 'new democracies' makes it difficult to improve the state of human rights. • Increased size creates bigger, more porous borders, creating problems with illegal immigration, drug smuggling and international crime.

members disagree fundamentally about Turkey joining. France and Germany are particularly opposed, while the UK leads Turkey's supporters.

The **benefits** of Turkey's admission include these:

- The introduction of a new state of over 70 million inhabitants would substantially increase the size of the single market.
- As Turkey is a Muslim state there are advantages in building bridges between the Western 'Christian' world and the Islamic world.
- Membership would be an incentive for Turkey to improve its democracy and human rights record.

The possible **problems** of Turkish entry include:

- Potentially large 'armies' of cheap Turkish workers might destabilise labour markets in Western Europe.
- Some suggest admission would make Europe yet more vulnerable to international terrorism.
- The standard of living in Turkey is considerably lower than in the rest of Europe. Thus Turkey would place yet another great strain on the finances of the EU.
- Turkey's entry might have the effect of increasing tension with the Islamic world rather than reducing conflict.

The possible admission of states such as Serbia, Croatia, Bosnia and Iceland suggests fewer problems and are more likely to proceed than Turkey's entry.

Beyond that, however, more problems might emerge. There is the general question of what constitutes a 'European' state – where does Europe begin and end? Thus should Ukraine, Israel or Armenia be admitted? Could the EU extend into the Middle East or even North Africa? The problems which have been encountered since 2004 and the possible entry of Turkey would be magnified further by unrestrained enlargement.

A COMMON DEFENCE, SECURITY AND FOREIGN POLICY FOR EUROPE

When the Maastricht Treaty was negotiated in 1992, a general intention to forge a common system of foreign and defence policy was made. The impetus for this initiative came from the conflict which had broken out in the Balkans in the 1990s following the collapse of Yugoslavia.

The Balkan war was the first major armed conflict to break out in Europe after the Second World War. It had the effect of alerting political leaders to the fact that Europe was going to have to take greater responsibility for its own internal security. External defence would continue to be provided by NATO; but NATO had proved to be an unwieldy organisation to deal with a complex issue like the Balkans war. Attempts to adopt a common European position in Bosnia had largely failed, so that a more permanent apparatus had to be found. There was an organisation in place to deal with such issues – the Organisation for Security and Co-operation in Europe (OSCE) – but it proved to be a toothless body, lacking the authority of the European Union or NATO. Progress has been slow, but this is likely to be an issue for many years to come. The conflicts on Kosovo and Macedonia which followed Bosnia have served as reminders to EU leaders that a long-term solution needs to be found.

Foreign policy

The Common Foreign and Security Policy (CFSP) was confirmed by the Amsterdam Treaty in 1997. Two years later a new post of **CFSP High Representative** was created and its first holder, Javier Solana, was appointed. This was an important first step, as it is vital for the EU to be able to negotiate with other states and organisations through a single individual, otherwise any messages are likely to become confused and lack authority. Solana has a planning unit to assist him, but the development of an extensive, permanent, *supranational* body in charge of foreign policy is slower in coming.

Foreign policy remains in the hands of *intergovernmental* bodies – the Council of Foreign Ministers and the European Council (of heads of government) as well as the **Policy Planning and Early Warning Unit** and the **Political and Security Committee**. This renders foreign policy making difficult. Key decisions require unanimous approval in these councils and every issue becomes an *ad hoc* negotiation, in other words each is treated separately. The requirement to reach agreement among foreign ministers and heads of governments presents a number of serious problems.

- Member states have existing alliances of their own which may cut across European Union interests. Britain, for example, has a close relationship with the USA and Israel and has loyalties to Commonwealth countries. Italy and France have close links with Arab countries in the Middle East, while Germany has a special interest in Turkey and the Balkans.
- Some countries, such as Sweden, Ireland and Austria now have traditions of neutrality which may be compromised by a common European foreign policy.
- The simple fact that countries have to reach agreement on very sensitive subjects is a huge stumbling block to decisive policy making.
- When foreign policy requires military backing – or at least the threat of it – there may be no guarantee that member states will support their intentions with such a commitment.
- Some states are, quite simply, less committed to European integration than others. This phenomenon is likely to vary as governments change, which they inevitably do. The British and Danish governments have, for example, been traditionally 'standoffish'.
- Although the European project is designed to end conflict, we have to accept that old rivalries die hard, making the reconciliation of foreign policy difficult. France – normally a fiercely nationalistic state – finds it hard to come to agreement with Germany and the UK, the Dutch are naturally suspicious of Germany, while Scandinavian countries have traditionally little interest in southern Europe.

Thus, until most of the members are willing to sacrifice this highly sensitive aspect of national sovereignty to supranational bodies, foreign policy is likely to remain a problematic subject. Some examples illustrate the remaining issues.

The Balkans. When the former multinational state of Yugoslavia broke up in the early 1990s a number of wars broke out in the region as the new states were forming and the old federation was collapsing. Apart from the fighting, there were a number of examples of genocide, ethnic cleansing and human rights abuses. The response of the EU was widely seen as inadequate and weak. Attempts to bring Serbia to justice for its criticized behaviour in various Balkans conflicts failed and there was a complete failure to put together a peace-keeping force. In the event it was left to the USA and the UK to intervene militarily, mainly in Bosnia and Kosovo, with the United Nations playing a support role.

The 'War on Terror'. The conflicts which broke out after 2003 in Iraq and Afghanistan demonstrated the EU's failure to establish a common response to the threat of terrorism. The military interventions in the Middle East were, in the event, organised by NATO rather than the EU. Germany and France in particular opposed military intervention in Iraq so a common EU response became impossible. The same has been true of military action in Afghanistan, though a wide range of EU states has provided modest support to the USA and the UK.

The Middle East. The EU has failed to play any significant *collective* role in attempts to solve the Arab–Israeli conflict or to manage the threat posed by a resurgent Iran. Here again it is the USA which has become the key player in attempts to broker a settlement, particularly after the election of President Barack Obama.

There are two main challenges for the future of a common EU foreign policy other than those described above. These concern relations with Russia and China. Here there is more room for optimism as these are unlikely to be military and diplomatic issues. To a great extent they concern trade and economic relations. As a single market the EU has found itself more capable of reaching common positions than it has in the general field of foreign relations.

Security and defence

Security became a major European concern after the attacks on the World Trade Center in New York in 2001 and further serious attacks in Madrid in 2004 and London in 2005. Following '9/11' in 2001, a **European Security Strategy** was agreed. However, Britain, which saw itself as the most threatened country, undermined the agreement by refusing to share intelligence information. This failure to establish a common policy and intelligence system extended to responses to organised crime and nuclear proliferation, both of which were seen as connected to terrorist threats.

The major problem in developing common security strategies has been the varying nature of the protection of civil liberties in different countries. Thus, attempts to organise the tracing of emails, mobile phone and other communication records and methods of tracing the movements of certain individuals have fallen foul of various legal challenges in member states, Similarly attitudes to the ways in which terrorist suspects can be interrogated vary from state to state. Since terrorism, organised crime and the movement of weapons does not recognise national borders, a purely nation-by-nation response remains inadequate.

The fact that co-operation over security has been difficult to achieve and that individual countries have tended to develop their own strategies, with minimum reference to fellow members, has led to the description **soft security** in the EU context.

The difficulties involved in a common defence policy for the EU are perhaps more acute than those involved in foreign policy or even security. Yet, surprisingly, progress has been more slightly more significant. At a series of meetings in **St Malo** (hence the term 'St Malo process'), Cologne, Washington and Helsinki in 1998–99 the idea of how Europe could move towards an independent, integrated defence capability was thrashed out. The agreement of the USA was sought and obtained, with various conditions, mainly safeguarding the role of NATO.

It was Britain's Tony Blair who solved the inevitable misgivings which some members had. He proposed a small, highly flexible force of about sixty thousand soldiers. This was far from being a 'European Army' which opponents, mainly Conservatives, had suspected. It was described instead as a 'rapid reaction force'. This proposal became known as the **Petersburg Tasks**. For larger operations it was agreed that the European force should be effectively the armed forces of the Western European Union (WEU) which is a section of NATO without the USA. By insisting that the WEU would be the major European force, the relationship with NATO was preserved and protected. The WEU cannot act without the wider agreement of NATO as a whole. In this way the USA retains an interest in European defence issues.

At Helsinki in 2000 a permanent defence establishment was created and represents a considerable amount of progress. The bodies which came into existence are:
- the Political and Security Committee
- the European Military Committee
- the European Military Staff.

Despite the apparently successful outcome of the negotiations, there remain a number of problems with control of a European force.
- The command structure of the force is a major problem, despite the existence of the European Military Staff. It may be difficult for armed forces to accept the command of officers who are not of the same nationality. This may not be a problem in peacetime, but could be a major concern on the battlefield.
- Armed forces need political direction. Although the foreign policy establishment of the EU appears to have been developed in the form of the Political and Security Committee and the Western European Union, in practice a coherent political direction may be difficult to achieve.
- There may still be occasions when the interests of NATO clash with those of the European Union. One might speculate that Middle East tensions, which

spill over into Turkey or Cyprus and southern Europe, may evoke a very varying response from the USA and the EU.
- A key aspect of defence (and foreign) policy concerns intelligence. It may be difficult for European powers to share intelligence, an area where there is a notorious amount of secrecy and national self-interest.

The permanent defence force had not come into existence by 2009. However, some progress has been made in the creation of a **Capabilities Catalogue**.

The Capabilities Catalogue

Rather than a permanent military force, which has proved too problematic, the Capabilities Catalogue is a recognised series of groups, drawn from member countries, which could, if needed, be quickly deployed to counter a military threat. Agreed in 2003, it includes the following:
- a group of experienced 'commanders'
- a group of military and logistics specialists
- military equipment.

Sadly, as with much of the European Security and Defence Policy, the Capabilities Catalogue remains a theory rather than a reality. There is, in other words, no guarantee that any participating state will actually supply the contribution which has been agreed. This is partly an issue of national sovereignty, but also reflects a view that there is no foreseeable 'conventional' military threat to Europe.

European Union defence and foreign policy abbreviations and definitions

- **NATO**: North Atlantic Treaty Organisation. Responsible for the collective security of Europe and the Western world. Comprises most European states plus the USA and Canada.
- **WEU**: Western European Union. The section of NATO comprising only European states.
- **CFSP**: Common Foreign and Security Policy. The European Union's commitment to adopt agreed common foreign policies.
- **CESDP**: Common European Security and Defence Policy. The agreement to co-operate on internal defence matters.
- **PSC**: Political and Security Committee. A permanent body whose role is to provide political direction for any military actions.
- **EMC**: European Military Committee. A committee of officials who have the task of co-ordinating military policy.
- **EMS**: European Military Staff. Officers of European armed forces who co-ordinate military arrangements.

EUROPEAN RIGHTS AND CITIZENSHIP

Civil rights and liberties

Most European states have adopted the European Convention of Human Rights. However this does not mean that the principle of human rights has been fully established throughout Europe. Some states, including the UK, do not treat it as binding and it is not fully comprehensive.

Civil rights campaigners have, as two of their goals, the establishment of a European Bill of Rights and a universal concept of European citizenship. At Maastricht this idea was built into the objectives of the EU, although little progress has been made since. What does this mean in principle?

- It implies that there will be a codified set of rights to which all citizens of the European Union will be entitled. These rights would include those contained in the European Convention plus the economic and social rights which are contained in the EU Social Chapter.
- These rights would be binding on all EU members, so that all laws and executive actions would have to conform.
- A European Court – presumably the existing Court of Justice – would have powers to enforce these rights.
- All citizens of member countries would gain all the rights contained in the Bill of Rights.
- The rules for citizenship, i.e. who is entitled to call himself or herself a citizen of the European Union, would be common to all member states.
- There would have to be common rules of naturalisation and other means of acquiring citizenship which would apply throughout Europe.

On the face of it, there might be little problem in codifying such a set of principles. Most countries already conform to most of the same rules and there would be little argument over those terms already contained in the European Convention and the Social Chapter. Nevertheless there are potential problems. Some of the main ones are as follows.

- Those countries and politicians who are worried about the growing power of the EU and the loss of national identities would perhaps object to the concept of European citizenship. They would place national identity above a European identity, and would be concerned if Europe were placed above the nation in this matter.
- There are likely to be disagreements about the rules by which individuals could become citizens of Europe. What, for example, would be the future status of refugees and asylum seekers? Who would decide whether such people should be entitled to apply for citizenship? It has to be remembered that, if citizenship were granted, the person concerned would have the right to live and work in any part of the Union.

- There might not be total agreement about what rights should be granted to all citizens. Most would be agreed, but perhaps not all. This may be a particular problem for new members who do not have the same tradition of rights as the rest of western Europe.
- Some countries, notably the UK with its doctrine of parliamentary sovereignty, might be unwilling to accept that a European Court could overrule elements of its legislation or could overturn the actions of its government.

The Charter of Fundamental Human Rights had been established as part of the 2001 Nice Treaty and member countries eventually all signed up to it. However it remained only advisory and did not have the force of law. The next step was to attempt to give it that force of law.

All these issues were brought together when the Lisbon Treaty was finally signed in 2009. The Treaty contained, effectively, a European Bill of Fundamental Rights. Its full implementation, however, remains in some doubt.

Social and economic rights and the Social Chapter

The Social Chapter was an addition to the Maastricht Treaty which was signed in 1992. It contains far-reaching regulations and agreements concerning the economic and social rights of workers throughout the EU. Indeed, so far-reaching were its terms that the UK, led by John Major, refused to sign the Social Chapter of Maastricht on the grounds that it involved too great a loss of national sovereignty. Thus it became an 'opt-out', a condition of Britain agreeing to the rest of the treaty. The Labour Party strongly supported the Social Chapter so it was no surprise that one of the first actions of the Labour government that came to power in 1997 was to sign the Social Chapter.

Among the main provisions of the Social Chapter are:
- A maximum working week of 48 hours for all workers unless they agree voluntarily to work longer hours.
- A minimum working age of 16.
- Totally equality of treatment, pay and conditions for women.
- Protection of the rights of disabled workers.
- Various health and safety conditions.
- Protection of the rights of workers to form and join trade unions or other associations.
- Minimum pension rights for most workers.
- Rights to maternity and paternity leave.
- Rights to training for most workers.
- Rights to minimum redundancy payments.
- Right to work flexible hours.

All these rights are enforceable within member states and may be further enforced on appeal by the European Court of Justice. Any member who has signed the

Social Chapter must agree to all its terms. The purposes of the Social Chapter are twofold. One is to reinforce equal economic and social rights for all workers. The other is to ensure that, in the single market, all member states operate the same labour laws. In this way no member can gain an unfair advantage, in terms of labour costs, by not enforcing the Chapter. All new member states must also sign the Social Chapter as a condition of entry.

Critics have argued that the Social Chapter is an undesirable set of regulations on business. They say it puts up labour costs, reduces flexibility and actually causes unemployment as employers are less willing to employ labour with all its additional costs. They claim it gives a competitive advantage to countries which do not operate such tight labour regulations, such as China, India, Russia and the USA. They also point out that it is a denial of national sovereignty.

Supporters, on the other hand, argue that it has considerably improved working conditions throughout the EU. They also suggest that workforces which enjoy better conditions are likely to be more productive. It is also, as we have seen above, essential to create a 'level playing field' in the single market.

THE SINGLE CURRENCY

The development of the single currency has, of course, been of great importance to the European project. However, it is no longer a live political issue. The single currency is here to stay for the time being and its successful introduction in early 2002 confirms that there is little point in discussing its advantages and disadvantages. For the UK and Denmark who did not enter the system in 2002 it is still a contentious matter, but for the thirteen existing members of the eurozone the discussions are over.

But the effects of the single currency will still be far-reaching. It is worth, at this stage, reminding ourselves what problems and difficulties are likely to arise.

- The role of the European Central Bank, which will control interest rates and, indirectly, the fiscal policies of member states, is likely to become controversial, especially as it is unelected and unaccountable.
- If there is an economic crisis or serious recession, there will be those who suggest that it is the single currency which is the culprit.
- Similarly, if any individual states run into economic difficulty and discover that the European Bank cannot help them, and that their own governments find their hands tied by centralised policies, their own public may become disenchanted with the single currency system.
- If the external value of the Euro declines, resulting in European inflation, support for the Euro may ebb away (the opposite has actually occurred during 2008–9).

- As economic harmonisation increases while the currency has its effect, there may be a reaction against the uniformity and loss of national sovereignty which has arisen from the single currency.

Yet, despite all this, the problems of returning to twenty-five or more individual currencies would seem to be now impractical, so discussion of such issues remains largely academic and speculative. All new member states must make a commitment to adopting the Euro as their currency and so, as the EU expands, there is every likelihood that the single currency will become even more established and influential in world financial markets.

The robustness of the single currency and the financial regulation of the European Central Bank has been severely tested during the economic crisis of 2007–9. The evidence suggests that the Euro has successfully come through this ordeal with some credit. Above all, while the value of the US dollar and UK sterling fell in 2008–9, the Euro remained strong. In a time of great financial and economic uncertainty, the fact that member states did not have to concern themselves with fluctuating exchange rates was a considerable advantage. By contrast the UK suffered a falling currency resulting in rising import prices.

SAMPLE QUESTIONS

Short questions

1 Why is the Common Agricultural Policy still a contentious issue?

2 Why is the possible admission of Turkey to the EU so contentious?

3 What are the main obstacles to a common defence and foreign policy in the EU?

4 In what ways has the single currency been a success?

5 Assess the success of the policy on the free movement of labour within the EU.

Essay questions

1 Assess the effects of enlargement of the EU since 2004.

2 To what extent has the Common Agricultural Policy been successfully reformed?

3 Is there such a thing as a common European environmental policy?

4 How has the single currency affected economic policy making in the EU?

5 Is there now an effective single market in the EU?

Britain and the European Union *10*

BACKGROUND

In the immediate post-Second World War period Britain played a leading role in the developing the idea of a politically integrated Europe. This was a response to the frequency costs of conflicts which had bedeviled Europe for centuries past. The Conservative leader Winston Churchill was a leading figure in the creation of the Council of Europe, a body which, it was hoped, would lead the way towards closer integration. The Council proved, however, to be a false dawn. Though it still exists today (most importantly administering the European Convention on Human Rights), it is a relatively insignificant body. It was the French Schuman–Monnet plan for economic integration that proved to be more enduring.

Britain was cautious about joining the new community and did not sign the Treaty of Rome, establishing the European Community, in 1957. Nevertheless the Conservative Prime Minister Harold Macmillan was a pragmatist who understood that European economic integration was inevitable and that Britain's place had to be in a new European community. This was becoming especially important as Macmillan was starting the process of dismantling most of the remaining British Empire. Britain had created a rival to the European Community in 1959. This was the **European Free Trade Association (EFTA)**, a group of mostly smaller countries around the fringes of Europe. But EFTA was never going to be a serious competitor for the main European Community and Macmillan realized this. He therefore entered negotiations for entry in 1961.

The main stumbling block to entry was the attitude of France under its nationalistic president, Charles de Gaulle. De Gaulle opposed Britain's application on a number of grounds:

- As a still economically powerful state, Britain might attempt to become the dominant player in Europe, possibly forging a powerful alliance with West Germany (Germany was still partitioned at that time).
- Britain's close alliance with the USA and NATO (de Gaulle had withdrawn France from the NATO alliance in order to remain an independent nuclear power) was seen as a major distraction from European integration.
- Britain had many special trade agreements with its Commonwealth allies, notably Australia, New Zealand, Canada and India, and wished to retain them. This would cause major problems in the search for a single European market. It also would give Britain an unfair advantage over other members.

Then, as now, the admission of a new member requires the unanimous approval of existing members. France was therefore able to veto Britain's application. It was to be a further ten years before relations between Britain and France were repaired, helped by de Gaulle's fall from power in 1969.

BRITISH ENTRY

The Labour Party which held power in Britain under Harold Wilson between 1964 and 1970 was divided over the issue of whether to re-apply for membership. The left wing of the party was opposed on the grounds that the community was seen as a 'capitalist club of nations'. More moderate members of the party supported a fresh application, but in the event the party was too divided to make a new application. That task was left to the extremely pro-European Conservative leader Edward Heath, who came to power in 1970. Heath quickly entered negotiations for British entry.

By 1972 the negotiations were complete. Britain succeeded in agreeing some 'transitional arrangements' to smooth over the loss of special trade arrangements with Commonwealth countries. There was a parliamentary majority in favour of entry and so, once the necessary legislation had been passed, Britain became a member of the European Community on 1 January 1973.

Heath lost power in 1974 and the incoming Labour Party, still led by Wilson, found itself in a dilemma. Powerful forces in its own left wing were pressing for British withdrawal. A coalition of dissident anti-European Conservatives and the Labour left were a powerful combination. Wilson then pulled off a major political coup to head off the opposition. First, he 'renegotiated' the terms of British membership. Though this was a largely 'cosmetic' exercise, he was able to claim that he had wrung important concessions out of his European partners, in particular reducing Britain's financial contributions to Europe. Wilson then called a national referendum in 1975 on the issue of whether Britain should remain a member. After a hard-fought, bitter campaign in the country's first ever national referendum, the 'yes' campaign won a resounding victory by a two-to-one majority. It was the combination of a majority of government ministers and key members of the business community, who were very much in favour of membership, which had carried the day. Thus, British membership of the community seemed to have been firmly established for the foreseeable future.

MARGARET THATCHER AND EUROPE

Margaret Thatcher's attitude to the European Union was, at first at least, double-edged. On the one hand she was by instinct a neo-liberal who believed in the importance of free markets and competition. This she saw as essential in the creation of greater efficiency, lower prices and controlled wage levels. On the other hand she was a nationalist who wished to place British interests first and who was not prepared to sacrifice sovereignty to any external body such as the European Union. To add to the political mixture in the mid-1980s, the Labour Party had swung violently to the left and its leaders were talking actively of Britain leaving the EU altogether. On the basis that 'my enemy's enemy is my friend', Labour's anti Thatcher European stance led to warm to closer integration.

In 1985–86 the EU members negotiated the **Single European Act (SEA)**. Although this represented many problems for the Thatcher government she was willing to sign up to it for one overwhelming reason. That was that the SEA was a commitment to a single market in Europe, signalling the future free movement of goods, finance and labour throughout the Union. As an ardent free marketer Thatcher could not resist the attractions of a completely free European market. The SEA did contain some problems. It introduced new functions to the EU, notably environmental protection and greater economic cohesion, and extended the use of qualified majority voting in a number of areas concerning the economic field. These developments were further erosions of British sovereignty. The SEA also contained a future commitment to monetary union. Thatcher largely ignored the last provision, mainly

monetary union
Established in 2000, monetary union refers to the adoption of a single European currency – the Euro – to replace various national currencies. Eleven states originally entered monetary union (Greece joined a year later to make twelve). It also implies that there will be close economic union between states who adopt the currency.

on the grounds that she did not believe it would come about. In 1986 she signed the SEA and so brought Britain closer into the European fold. Two years later, however, the whole European landscape had changed.

Three main factors caused Thatcher to change her stance on Europe in a radical manner. First, the President of the Commission was now Jacques Delors, a former French socialist politician who was committed to closer political integration in Europe and who hoped that the EU could become a vehicle for improving the rights of workers. Second, there was now serious talk of a single currency coming into effect within ten years. Third, Delors signalled that a new treaty (which turned out to be the Maastricht Treaty of 1992) would promote greater *political* union to match economic integration. In September 1988 Thatcher travelled to Bruges in Belgium and delivered a speech (forever known as the 'Bruges Speech') which was to influence Conservative attitudes to Europe for the next twenty years. In the speech she railed against the 'socialist' tendencies of the Commission. She also ruled out any notion that Britain would be any party to a single currency or to closer political union. This was effectively the birth of Conservative 'Euro-scepticism' and it became both the dominant attitude of the party in the 1990s and the policy which set up an internal party conflict, sending the Conservative Party into the political wilderness through most of that decade and beyond.

Margaret Thatcher lost power in 1990, giving way to John Major who was also a Euro-sceptic but was, above all, a pragmatist. Meanwhile change was afoot in the Labour Party, change which would eventually lead to the emergence of New Labour and a much changed attitude to Europe.

JOHN MAJOR, MAASTRICHT AND NEW LABOUR

When negotiations began in 1991 towards an important new European Treaty, Britain's new Prime Minister was faced by a serious dilemma. On the one hand he realised that Britain would have to co-operate with its European partners or face being marginalised at best, thrown out of Europe at worst. But he faced huge difficulties at home. The Conservative Party, still under the influence of Margaret Thatcher, was moving ever further to a Euro-sceptic approach. They wanted him to make it clear that Britain would not tolerate any further loss of national sovereignty and would resist moves towards closer political integration in Europe. He was, however, faced by France and Germany who were now committed to political union and to the development of a single currency. Furthermore there was talk of a common defence and security policy, of a binding European bill of rights and – most abhorrent of all to most Conservatives – of a new 'social dimension' which would establish common economic and social rights for all workers binding on all member states.

Major did sign the Maastricht Treaty in 1992 (the formal name of the treaty was **The Treaty on European Union**), having negotiated important opt-outs for Britain. The most important opt-out concerned the Social Chapter. Britain was exempted from this and did not sign until Labour came to power in 1997. Major also made it clear that Britain had no intention of joining any future monetary union. But signing the Treaty was only the start of Major's troubles.

The Maastricht Treaty created a huge political conflict within the Conservative Party. Furthermore, in the 1992 general election, Major's Conservatives had won, but with a narrow parliamentary majority of 21. This small majority was gradually whittled away as some Conservative MPs defected to other parties and by-election defeats further eroded the Conservative advantage. Major did just succeed in gaining parliamentary approval for the Maastricht Treaty, though he came very close to losing power over the issue. The first Commons vote in 1993 went against ratification by a majority of 40. Major called a fresh vote the following day, declaring that it was a vote of no confidence in the government. In other words, if he lost the second vote he would resign. This brought the Conservative rebels temporarily into line and, in a close vote, Maastricht was approved. But this did not end the conflict. The prominent Euro-sceptics, led by such figures as John Redwood, Bill Cash and Norman Lamont, continued to plot against Major. The fact that John Major led a totally divided party was a major contributing factor to the Conservative Party's traumatic and decisive defeat at the 1997 general election.

While the Conservative Party was tearing itself apart over Europe, New Labour was uniting behind Tony Blair and a considerably more positive attitude towards the EU. Conservative hopes that a generally Euro-sceptic British public would not support a pro-European Labour Party were unfounded. Though a considerable majority of the electorate were opposed to closer European integration, they did not consider it a political priority compared to economic policy and the state of public services. As a choice between a Conservative Party in disarray and a determined, united Labour Party, the 1997 election was no contest.

BLAIR, BROWN AND THE EUROPEAN UNION

When New Labour came to power in 1997 the principal European issue concerned whether Britain should join a new monetary union, scheduled to come into being at the end of the century. Tony Blair was enthusiastic for the Euro, but his Chancellor, Gordon Brown, was less convinced. In any event, the new government had promised that Britain would not enter monetary union unless there was a positive vote in a national referendum.

It was Brown who won the day over the Euro. He argued that the economic conditions were not favourable for British entry. He produced five 'conditions for entry' which introduced several very high economic hurdles. These were as follows.

1 The economies of Britain and most of the other major members of the EU would need to be 'converged, in other words would be at the same point in their 'economic cycle'. In particular British interest rates would need to be close to those operating in the eurozone (they were normally considerably higher in Britain).

2 European labour markets would need to be as deregulated and flexible as British labour markets, a process which was under way but being seriously resisted by France in particular.

3 The government would have to be satisfied that British adoption of the Euro would be a benefit to business.

4 Adoption of the Euro would have to be seen as beneficial to the financial establishment in Britain.

5 The British government would need to be convinced that adopting the Euro would have a positive effect on employment.

> **labour markets**
> The term labour market refers to the processes whereby labour of all kinds offers itself for work and is employed. It also refers to the determination of wages through the forces of demand for, and supply of, labour. Under EU rules labour markets must be free and not subject to any national-based restrictions. It also implies that workers of all kinds in Europe should be free to seek employment anywhere in the EU without restriction.

Cynics argued that Brown's five conditions were both vague and demanding and were effectively a device by which he could resist Blair's plans for British participation. Furthermore, unlike Blair, Brown was convinced that the British people would not vote for the Euro in a referendum.

Brown won the day on the Euro and, by the time he became Prime Minister in 2007, the prospect of British entry into the eurozone was a very distant one. The economic crisis which engulfed Europe in 2008 did not clarify the issue. The strength of the Euro in the currency markets at a time when sterling was weak seemed to strengthen the pro-Euro argument. As the value of the Euro and pound crept gradually towards parity (i.e. one-to-one) during late 2008 and 2009, the possibility of British entry grew. On the other hand it was argued that the middle of a serious economic slump was not the right time for any major financial upheaval.

While Blair was losing the argument with Brown over the Euro, he was busily planning to place Britain at the centre of the EU and to play a leading role in reform of the Union. Blair saw Britain as a potential 'bridge' between the EU and the USA. He also saw enlargement as a key way to promote peace and to build a further bridge with the Middle East (largely through Turkish entry). Above all Blair shared a common view in Europe that the future success of the Eu depended on reform of its institutions and improvements in its democratic arrangement. He therefore supported the plan to negotiate a new constitutional treaty in 2006–7.

Though less enthusiastic about European integration, Brown, who took over as Prime Minister in 2007, also supported the idea of a new treaty and he signed the draft Lisbon Treaty in 2008. While lamenting its ultimate demise, it could be argued that Gordon Brown was somewhat relieved that the Irish referendum defeat for the Lisbon Treaty set back the process of reform. Europe remains a dangerous political issue in Britain. Any suspicion that national sovereignty might be sacrificed is greeted with great opposition. It is not surprising therefore that Brown has always insisted that there are certain 'red lines' representing developments to which he will never agree. Thus Gordon Brown has always declared his intention to veto any moves towards harmonisation of tax in the EU. He has also declared such areas as social policy, law and order and welfare as 'no-go areas' for Britain.

PARTY IDEOLOGY, POLICY AND THE EUROPEAN UNION

At this point we can summarise British political attitudes towards the European Union. First it is worth reconsidering the various ideological attitudes to Europe. These do not coincide with specific party policies and, in some cases, cross party lines.

Right-wing conservatism (also referred to as neo-conservatism) is deeply suspicious of the European Union. For many the only response to integration should be for Britain to leave altogether. Certainly the UK Independence Party (UKIP) takes this view. There are also some members of the Conservative Party who consider themselves to be Europhobes of this kind.

Traditional (mainstream) conservatism is currently represented by David Cameron and his leadership group. They are fundamentally suspicious of European integration, but accept that the UK must remain a full member. As a compromise position, mainstream conservatives envisage a 'two-speed' Europe where some members are more fully integrated than others (Britain being in the latter category).

Pro-European conservatives. There is a small group of traditional conservatives, led by former Chancellor of the Exchequer, Kenneth Clarke, who see Britain at the centre of a closely integrated Europe. They believe that Britain's long-term interests lie with closer integration with European partners.

Neo-liberals. These 'Thatcherite' economic liberals, who belong mostly in the Conservative Party, argue that the European Union should certainly be a free trade area with Britain as a member, but that there should be the very minimum of political integration and little regulation by the institutions of the EU.

Socialists and democratic socialists remain suspicious of the European Union. They see it as a vehicle for capitalism rather than a guarantor of workers' rights. They see the free market as a means by which competition will depress wages, create competition between workers and so weaken the power of organised labour. They also believe that the European free market will open opportunities for large multinational companies to dominate the economy and so operate against the interests of workers and consumers. In theory a 'socialist' European Union would be desirable, but there is no realistic possibility of this coming about.

Liberals and liberal democrats are the most enthusiastic supporters of the European Union. They support the concept of free markets and of regulation which would ensure that all members of the Union should enjoy equal access to those markets. They see European integration as an opportunity to spread the cause of civil, economic and social rights more widely. In contrast to many Euro-sceptics, they believe that the EU is a means by which power can be dispersed towards regions and localities rather than being over-centralised in Brussels as most conservatives claim.

Environmentalists are divided over European integration. Some are supportive, taking the view that the environment is an international issue requiring international solutions. If co-operation between members of the EU can be achieved, there may be significant progress towards better environmental protection. More radical ecologists are largely Euro-sceptic. They see the EU as business-dominated and, since business is largely opposed to environmental protection measures, the EU will not advance environmental causes.

As we have said, these ideological distinctions do not match party policy so it is also worth summarising the policies towards Europe of large and small parties in 2009.

Labour still sees Britain at the centre of the EU. However, the party supports very little further transfer of functions to the Union. For example it believes that taxation, social and welfare policy and law and order should remain in the control of national governments. The party intends that Britain should eventually adopt the Euro, but imposes tight criteria on British membership of monetary union. Labour has supported the plan for a new constitutional treaty, largely on the grounds that it may prevent any further drift towards centralisation and may help to make the EU more democratic. There remains a small left-wing group in the party which does not see Britain's future being in Europe.

The Conservative Party firmly opposes any further political integration and has ruled out any possibility that Britain should adopt the Euro in the future. It would also attempt to negotiate more 'opt-outs' for Britain, in particular proposing that the Social Chapter should no longer apply in the UK. If further integration is proposed, they support the idea of a two-speed Europe, with some countries, including Britain, being part of the single market, but exempt from full political integration. A small group of moderate conservatives shares Labour's policies towards Europe.

> **single market**
> A key principle of the European Union. The single market is a major aspiration and seeks to establish one European market for all goods, labour and finance. This is being achieved by the gradual removal of barriers to trade or any practices which discriminate in trade matters against a member state. Effectively it implies the creation of one economic union.

The Liberal Democrats are the most enthusiastic party. They would wish to see Britain adopt the Euro as soon as possible. They also support further European integration, including more tax harmonisation and co-operation on social policy. They also see Europe as a future vehicle for the further protection of civil, economic and social rights. They support strongly the principle of 'subsidiarity' which would disperse power downwards towards regions and local communities. The condition for closer integration, however, has to be democratisation of European institutions. There is a small group of dissidents who are suspicious of further integration, but all members of the party are broadly supportive of the European Union.

Nationalist parties, notably the Scottish Nationalists and Plaid Cymru, are pro-European. They see the EU as a 'Europe of the regions' where there are opportunities to support areas like Wales and Scotland. They also believe that, if Scotland and Wales were to gain full independence, they would need the support of the EU to survive. The regional and structural funds, the CAP and rural development grants would be of huge benefit to these countries as they have been to Ireland.

UKIP and the BNP are anti-European Union parties. For them European political union is a denial of British national sovereignty. For them, the nation state is sacred and must be protected from the centralising forces of the EU. They also oppose the free movement of people in general and workers in particular as they see them as threats to employment and to social harmony.

The Green Party, as we have seen, has been divided over Europe. Its official policy is to support the EU, seeing it a key vehicle for environmental protection. However, it recognises that the EU is undemocratic and wishes to see radical reform of the kind envisaged in the first failed Constitution Treaty. A substantial minority in the party believe that the EU is fundamentally incapable of protecting the environment and so oppose it.

THE EUROPEAN UNION AND BRITISH SOVEREIGNTY

Despite the wide variety of political controversy over Europe in Britain, the fundamental problem lies with the issue of national sovereignty. To some extent this is a reflection of a British 'obsession'. Britain is a unitary system where power is concentrated at the centre. It is also a basic principle of the Constitution that Parliament is sovereign. It is a British political tradition to see sovereignty as a very 'hard concept'. This means that there is very little room for compromising with sovereignty. Ultimate power lies in one central location – Westminster – and any variation from that reality is seen as extremely dangerous.

By contrast many European nations have a 'softer' view of sovereignty. They are used to the idea of power being dispersed more widely within their political systems. Thus Germany, for example, is a federal state. France divides executive power quite evenly between its Parliament, its President and its Prime Minister. Italy is a more politically unstable country with governments coming and going with great regularity and with a parliament which is not afraid to dismiss governments and prime ministers. Thus, when the European Union requires the transfer of sovereignty from member states to central, supranational institutions, as was the case at Maastricht, European politicians and electorates are less alarmed than they are in Britain. Most Europeans are used to the idea of shifting power bases and the idea that power or sovereignty can be 'shared'. It is also true that European states are historically used to more economic and social intercourse with each other than the more isolated British. The British are reluctant to share power and have a long tradition of political independence. Thus, when more power is transferred to Brussels it is seen in Britain as a *loss* of sovereignty, rather than *pooling* of sovereignty.

The main British concerns over sovereignty lie in the following areas:

- Parliamentary sovereignty is a closely guarded principle. The European Union erodes parliamentary sovereignty as EU laws are superior to British domestic law. Some comfort can be taken from the fact that parliamentary sovereignty could be completely restored if the UK were to leave the EU.
- Where decisions require a unanimous approval in the Council of Ministers, such as over taxation, major foreign policy initiatives and the admission of new members, Britain is not afraid to use its veto even if this incurs the wrath of other large nations such as France and Germany. Indeed British

representatives have taken some pride in the country's reputation as the 'awkward partner'.

- The extension of qualified majority voting which has gradually occurred since 1986 has meant that British influence has gradually diminished. This has been especially true since the extensive enlargement in 2004.

> **enlargement**
> Simply, the process where new members are admitted into the European Union. The biggest enlargement occurred in 2004 when ten states entered the EU.

- The 1990 Factortame case (when the UK Merchant Shipping Act was declared contrary to EU law allowing international shipping rights) was a major shock for Britain. Its implication – that EU law always takes precedence over British law even if this means a threat to British national interest – had not been fully foreseen. It had been assumed that the British courts would administer European law. It became clear that the European Court of Justice was now the highest court of jurisdiction in a wide range of issues. British law and policy makers would now have to take notice of 'foreign' judges, something which was completely anathema to them. Civil servants, ministers and the drafters of UK laws would now have to take into account the question of whether their initiatives would be compatible with European law.

PRESSURE GROUPS AND THE EUROPEAN UNION

Opportunities and challenges

Closer European integration has created both opportunities and challenges for pressure groups. The opportunities relate especially to those groups whose concerns cross national boundaries such as environmentalists, rights campaigners, development campaigners and multinational industries. The decision-making institutions in the EU are in a position to effect change which will affect a huge community and so any influence on them has far-reaching consequences.

It is also true that pressure groups have a special part to play within the EU's democratic system. Within the EU it is acknowledged that both representation and accountability are relatively weak. The party system in Parliament is weak, there is no sense of a democratic mandate for decision makers and the lines of accountability between the executive bodies and the citizens of Europe is long, tenuous and fragile. Thus pressure groups provide alternative lines of representation and accountability. Citizens can participate directly or indirectly in group politics in a way that is lacking in European party politics. The absence of conventional party politics also means that decisions are often made on the basis of consensus rather than ideology. This gives much greater potential access to non-partisan groups. Similarly European decision makers can be made accountable to relevant groups with which they have contact in a way that they cannot with loose party confederations. Accountability through the European Parliament has been strengthened in recent years, but it still remains imprecise and weak. On the other hand, where a pressure group has direct access to the decision makers, there is a stronger sense of accountability.

The challenges are that many groups can no longer operate within the relatively narrow confines of national government. Wherever power has passed to European institutions the politics of influence has become more costly and more complex. The political system of the EU is considerably more intricate and multilayered than within individual nations so the task of accessing decision makers becomes more difficult and technical.

In terms of Britain specifically, pressure groups have had to respond in a number of ways.

First, where an issue is genuinely supranational, British groups have tended to join with European groups, working together in a common cause. That said, of course, some groups have specifically *national* concerns and so will be reluctant to adopt a supranational approach to political influence. The most common examples of such 'federated' groups occur in business and industry groups such as motor manufacturing, engineering, energy production or aerospace, as well as trade unions.

Second, groups must recognise that much decision making has now shifted from British to European institutions. This is especially true of environmental concerns, agriculture, fisheries, trade, consumer protection, workers' rights and regional development. The response must therefore be to shift operations to Europe, often setting up permanent offices with professional lobbyists in place.

Third, so-called 'outsider' groups normally pursue an issue rather than an economic interest. These groups may not have direct access to decision makers and so engage in 'direct action' to mobilise public opinion in order to put pressure on decision makers. Their challenge is the mobilisation of action across national borders as well as the sheer problem of moving large numbers of people across Europe for campaign purposes. Environmentalist, development world campaigners, free trade supporters and the like are typical examples. Fortunately for them, communications have improved so much since the development of the Internet that international action has become more feasible.

Fourth, it is important for groups to understand *where* decisions are to be made. Where a policy requires unanimous voting in the Council, a group may choose to concentrate on working with the British government. On the other hand, where a decision is subject to qualified majority voting, campaigns must become supranational, which may involve co-operating with other groups throughout Europe. Pressure groups must also consider the extent to which working with the European Parliament might yield results. Here the question is whether the policy is subject to codecision or not. If co-decision applies, the Parliament becomes an important source of influence. In such a case pressure on members of the UK Parliament and various domestic party leaderships may also be fruitful.

Points of access

As we have seen, there are many more points of access in the EU for groups seeking to gain influence. Among them are these:

The European Council, or meeting of heads of government up to four times a year, generally attracts the attention of large, supranational cause groups who seek to gain maximum publicity. As there is so much media attention on such European 'summit meetings', cause groups often seize the opportunity to ride on the back of such publicity. Thus environmentalists such as Friends of the Earth and Greenpeace, anti-war protesters, anti-world-poverty campaigners and the like organise mass rallies and civil disobedience campaigns at the meeting venues.

The Council of Ministers is perhaps the least fertile ground for group influence. By the time ministers meet to ratify decisions it is too late. The real negotiations have already taken place among ministers and their officials, often in COREPER, and so there is usually little lobbying activity here.

The Commission is the key institution for group pressure. This is mainly because it is here that policy is first formulated. It is also true that the Commission welcomes the input of legitimate interest groups as this represents an effective means of consultation. It maintains a **Register of Representatives** on which over 1400 groups were registered at the start of 2009. This is a voluntary register which enables groups to be officially recognised, to receive briefing papers on policy, to be invited to make submissions on policy and to be invited to take part in policy meetings. In other words there is a two-way flow of information and an open-access policy operating at the Commission.

Parliament has become increasingly important. Many key policies are now the subject of codecision, which gives Parliament the opportunity to veto proposals and to propose amendments. The areas subject to codecision are listed above in the section on the European Parliament. It can be seen how extensive these are, and among the key areas are environmental issues, trade, employment and consumer protection. In all these policy categories there are many groups which have an interest in influencing MEPs. Much of the work is done in committees, which have regular contacts with the Commission.

The European Court of Justice (ECJ). On a regular basis the ECJ hears cases where it is required to interpret an aspect of European law. In some cases interest and cause groups will have an interest in the outcome. Indeed, in some cases it is a pressure group which brings the case to the court in the first place, hoping for a favourable outcome.

Typical examples are cases concerning the application of the Social Chapter. Trade unions often have a vested interest in judgements which may be favourable for workers' rights and conditions. Producer and business groups also often seek favourable judgements. In such cases a group may hire lawyers and lobbyists to give evidence which may affect a decision.

The Economic and Social Committee. Though this committee has no power, it does discuss policies at the very early stages of their formulation. It therefore represents an opportunity for groups to influence policy before decisions are actually made.

The Committee of the Regions. This important body is influential in the distribution of funds for regional development. Clearly it is important for any groups which represent regional interests, such as specific industries, farmers, local government groups and trade unions. The competition for scarce funds is a key process for pressure groups who have to press their claims against alternative pressures.

At this point it will be illustrative to show prominent examples of groups which are included in the Commission's Register of Representatives (Table 10.1).

The range of bodies identified above demonstrates how extensive and complex pressure group operations have to be in Europe. The important principles are that groups should seek to gain influence at the *early* stages of policy consideration, so that they should be able to identify the key players in policy development and convince decision makers that their demands are compatible with the wider interests of the European Union as a whole.

Table 10.1　Some groups from the Committee of the Regions Register of Representatives

Federated European groups	Specifically British groups
European Federation of Public Service Unions	British Bankers' Association
Eurogroup for Animals	British Retail Consortium
European Anti-Poverty Network	London Investment Banking Association
European Chemical Employers Group	Scotch Whisky Association
European Farmers Group	Institute of Chartered Accountants for England and Wales
European Newspaper Publishers' Association	East of England Regional Assembly
Greenpeace European Unit	

SAMPLE QUESTIONS

Short questions

1 Why have Liberal Democrats been consistently enthusiastic about European integration?

2 To what extent has the Labour Party lost its enthusiasm for the European Union?

3 Why do Conservatives oppose further European integration?

4 In what ways have British ministers resisted further European integration since 1997?

Essay questions

1 To what extent does the issue of Europe remain a key political issue in Britain?

2 Why has Britain failed to enter monetary union in Europe?

3 Explain Britain's ambivalent attitude towards a new constitutional treaty for the EU.

Further reading

UNITED KINGDOM

General

Gordon Brown Prime Minister. T. Bower. HarperCollins, 2009
Blair's Britain, 1994–2007. A. Seldon and P. Snowdon (eds). Pearson, 2007
New Labour. S. Driver and L. Martell. Polity, 2006
Policy Making in Britain: An Introduction. P. Dorey. Sage, 2005
Governing before New Labour. A. Seldon (ed.). Macmillan, 2004
Britain Under Thatcher. A. Seldon and D. Collings. Pearson, 2000
The Major Effect. D. Kavanagh and A. Seldon. Macmillan, 1994

Economic policy

Global Financial Meltdown. C. Read. Palgrave, 2009
A Brief History of Neoliberalism. D. Harvey. Oxford University Press, 2005
Economic Policy in Britain. W. Grant. Palgrave, 2002

The Welfare State

Education Policy in Britain. C. Chitty. Palgrave, 2009
Health Policy in Britain. D. Han. Palgrave, 2009
Welfare Benefits and Tax Credit Handbook. C. George. CPAG, 2009
Modernising the Welfare State: The Blair Legacy. M. Powell (ed.). Policy, 2008
Pensions. Michael Hill. Policy, 2007
Beyond the Welfare State? C. Pierson. Polity, 2006
Housing Policy in the UK. D. Mullins and A. Murie. Palgrave, 2006
The Welfare State We're In. J. Bartholomew. Politicos, 2006
Understanding Social Policy. Michael Hill. Blackwell, 2003
The Widening Gap. M. Shaw, D. Dorling, D. Gordon and G. Davey-Smith. Policy, 1999

Law and order

The British Crime Survey, 2007–8. Home Office, 2009
Law and Order. R. Reiner. Polity, 2007
The Politics of Crime and Community. G. Hughes. Palgrave, 2006

Environment

The Politics of Climate Change. A. Giddens. Polity, 2009
The Politics of the Environment. N. Carter. Cambridge University Press, 2007
Environmental Policy Making in Britain, Germany and the European Union. R. Wurzel.
Manchester University Press, 2006

Northern Ireland

The Northern Ireland Peace Process. P. Dixon. Routledge, 2010
Northern Ireland: A Triumph of Politics. F. Millar. Irish Academic Press, 2009
Northern Ireland Politics. A. Aughey and D. Morrow. Pearson, 1996

Women and politics

Women and British Party Politics. S. Childs. Routledge, 2008
Feminizing Politics. J. Lovenduski. Polity, 2005
Women in Contemporary Politics. W. Stokes. Polity, 2005

EUROPEAN UNION

General

What's Wrong with the European Union and How to Fix it. S. Hix. Polity, 2008
The European Union: A Very Short Introduction. J. Pinder and S. Underwood. Oxford
University Press, 2007
European Union Politics. M. Cini. Oxford University Press, 2007

Britain and the European Union

The Europeanization of British Politics. I. Bache and A. Jordan. Palgrave, 2008
Britain and the European Union Today, 3rd ed. D. Watts and C. Pilkington. Manchester
University Press, 2005

Integration

Constitutionalizing the European Union. T. Christiansen and C. Reh. Palgrave, 2009
Ever Closer Union. D. Dinan. Palgrave, 2005
Theories of European Integration. B. Rosamond. Palgrave, 2005
Multi-Level Governance. I. Bache and M. Flinders. Oxford University Press, 2004

Issues

Monetary Integration in the European Union. M. Chang. Palgrave, 2009
Understanding the Common Agricultural Policy. B. Hill and S. Davidova. Earthscan, 2009
European Union Foreign Policy in a Changing World. K. Smith. Polity, 2008
Politics in the European Union. I. Bache and S. George. Oxford University Press, 2006
European Union Enlargement. N. Nugent (ed.). Palgrave, 2004

Institutions

Governing Europe. W. Walters and J. Haahr. Routledge, 2006
The Government and Politics of the European Union. N. Nugent. Palgrave, 2006
The European Union: How Does it Work? C. Blomberg. Oxford University Press, 2003

WEBSITES

All government departments and issues: www.number10.gov.uk
Environment: www.greenparty.org.uk
European Union: http://europa/abc/index_en.htm
Law and order: www.homeoffice.gov.uk/rds/bcs1.html
Northern Ireland: www.nio.gov.uk
Women's Issues: www.equalityhumanrights.com

Index